JOURNAL FOR THE STUDY OF THE OLD TESTAMENT SUPPLEMENT SERIES
220

Sheffield Academic Press

In Conversation with Jonah

Conversation Analysis, Literary Criticism, and the Book of Jonah

Raymond F. Person, Jr

Journal for the Study of the Old Testament
Supplement Series 220

Copyright © 1996 Sheffield Academic Press

Published by Sheffield Academic Press Ltd
Mansion House
19 Kingfield Road
Sheffield S11 9AS
England

Printed on acid-free paper in Great Britain
by Bookcraft Ltd
Midsomer Norton, Bath

British Library Cataloguing in Publication Data

A catalogue record for this book is available
from the British Library

ISBN 1-85075-619-8

CONTENTS

PREFACE

As to the making of many books, there is no end.
Ecclesiastes 12.12
It is a matter of competence.

Wolfgang Iser[1]

These two quotes represent the two opposing views I have of this work. On the one hand, I know that this work is simply one of many books that have been and will be. It certainly does not exhaust the meaning of the Jonah narrative as it interacts with its readers. Therefore, I am conscious that 'the fictional text refuses to be sucked dry and thrown on the rubbish heap'[2] and, so, defies all attempts to completely describe its meaning. Therefore, my own work is simply one attempt to aid other readings of the Jonah narrative and, indirectly through my method, other narratives. On the other hand, my motivation for writing this book emerges from an assumed degree of competence in my reading of the book of Jonah due to my particular approach. This motivation probably drives all of us who are compelled to write books that attempt to describe the interactions between texts and readers and, therefore, as expressed well in Ecclesiastes, there is no end to our writing such books.

Why do I make the assumption about my competence? This question can be answered in various ways, all of which are summed up in the title, *In Conversation with Jonah*. Conversations are what this book is all about and my study of these various conversations is the basis of my particular competence. These conversations include those between the characters in the narrative and those 'conversations' that constitute the interactions between the text and its readers.

The place to start in any such study is conversation analysis, and I have profited greatly from my esteemed teacher and friend, William

---

1. In E. Bloom, 'In Defense of Authors and Readers', *Novel* 11 (1977), pp. 2-25 (25).

2. W. Iser, *The Act of Reading: A Theory of Aesthetic Response* (Baltimore: The Johns Hopkins University Press, 1978), p. 7.

(Mack) O'Barr, and the writings of other conversation analysts, especially John Heritage, Stephen Levinson, and Deborah Tannen. Mack introduced me to the field of sociolinguistics, including conversation analysis, and has supported me in this project from its inception. Without his contribution, the following observations on method and their application to the Jonah narrative would never have occurred to me.

In order to understand how conversations operate within literary texts, a knowledge of literary theory is important. Wesley A. Kort has taught me much about literary theory, especially concerning narrative; his contribution is especially obvious in Chapter 3. In addition, the work of Wolfgang Iser significantly influenced my method as developed in Chapter 4.

My competence in biblical studies has been nurtured by various teachers, including especially James L. Crenshaw, Eric Meyers, Leo G. Perdue, M. Eugene Boring, and Melvin K.H. Peters.

To all of these teachers and friends I owe special thanks.

The first draft of this work was undertaken while I was a participant in a National Endowment for the Humanities Summer Seminar on Oral Tradition in Literature hosted by the University of Missouri at Columbia. I profited from my interactions with all of the seminar participants, but especially from my conversations with the director, John Miles Foley. John carefully read the first drafts, made helpful comments on content and style, and otherwise supported my work. Others who read and commented on this project are William M. O'Barr, James L. Crenshaw, and Mary Gerhart. I thank all of them for their time and support. I also want to thank my wife, Elizabeth Kelly, who has supported me in my work.

ABBREVIATIONS

AB	Anchor Bible
ATAT	Arbeiten zu Text und Sprache im Alten Testament
BZAW	Beihefte zur *ZAW*
CBC	Cambridge Bible Commentary
HAR	*Hebrew Annual Review*
ICC	International Critical Commentary
JBL	*Journal of Biblical Literature*
JQR	*Jewish Quarterly Review*
JSOT	*Journal for the Study of the Old Testament*
JSOTSup	*Journal for the Study of the Old Testament*, Supplement Series
OTL	Old Testament Library
OTS	*Oudtestamentische Studiën*
UBS	United Bible Societies
VTSup	*Vetus Testamentum*, Supplements
ZAW	*Zeitschrift für die alttestamentliche Wissenschaft*

INTRODUCTION

Narratives contain descriptions of the interaction between various characters, and these, like most human interactions, involve conversation. An entire field of study is devoted to understanding how conversation is organized and structured: conversation analysis. Nevertheless, few studies in literary theory and criticism have drawn from the wealth of information which conversation analysts have gathered and few conversation analysts have examined literary texts.[1] This study, in contrast, draws

1.　Some that use conversation analysis to interpret literature are the following: C.D. Baker and P. Freebody, 'Representations of Questioning and Answering in Children's First School Books', *Language in Society* 15 (1986), pp. 451-84; K.S. Campbell, 'A Lesson in Polite Compliance: Gawain's Conversational Strategies in Fitt 3 of Sir Gawain and the Green Knight', *Language Quarterly* 28 (1990), pp. 53-62; K.K. Gautam, 'Pinter's *The Caretaker*: A Study in Conversational Analysis', *Journal of Pragmatics* 11 (1987), pp. 49-59; R.T. Lakoff and D. Tannen, 'Conversational Strategy and Metastrategy in a Pragmatic Theory: The Example of *Scenes from a Marriage*', *Semiotica* 49 (1984), pp. 323-46; C.L. Miller, 'Reported Speech in Biblical and Epigraphic Hebrew: A Linguistic Analysis' (PhD dissertation; University of Chicago, 1992); R.F. Person, Jr, 'Restarts in Conversation and Literature', *Language and Communication* 16 (1996), pp. 61-70; M. Toolan, 'Analysing Conversation in Fiction: The Christmas Dinner Scene in Joyce's *Portrait of the Artist as a Young Man*', *Poetics Today* 8 (1987), pp. 393-416; *idem*, 'Analysing Fictional Dialogue', *Language and Communication* 5 (1985), pp. 193-206; *idem, The Stylistics of Fiction: A Literary–Linguistic Approach* (London: Routledge & Kegan Paul, 1990); K.L. Wadman, '"Private Ejaculations": Politeness Strategies in George Herbert's Poems Directed to God', *Language and Style* 16 (1983), pp. 87-106.
　　Also see the works by D. Tannen who argues convincingly that literature is closely related to ordinary conversation: 'Ordinary Conversation and Literary Discourse: Coherence and the Poetics of Repetition', in E.B. Bendix (ed.), *The Uses of Linguistics* (New York: New York Academy of Sciences, 1990), pp. 15-32; 'Oral and Literate Strategies in Spoken and Written Narratives', *Language* 58 (1982), pp. 1-21; 'Relative Focus on Involvement in Oral and Written Discourse', in D.R. Olson, N. Torrance and A. Hildyard (eds.), *Literacy, Language and Learning: The Nature and Consequences of Reading and Writing* (Cambridge: Cambridge

heavily upon conversation analysis in order to develop further the theories of both narrative art and the reading process.

In order to illustrate fully the application of these theoretical methods, a narrative has been chosen which suits this purpose well—that is, the book of Jonah, in which the narrator satirically manipulates readers in the selection and arrangement of the characters' speeches. Although previous studies on the Jonah narrative have utilized literary theory,[2] this study is the first in which observations from conversation analysis are used to inform the interpretation of its narrative art and its interaction with readers, thereby opening up new insights into the Jonah narrative.

Before discussing the Jonah narrative, some background information in conversation analysis is necessary. Therefore, in Chapter 1 I summarize the theoretical background and basic observations of conversation analysis. I then present my theoretical defense of applying this approach, which primarily deals with ordinary conversation, to oral narratives and, finally, to written narratives. In Chapter 2, I apply the basic observations of conversation analysis to the Jonah narrative in the form of a verse-by-verse commentary. This analysis not only shows that the Jonah narrative consists of the structure called adjacency pairs (for example, question/answer, request/refusal) but also demonstrates the complex interweaving of the multiple parts of adjacency pairs in the conversations between the characters. In Chapter 3, I elaborate on how the narrated conversations and their structures are made up of adjacency pairs and how these structures contribute to the development of the different narrative elements of plot, character, atmosphere and tone.

University Press, 1985), pp. 124-47; 'Repetition in Conversation: Toward a Poetics of Talk', *Language* 63 (1987), pp. 574-605; 'Silence as Conflict Management in Fiction and Drama: Pinter's *Betrayal* and a Short Story, "Great Wits"', in A.D. Grimshaw (ed.), *Conflict Talk: Sociolinguistic Investigations of Arguments in Conversations* (Cambridge: Cambridge University Press, 1990), pp. 260-79; *Talking Voices: Repetition, Dialogue, and Imagery in Conversational Discourse* (Cambridge: Cambridge University Press, 1989).

2.   For examples, see K.M. Craig, Jr, *A Poetics of Jonah: Art in the Service of Ideology* (Columbia: University of South Carolina Press, 1993); A.J. Hauser, 'Jonah: In Pursuit of the Dove', *JBL* 104 (1985), pp. 21-37; J. Magonet, *Form and Meaning: Studies in Literary Techniques in the Book of Jonah* (Sheffield: Almond Press, 1983); J.A. Miles, 'Laughing at the Bible: Jonah as Parody', *JQR* 65 (1975), pp. 168-81; D.F. Payne, 'Jonah from the Perspective of Its Audience', *JSOT* 13 (1979), pp. 3-12; and J.M. Sasson, *Jonah* (AB, 24B; Garden City, NY: Doubleday, 1990).

Chapter 4 concerns another type of conversation, that which occurs in the interaction between text and reader. When discussing this type of conversation, one should refer to reader-response criticism, and I have profited greatly from the writings of various reader-response critics, most especially Wolfgang Iser. I first summarize Iser's thought and then develop it further by creating a dialogue between Iser's work and sociolinguistics, especially conversation analysis. After this dialogue reaches some consensus, at least in my mind, I identify the implied reader of Jonah and describe this reader's conversation with the text in another verse-by-verse commentary.

Although Chapter 4 concerns the interaction between the text and the implied reader of the Jonah narrative, there are various other conversations between the text and actual readers that have occurred over the centuries and deserve comment, many of which have had a strong influence on my own dialogue with the text. Thus, in Chapter 5, I analyze these other conversations by studying the writings of other actual readers and by referring to my own journey as a reader. These actual readers include not only modern biblical scholars but also ancient interpreters and modern popular interpreters. This chapter is also influenced by conversation analysis in that the differences between various actual readers can be explained by my extensions of its basic observations.

I hope that this study not only opens up new insights into the Jonah narrative but also provides an excellent illustration of how a greater sensitivity to the structure of ordinary conversation can enhance one's reading of any narrative.

Chapter 1

CONVERSATION ANALYSIS AND NARRATIVE

1. *Conversation Analysis*

Conversation analysis[1] developed from the field of ethnomethodology, which seeks to understand the 'ethnic' methods (that is, the participants' own common-sense skills and abilities) which enable participants to produce and recognize meaningful social interaction. Conversation analysis thus shares with ethnomethodology a commitment to naturally occurring interaction and the avoidance of premature, theoretical constructs. However, increasing evidence suggests that the basic observations of conversation analysis are not culturally limited, but rather are universal in relation to the basic organization of all language.[2]

1. For good overviews on conversation analysis, see J.C. Heritage, 'Current Developments in Conversation Analysis', in D. Roger and P. Bull (eds.), *Conversation: An Interdisciplinary Perspective* (Intercommunication, 3; Clevendon: Multilingual Matters, 1989), pp. 21-47; J.C. Heritage and J.M. Atkinson, 'Introduction', in *idem* (eds.), *Structures of Social Action: Studies in Conversation Analysis* (Cambridge: Cambridge University Press, 1984), pp. 1-15; S.C. Levinson, *Pragmatics* (Cambridge: Cambridge University Press, 1983), pp. 294-364. For an excellent discussion concerning the relationship between conversation analysis and ethnography, see M. Moerman, *Talking Culture: Ethnography and Conversation Analysis* (Philadelphia: University of Pennsylvania Press, 1988), pp. 1-18.

2. Early criticisms of the universalizing tendencies of conversation analysis were well founded because the earliest studies were limited primarily to English-speaking Americans. However, studies have now analyzed various unrelated languages and have concluded that these languages have the same basic organization identified in earlier studies. For example, on the Mayan language of Tzotzil, see J.B. Haviland, '"We Want to Borrow Your Mouth": Tzotzil Marital Squabbles', *Anthropological Linguistics* 30 (1988), pp. 395-447. On an Aboriginal language of Australia, see *idem*, 'Guugu Yimidhirr Brother-In-Law Language', *Language in Society* 8 (1979), pp. 365-93. On Thai, see Moerman, *Talking Culture*. On Arabic, see O.M. Hafez, 'Turn-Taking in Egyptian Arabic: Spontaneous Speech vs Drama Dialogue', *Journal of Pragmatics* 15 (1991), pp. 59-81. On Hebrew, see B. Spolsky and J. Walters,

One of the most basic observations of conversation analysis concerns preference organization. 'Preference organization' is a potentially misleading term, for it in no way refers to the 'preferences' of individual speakers, but rather to *linguistic structures*. 'Preference' here refers to the observation that language is organized in such a way that linguistically 'preferred' actions are encouraged, while linguistically 'dispreferred' actions are discouraged, thereby limiting conflict.[3] For example, students may verbally agree with a professor's assessment in a class lecture (the linguistically preferred response of agreement), even though they strongly disagree with it. Thus, the term 'preferred' does not refer to the students' opinions, but rather to the linguistic structure that is characteristic of agreements to assessments. Preference organization is best illustrated within the structure called adjacency pairs, such as assessment–agreement, question–answer, and invitation–refusal. Adjacency pairs, which are fundamental to conversational organization, can be characterized as follows:[4]

Adjacency pairs are sequences of two moves (verbal or non-verbal) that are:

(i)   adjacent or containing an insertion sequence (for example, a clarifying question between question and answer)

(ii)   produced by different individuals

(iii)   ordered as a first part and a second part

(iv)   typed, so that a particular first part has a range of second parts: those which are linguistically preferred and those which are linguistically dispreferred.

There are two types of adjacency pairs: (1) those with preferred second parts and (2) those with dispreferred second parts. Preferred seconds are

'Jewish Styles of Worship: A Conversational Analysis', *International Journal of the Sociology of Language* 56 (1985), pp. 51-65.

    For an excellent discussion on the universality of the basic observations of conversation analysis, see Moerman, *Talking Culture*, pp. 3-4.

3.   Heritage, 'Current Developments in Conversation Analysis', pp. 26-27.

4.   This characterization borrows heavily from Levinson's discussion of adjacency pairs (*Pragmatics*, pp. 303-307), which is in turn heavily influenced by that of E.A. Schlegloff and H. Sacks ('Opening Up Closings', *Semiotica* 7 [1973], pp. 289-327). Levinson's revision of Schlegloff and Sacks incorporated observations from other studies (e.g. M. Merritt, 'On Questions Following Questions in Service Encounters', *Language in Society* 5 [1976], pp. 315-57), thereby allowing for more complexity and flexibility. My revision takes into account the possibility of non-verbal elements in adjacency pairs.

generally brief utterances given without delay and are unmitigated.[5] The following adjacency pair (invitation–acceptance), taken from an actual conversation, illustrates well all of the characteristics of adjacency pairs with preferred seconds. Note that the slash marks and indentation indicate where the second utterance began, overlapping the first utterance.[6]

A: Why don't you come up and see me some//times?
B: I would like to.

Speaker A produces a first part which is followed by the adjacent second part of B (i, ii and iii). Speaker B's second part exhibits the characteristic of preferred seconds (iv). It occurs without delay (in fact, it overlaps the second part) and is brief and unmitigated. Thus we can see in this example all of the characteristics of adjacency pairs with preferred seconds.

In contrast, dispreferred seconds are far more elaborate; they are generally lengthy, given after a delay, and respond to the first part of the adjacency pair indirectly. Thus, dispreferred seconds generally contain the following four characteristics:[7] 1. a *delay*, 2. a *preface*, 3. an *account* for why the dispreferred response is given, and 4. a *declination component*, which is often indirect or mitigated. Some examples of different types of delays include pauses before delivery, the use of a preface and the initiation of insertion sequences (for example, a clarifying question between request and refusal). Some examples of prefaces include the use of announcers (for example, 'Well...' and 'Uh...'), token agreements before disagreements, appreciations before refusals, and qualifiers and hedges (for example, 'I don't know for sure, but...'). An account is an explanation for why the preferred response is not given and a declination component is generally an indirect or mitigated manner of expressing the dispreferred response. The following adjacency pair (invitation–refusal), taken from an actual conversation, illustrates well all of the characteristics of adjacency pairs with dispreferred seconds:

5.   Heritage, 'Current Developments in Conversation Analysis', p. 26; Levinson, *Pragmatics*, p. 333.

6.   J.M. Atkinson and P. Drew, *Order in Court: The Organization of Verbal Interaction in Judicial Settings* (London: Macmillan, 1979), p. 58, cited in Levinson, *Pragmatics*, p. 333. This and the following examples have been made more reader-friendly in that I have edited them, removing some of the standard transcription conventions used by conversation analysts.

7.   See P. Drew, 'Recalling Someone from the Past', in Roger and Bull (eds.), *Conversation*, p. 111; Heritage, 'Current Developments in Conversation Analysis', p. 26; Levinson, *Pragmatics*, pp. 334-35.

A: Uh, if you'd care to come and visit a little while this morning,
    I'll give you a cup of coffee.

B: (*pause*) Well, that's awfully sweet of you.
    I don't think I can make it this morning,
    (*pause*) Uhm, I'm running an ad in the paper and...and, uh, I
    have to stay near the phone.[8]

The invitation is refused. However, we can see how the refusal is
softened with the use of the characteristic elements of dispreferred
seconds. The refusal begins with a *delay* in the form of a pause and a
preface (the particle, 'Well') as well as an appropriate appreciation
('that's awfully sweet of you'). This preface introduces the mitigated
declination component ('I don't think I can make it this morning')
which is followed by the *account* ('I'm running an ad...and I have to
stay near the phone').

The two previous examples follow closely the paradigmatic structure of
adjacency pairs—that is, the first and second parts were actually adjacent.
However, the second part of an adjacency pair can occur after a sub-
stantial insertion sequence—that is, the first and second parts are not
immediately adjacent, but the adjacency pair structure is nevertheless
evident. The following example illustrates this possible complexity.[9] (The
following abbreviations are used: R = Request, Q = Question, Ans =
Answer.)

B: I ordered some paint from you uh a couple of weeks ago,
    some vermilion.

A: Yuh.

B: And I wanted to order some more. The name's Boyd.   (R1)

A: Yes. How many tubes would you like sir.   (Q1)

B: Uhm...what's the price now eh with V.A.T...
    Do you know? Eh?   (Q2)

A: Er I'll just work that out for you.   (Hold)

B: Thanks.   (Accept)

A: Three pounds nineteen a tube, sir.   (Ans2)

B: Three nineteen is it?   (Q3)

A: Yeah.   (Ans3)

B: Eh. Yes, uhm. Eh. Jus–justa think. That's what?
    Three nineteen?   (Q4)

8.   Atkinson and Drew, *Order in Court*, p. 58, cited in Levinson, *Pragmatics*,
pp. 333-34.
9.   Cited in Levinson, *Pragmatics*, p. 305.

A: Well, yeah. It's the thirty seven c.c.s.   (Ans4)
B: Er, hh. I'll tell you what. I'll just eh eh ring you
     back. I have to work out how many I'll need.
     Sorry, I did–, wasn't sure of the price you see.   (Account
                                                        for No Ans1)

This example demonstrates some of the complexity found in conversation that nevertheless contains adjacency pairs. First, the adjacency pair begun with the request (R1) is aborted in that speaker B later withdraws the request, disallowing the salesperson from completing the adjacency pair with the preferred response of acceptance. The abortion of this adjacency pair does not occur immediately but comes only after the insertion sequence begun by the question 'how many tubes?' (Q1) and closed by the dispreferred response of non-answer (Account). Even within this adjacency pair there are other adjacency pairs as insertion sequences concerning the price of the paint (Q2–Ans2, Q3–Ans3, Q4–Ans4) and within one of these adjacency pairs (Q2–Ans2) is an insertion sequence (Hold–Accept). The repeated questions of the cost of the paint (Q3, Q4) function as a delay and preface to the dispreferred second explicitly given in the account for the non-answer to Q1. Thus, here we have an example of the possible complexity of conversation that includes insertion sequences.

As we will see below, adjacency pairs are used in the Jonah narrative. Interestingly, the content within the adjacency pairs of the Jonah narrative, not only their structure, is significantly similar to adjacency pairs found in modern, English conversation.[10] The following table is taken from Levinson's discussion of preference organization:[11]

FIRST PARTS:	request	offer	assessment	question	blame
SECOND PARTS:					
Preferred:	acceptance	acceptance	agreement	expected answer	denial
Dispreferred:	refusal	refusal	disagreement	unexpected answer or non-answer	admission

(Note that the linguistically preferred response to blame is not admission, but denial: the blamer may have so much evidence of the accused's guilt that he or she expects the accused to admit his or her fault; however, this

---

10. This is not necessarily the case in all cultures.
11. *Pragmatics*, p. 336.

expectation does not correspond with the linguistically preferred response of denial. Even in such a case, the accused's admission would adhere to the linguistic characteristics of dispreferred seconds.) Throughout this work, terminology concerning adjacency pairs will consistently follow that given in this table; however, for the sake of stylistic variation sometimes this terminology will be given in verbal rather than nominal form (for example, 'refused' rather than 'refusal').

Below, we will see how knowledge of adjacency pairs and their constituent parts (especially those of dispreferred seconds: delay, preface, declination, account) can elucidate the Jonah narrative, its structure, and the reading process. However, before this knowledge can be used in the interpretation of the book of Jonah, the relationship between ordinary conversation and narrated conversation must be explicated in its similarities and differences.

2. *From 'Ordinary' Conversation to Narrated Conversation*

John Heritage has summarized the basic orientation of conversation analysis in four fundamental assumptions:

> (1) interaction is structurally organized; (2) contributions to interaction are both context-shaped and context-renewing; (3) these two properties inhere in the details of interaction so that no order of detail in conversational interaction can be dismissed a priori as disorderly, accidental or inter-actionally irrelevant; and (4) the study of social interaction in its details is best approached through the analysis of naturally occurring data.[12]

Given the emphasis upon interaction in the first three of these assumptions, it should be of no surprise that the fourth assumption is an insistence on naturally occurring conversation as data. There is also a presumption that 'ordinary' or 'everyday' conversation between peers is the foundational form of conversation upon which other forms of social interaction are based. In other words, in order to understand the use of language in institutionalized settings (for example, the courtroom), one must first understand how ordinary conversation is structured and then discern how the institutional setting impacts the use of language.

Conversation analytic studies can, thus, be roughly divided into two groups: (1) studies that focus on ordinary conversation and (2) studies that emphasize the impact of institutional settings upon conversation. The

---

12. 'Current Developments in Conversation Analysis', p. 22. See further his excellent discussion of each of these basic orientations.

first group consists of the studies that defined the basic observations of conversation analysis[13] as well as the more recent studies concerning non-lexical speech (such as 'mm hm') and non-vocal activities (such as nods). The second group consists of the more recent studies that have looked at the use of language in various settings in contrast to ordinary conversation—for example, courtrooms, classrooms, service encounters, news interviews, worship. These studies have not only helped to refine the basic observations of conversation analysis, but have also demonstrated how ordinary language can be transformed in institutionalized settings.

Although language has been analyzed in various institutionalized settings, conversation analysts have generally avoided written texts, which could be understood as another institutionalized setting for language. Recently, however, some analysts have studied written texts in relation to ordinary conversation. These studies take seriously the contention by J. Maxwell Atkinson, 'that an adequate understanding of how texts are produced and responded to may remain elusive so long as the issue is pursued without making close comparative reference to how talk works'.[14] They analyze written texts that are understood as closely resembling ordinary conversation and can be placed into two categories, according to the types of written texts analyzed and the different understandings of what 'closely resembling ordinary conversation' means. The first category concerns those groups of texts that contain direct address, involve turn-taking, and include more than one participant—for example, letters and public speeches.[15] The second category concerns

---

13. This group especially includes the work of Harvey Sacks and his earlier students (J. Maxwell Atkinson, Gail Jefferson, Anita M. Pomerantz, E.A. Schegloff). The seminal article in the field certainly belongs in this group—H. Sacks, E.A. Schegloff and G. Jefferson, 'A Simplest Systematics for the Organization of Turn-Taking for Conversation', *Language* 50 (1974), pp. 696-735.

14. J.M. Atkinson, 'Two Devices for Generating Audience Approval: A Comparative Study of Public Discourse and Texts', in K. Ehlich and H. van Riemsdijk (eds.), *Connectedness in Sentence, Discourse and Text* (Tilburg Studies in Language and Literature, 4; Tilburg: Tilburg University, 1983), pp. 199-236 (230). Cited in M. Mulkay, 'Agreement and Disagreement in Conversations and Letters', *Text* 5 (1985), pp. 201-27 (202); *idem*, 'Conversations and Texts', *Human Studies* 9 (1986), pp. 303-21 (303); *idem*, *The Word and the World: Explorations in the Form of Sociological Analysis* (London: Allen and Unwin, 1985), p. 79.

15. Atkinson analyzed political speeches and newspaper reports of these speeches ('Two Devices for Generating Audience Approval'). Mulkay has analyzed scientific

literature that similarly contains direct address, involves turn-taking, and includes more than one participant, however, this time in the form of different characters.[16] Both groups of studies have been successful in demonstrating how fruitful the basic observations of conversation analysis can be in interpreting written texts. With the intention of continuing on this path, this study analyses another literary work, the book of Jonah.

Although narrated conversation closely resembles ordinary conversation in some ways, there remain some significant differences, primarily related to the control over the narrative that an author (through the narrator) asserts.[17] Two such significant differences—those which particularly apply to the Jonah narrative—are the use of constructed dialogue and the omission of dialogue.

letters ('Agreements and Disagreements in Conversations and Letters', 'Conversations and Texts', *The Word and the World*) as well as prepared speeches given in Nobel ceremonies ('Conversations and Texts', *The Word and the World*).

16. For example, Campbell, 'A Lesson in Polite Compliance'; Gautam, 'Pinter's *The Caretaker*'; Toolan, 'Analysing Fictional Dialogue'; Wadman, '"Private Ejaculations"'.

17. See also R. Bishop, 'There's Nothing Natural About Natural Conversation: A Look at Dialogue in Fiction and Drama', *Oral Tradition* 6 (1991), pp. 58-78. Bishop emphasizes the differences between ordinary conversation (his 'everyday conversation') and narrated conversation (which he limits to 'the literary mode') concerning difficulties in making a transition from oral discourse to written discourse. However, his stark conclusion ('there's nothing natural about natural conversation… in [written] fiction and drama') needs to be moderated for two reasons: (1) The studies in oral and written discourse to which he refers are older studies in which oral and written discourse were generically viewed as polar opposites. More recent studies have emphasized that the relationship between the varieties of both oral and written discourse is best understood as a matrix of continua. A hastily written love letter, for example, may preserve some features more closely related to ordinary conversation than an oral classroom lecture. See D. Tannen, 'Oral/Literate Continuum in Discourse', in *idem* (ed.), *Spoken and Written Language: Exploring Orality and Literacy* (Advances in Discourse Processes, 9; Norwood: ABLEX, 1982), pp. 1-16. (2) The difference between ordinary conversation and narrated conversion is not only found between oral ordinary conversation (his 'everyday conversation') and (written) narrated conversation (his 'natural conversation'): it is also found within oral discourse itself. In fact, (oral) ordinary conversation may include (oral) narrated conversation. For further discussion of the use of narrated conversation within ordinary conversation, see the following sections.

Constructed Dialogue

What is often referred to as 'reported speech'—that is, speech that is attributed by conversants to someone other than themselves—is here referred to as 'constructed dialogue' because, as Deborah Tannen puts it,

> [r]eported speech is a misnomer…What is commonly referred to as reported speech or direct quotation in conversation is constructed dialogue, just as surely as is the dialogue created by fiction writers and playwrights.[18]

Tannen notes that the idea of reported speech or direct quotation in conversation is really a literate manner of viewing oral discourse for, when participants in ordinary conversation hear an utterance, they focus not on the words themselves, but rather on the meaning of the utterance.[19] That is, in the words of Hildyard and Olson,[20] hearers focus upon the 'speaker's meaning' whereas readers focus upon the 'sentence's meaning'; therefore, when asked to recall the meaning of an utterance, readers are more likely to reproduce the exact wording than hearers. Thus, the idea represented by the phrase 'reported speech' is the imposition of a literate mentality (with emphasis on the 'sentence's meaning') upon conversation and should be avoided. Rather, constructed dialogue better applies to conversation and breaks down the too rigid distinction between oral narrative and written narrative, both of which include constructed dialogue.

Tannen provides examples taken from actual conversations to prove her point, including the following:

> You can't say, 'Well Daddy I didn't HEAR you'.
> And then all the Americans said, 'Oh in that case, go ahead'.
> He was sending me out to get tools or whatever (imitates father), 'Go get this and it looks like this and the other'.[21]

These three examples are clearly not 'quotations'. The first provides an utterance that, according to the introducer ('You can't say'), was never

18. D. Tannen, 'Introducing Constructed Dialogue in Greek and American Conversational and Literary Narrative', in F. Coulmas (ed.), *Direct and Indirect Speech* (Berlin: Mouton, 1986), pp. 311-32 (311). See also Tannen, *Talking Voices*, pp. 98-133.

19. Tannen, 'Constructed Dialogue', p. 313.

20. A. Hildyard and D.R. Olson, 'On the Comprehension and Memory of Oral vs. Written Discourse', in Tannen (ed.), *Spoken and Written Language*, pp. 19-33.

21. Tannen, 'Constructed Dialogue', pp. 313-14.

spoken and should not be spoken in such circumstances. The second implies that 'all the Americans' said the same thing in unison, in good (but unlikely) choral fashion. The third uses vague speech as a way of summarizing all the father's requests, each one of which certainly would have been more specific.[22] Thus, with these examples and others, Tannen demonstrates that 'reported speech is constructed dialogue'.[23]

Although reported speech is a misnomer, the two forms often discussed as reported speech still apply to constructed dialogue. Speech within constructed dialogue can take two primary forms: direct speech or indirect speech.[24] That is, the narrator can 'quote' the words attributed to a character (direct speech) or can paraphrase these same words (indirect speech). A narrator may even go one step further by omitting the speaker's words altogether and simply reporting the performative consequences of the communicative act (what I will call 'reported consequences'). These three options—direct speech, indirect speech, reported consequences—are respectively illustrated below in the second part of what is essentially the same adjacency pair of request/acceptance:

Request:	The parent said, 'Please, go to the store for me'.
Acceptance:	The child said, 'OK, I will go'.
	The child said that she would go.
	The child went.

When reading the second parts in the form of direct speech and indirect speech, the reader expects that the child will do what she agreed to do and this completed action would probably be reported by the narrator ('And she went'). When reading the reported consequences, the reader has been told by the narrator that the child performed the preferred response and the question as to whether or not the child verbalized this response would probably not even arise. Of course, these same three

22. Of Tannen's categories, those to which the last two examples belong—choral speech and vague references—are the most relevant to the study of the Jonah narrative. Choral speech is repeatedly used in the presentation of the sailors (Jon. 1.7-16), and vague speech is found the Lord's requests of Jonah (1.2; 3.2) and Jonah's oracle (3.4). See 'Omitted Dialogue' in Chapter 3 §4.

23. Tannen, 'Constructed Dialogue', pp. 313-14. Tannen's examples include other categories as well: 'illustrations of a general phenomenon', 'a line of dialogue that is constructed not by the storyteller but by a listener', reports of the inner thoughts of self or others and the fading of an indirect quote into a direct quote.

24. For an excellent discussion of direct and indirect speech, see F. Coulmas, 'Reported Speech: Some General Issues', in Coulmas (ed.), *Direct and Indirect Speech*, pp. 1-28.

options obtain for the first part of any adjacency pair as well. Hence, a narrator has a variety of options for expressing conversation while still preserving the basic characteristics of adjacency pairs.

Omitted Dialogue
As was seen above, a narrator not only constructs dialogue but may also withhold dialogue from the readers by simply reporting the consequences. In the example of reported consequences above, this omission is inconsequential, since the child performed the request made by the parent. However, a narrator may withhold information that could prove to be very significant in the development of the narrative in order to manipulate the reader's interest and provide emphasis to this information when it is presented out of its 'natural' sequential order.[25] Thus, constructed dialogue that is nevertheless *not* reported by the narrator may prove as significant as well as what *is* reported, and in some cases even more significant.

Constructed Dialogue and Adjacency Pairs
As we have just seen, a narrator has various possible ways to represent characters' conversations—direct speech, indirect speech and reported consequences—or may choose to omit certain aspects of the characters' speech. What are the effects of these various narrative strategies on preference organization when one moves from ordinary conversation to narrated conversation? In other words, how do these various narrative strategies relate to preference organization, especially adjacency pairs? These questions cannot be answered with any one description of this relationship, for there are probably other factors involved (for example, characterization, oral versus written discourse) which also influence this relationship.[26] However, I think that some general comments can be

---

25. See 'Omitted Dialogue' and 'Constructed Dialogue and Adjacency Pairs' in Chapter 3 §4.

26. In her dissertation, Cynthia L. Miller discusses the relationship of adjacency pairs to the three narrative strategies discussed here ('Reported Speech in Biblical and Epigraphic Hebrew'; see especially Chapter 5, 'Reported Speech in Conversation and Narrative'). Her dissertation is clearly the most thorough work on constructed dialogue in biblical Hebrew (Genesis–2 Kings) from a linguistic perspective. Her work emphasizes the descriptive task of constructed dialogue in Hebrew. The following comments are more theoretical and, to my knowledge, are without precedent; therefore, they are certainly preliminary and probably will require revision when other factors (for example, oral versus written discourse) are taken into account.

made. Below, I submit some suggestions concerning the relationship of these strategies in narratives with adjacency pairs. First, I discuss first parts and, then, preferred and dispreferred seconds respectively.

First parts not only begin adjacency pairs, but they define the range of possible second parts. For example, a request initiates an adjacency pair of either request–acceptance or request–refusal. Since first parts play such a defining role, it may be more probable that they occur within direct speech, which is closer to ordinary conversation in that it purports to 'quote' speech.

Given that preferred seconds are generally brief and unmitigated, they may be more likely to appear in reported consequences. This can be seen in a closer analysis of the example given above:

Request:	The parent said, 'Please, go to the store for me'.
Acceptance:	The child said, 'OK, I will go'.
	The child said that she would go.
	The child went.

As suggested above, the reader of the direct and indirect speech would expect the child to perform the request and, most likely, the narrator would report this performance similar to that of the reported consequences. Therefore, the complete narrative portrayal of the second part of this adjacency pair would probably be better represented by the following possibilities:

Direct speech:	The child said, 'OK, I will go'. And she went.
Indirect speech:	The child said that she would go and she did.
Reported consequences:	The child went.

As is now evident, we can discern a continuum based on brevity with reported consequences at one pole (briefest) and direct speech at the other (lengthiest) and indirect speech between the two, but much closer to direct speech. Hence, if reported consequences tend to be the most economical way of completing an adjacency pair, preferred seconds in written narrative may gravitate toward reported consequences.

But what about dispreferred seconds? Before trying to answer this question, which we will see in a moment is much more difficult, the above example has been modified to include a dispreferred second in the form of direct speech, indirect speech, and reported consequence, respectively. Once again we see a similar continuum based on brevity.

Request:	The parent said, 'Please, go to the store for me'.
Refusal:	The child said, 'Oh Dad, I want to go outside to play'.
	So she went outside and played.
	The child said that she would rather go outside to play,
	so she did.
	But the child went outside to play.

I suggest that there are two opposing tendencies at work here.

First, dispreferred seconds tend to be longer and more developed than preferred seconds; that is, they characteristically contain a delay, a preface, an account and a declination component. In order to include all of these characteristic elements, dispreferred seconds may gravitate towards the longer, direct speech in which delays and prefaces are more likely to be found. For example, delays and prefaces like the 'Oh Dad' in the above example are omitted in all cases of indirect speech and reported consequences. Thus, a narrator who wants to fully develop a dispreferred second with all of its characteristic elements, will necessarily choose direct speech as the medium to communicate this.

Second, dispreferred seconds are generally mitigated and indirect; that is, all of the characteristic elements of dispreferred seconds serve the purpose of mitigating the dispreferred response by easing into the declination component. The declination component generally comes after a delay and preface, which already are communicating to the hearer/reader that the utterance is a dispreferred second. Then an account is given for why the preferred response is not being given, thereby also indirectly implying that the utterance is a dispreferred second. All of this—delay, preface and account—generally precedes the most direct (yet still mitigated) characteristic of dispreferred seconds, the declination component. Thus, the very structure of dispreferred seconds tends to mitigate any possible conflict that could arise. Given this tendency, a narrator who wants to mitigate a report of a dispreferred second, may tend to 'hide' the character's own words by the use of reported consequences. In other words, narrators have a technique by which they can mitigate a dispreferred second more than participants in ordinary conversation: they can gloss over the dispreferred response altogether and simply report its consequences.

How do these narrative strategies relate to dispreferred seconds? As we have just seen, no one answer can be given to this question because the nature of dispreferred seconds creates two opposing tendencies. On the one hand, dispreferred seconds tend to be longer and more developed than preferred seconds; therefore, they may gravitate towards the longer, direct speech. On the other hand, dispreferred seconds are generally indirect and mitigated; therefore, they may gravitate towards reported consequences because the dispreferred second would be mitigated by the omission of the character's own words. Given these two opposing tendencies, narrators may choose either to develop the dispreferred second more fully in direct speech or to mitigate the dispreferred second in reported consequences or to combine to some extent both tendencies in the use of indirect speech. Thus, dispreferred seconds may show considerably more variation in narrative than preferred seconds.

In summary, some suggestions have been made above as to the possible relationships between the various elements of adjacency pairs and the three narrative strategies of direct speech, indirect speech and reported consequences: (1) first parts may gravitate towards direct speech, since they play a defining role in the adjacency pair; (2) preferred seconds may gravitate towards reported consequences, since both preferred seconds and reported consequences tend to maximize economy; (3) dispreferred seconds gravitate toward two opposing poles—they may gravitate either towards direct speech in order to permit elaboration or towards reported consequences in order to further mitigation.[27]

3. Summary[28]

The structure of ordinary conversation (that is, naturally occurring conversation without constructed dialogue) consists of adjacency pairs. When conversations are placed within narration, these conversations are also formed of adjacency pairs; however, their constituent parts may appear in a somewhat different form or they may be omitted altogether. That is, narrated conversation, as constructed dialogue, may appear to be just like ordinary conversation in the form of direct speech, but it differs in the forms of indirect speech and reported consequences and in its ability to omit dialogue. Hence, narrated conversation is structured in the same way as ordinary conversation, even though the parts of the adjacency pairs may be presented in somewhat different forms or not presented at all.

But what of the changes from oral, narrated conversation to written,

---

27. In the following analysis of the Jonah narrative, these suggestions find support. See especially the section 'Constructed Dialogue and Adjacency Pairs' in Chapter 3 §4.

28. See also Toolan, *Stylistics of Fiction*, pp. 273-77.

narrated conversation? Certainly, written narrative cannot fully represent various aspects of oral narrative. For example, written narrative cannot fully represent the performance qualities of oral narratives such as intonation and prosody. However, it can compensate, to some degree, for this difference, as is evident in the variety of expressive verbs and other modifiers found in written narrative in contrast to oral narrative.[29] In addition, written narrative can take advantage of its medium in that its audience is not immediately present, which allows for greater integration through 'hidden' revisions. That is, writers have the ability to 'create maximum effect with the fewest words'.[30] However, despite these differences, written narrative still preserves the different strategies used in oral narrative for constructed dialogue: direct speech, indirect speech, reported consequences and omitted dialogue. Written narrative is also similar to oral narrative in that it also depends on a sense of involvement; it involves the reader in its very being.[31]

> It is for this reason that literary discourse (short stories, poems, novels), rather than being most different from ordinary conversation, is, in fact, most similar to it: those features which are thought quintessentially literary (repetition of sounds and words, syntactic parallelism, rhythm) are all basic to ordinary spontaneous conversation.[32]

29. See Tannen, 'Constructed Dialogue', pp. 314-24.

30. Tannen, 'Oral and Literate Strategies in Spoken and Written Narratives', p. 2. See also W.L. Chafe, 'Integration and Involvement in Speaking, Writing, and Oral Literature', in Tannen (ed.), *Spoken and Written Language*, pp. 35-53.

31. See Tannen, 'Oral and Literate Strategies in Spoken and Written Narratives'. See also my discussion of Wolfgang Iser's understanding of the reading process at the beginning of Chapter 4.

32. Tannen, 'Oral and Literate Strategies in Spoken and Written Narratives', p. 2. See also Tannen, 'Relative Focus on Involvement in Oral and Written Discourse', pp. 137-40; Tannen, *Talking Voices*; L. Polanyi, 'Literary Complexity in Everyday Storytelling', in Tannen (ed.), *Spoken and Written Language*, pp. 155-70. For a brief, yet excellent, review of different stances of scholars from different fields towards the relationship between 'fictional and natural language', see N. Stucky, 'Unnatural Acts: Performing Natural Conversation', *Literature in Performance* 8 (1988), pp. 28-39 (29-30).

Tannen's conclusion is similar to that of (the early) Stanley Fish, who wrote,

> what philosophical semantics and the philosophy of speech acts are telling us is that ordinary language is extraordinary because at its heart is precisely the realm of values, intentions, and purposes which is often assumed to be the exclusive property of literature ('How Ordinary is Ordinary Language?', *New Literary History* 5 [1973], pp. 41-54 [51]).

Given these similarities between ordinary conversation and written narratives, it should be of no surprise that the foundational devices of adjacency pairs make the transition from ordinary conversation to conversations in oral narrative to conversations in written narrative, even though the narrated forms of conversation (direct speech, indirect speech, reported consequences, omitted dialogue) allow some variety of presentation.

In the following commentary on the book of Jonah, both constructed dialogue and omitted dialogue will be analyzed. This analysis will once again demonstrate the effectiveness of using the basic observations of conversation analysis as a paradigm for interpreting written texts as well as provide a fresh reading of the Jonah narrative.

However, Tannen would probably disagree with the implications Fish further drew:

> Literature is still a category, but it is an open category, not definable by fictionality, or by a disregard of propositional truth, or by a statistical predominance of tropes and figures, but simply by what we decide to put into it. The difference lies not in the language, but in ourselves ('How Ordinary is Ordinary Language?', p. 52).

She would probably disagree, because she still notes (in my opinion, correctly) that differences remain between literature (at least that which is written) and ordinary conversation. For example, see Tannen, 'Relative Focus on Involvement in Oral and Written Discourse', pp. 130-32.

Chapter 2

COMMENTARY ON THE BOOK OF JONAH FROM A CONVERSATION ANALYTIC PERSPECTIVE

The following commentary does not attempt to deal with all of the interpretive issues usually found in commentaries on biblical books—for example, the textual variants and history, prose versus poetry, composition, date, provenance. This does not, however, imply that these issues have not been given serious consideration in the preparation for this work; rather, my preparation has led me to very similar conclusions concerning composition and date as those of Jack Sasson, whose Anchor Bible commentary was clearly the most carefully argued and thorough commentary on the book of Jonah available at this writing. Like Sasson, I believe that there probably lie various oral and/or written traditions about Jonah (and possibly other ancient figures) behind the present work;[1] however, these traditions were consciously brought together by a skilled author to form the present narrative, which exhibits a superb literary unity. This skilled author was a Jew writing to a Jewish audience probably sometime during the post-exilic period (5th–3rd centuries BCE).[2]

The format used below is as follows: a new translation of the Hebrew text is followed by commentary upon that text. The text is divided into sections according to my own understanding of the structure of the narrated conversations. Versification follows that of the Hebrew text. Historical information is given only when it is deemed necessary for fully understanding the basic meaning of the text. Following the commentary are outlines summarizing the adjacency pairs that constitute the Jonah narrative.

1. See Sasson, *Jonah*, pp. 16-19.
2. See Sasson, *Jonah*, pp. 20-27.

1. *Translation*[3]

1.1 Now it once happened that[4] the word of the Lord came to Jonah, son of Amittai: **2** 'Get up. Go to Nineveh, that large city,[5] and call out against it,[6] for their wickedness is obvious to me.' **3** Jonah, instead, got up to escape to Tarshish from the Lord; and he went down to Jaffa and found a ship which had just come[7] from Tarshish. He paid its hire and sailed in it[8] to accompany them towards Tarshish away from the Lord.

4 The Lord, however, cast mighty winds towards the sea so that a mighty storm raged upon it. When the ship threatened to break up,[9] **5** the sailors became afraid and each prayed to his own gods. Then they cast the cargo which was on the ship into the sea in order to lighten it. Meanwhile,[10] Jonah went down into the vessel's hold, laid down, and went to sleep. **6** Then the helmsman approached him to ask, 'How could you sleep? Get up! Call out to your god! Perhaps that god[11] will

---

3.   As stated above, Sasson's commentary is the most thorough and careful study of Jonah published. As such, it contains most of the significant data relating to the translation of the Hebrew text. The following translation still draws substantially from Sasson's translation and notes, even where it disagrees with Sasson's actual rendering. Like Sasson, the Hebrew text used for this translation is *Biblia hebraica stuttgartensia*.

4.   Reading ויהי as opening a story, as with Josh. 1.1; Judg. 1.1; 13.2; 17.1; 19.1; 1 Sam. 1.1; 2 Sam. 1.1; Ruth 1.1; Est. 1.1. See H.W. Wolff, *Obadiah and Jonah: A Commentary* (trans. M. Kohl; Minneapolis: Augsburg, 1986), p. 95.

5.   See Sasson, *Jonah*, pp. 70-71.

6.   Sasson's various nuanced translations of קרא are excellent (*Jonah*, pp. 72-75), but are not followed here in order to show to the English reader the repetition of the word.

7.   See Sasson, *Jonah*, pp. 66, 82-83. Sasson notes that בא clearly means a ship's arrival in 2 Chron. 9.21 and, thus, convincingly argues that it should be translated 'had come from'.

8.   Reading וירד בה as an idiom meaning 'sail in it', rather than the usual translation of 'go down into it/board it'. See T. Pope, 'Notes on Selected Exegetical Issues in Jonah', *Notes in Translation* 3 (1989), pp. 45-50 (45).

9.   Reading ויהי as a temporal clause modifying the action which begins in v. 5. See Wolff, *Obadiah and Jonah*, pp. 105-106.

10.   E.R. Hope, 'Pragmatics, Exegesis and Translation', in P.C. Stine (ed.), *Issues in Bible Translation* (UBS Monograph Series, 3; New York: United Bible Societies, 1988), pp. 113-28 (120).

11.   Reading האלהים with the article functioning like a demonstrative pronoun. This reading is given as a possibility in Sasson, *Jonah*, p. 104.

intercede[12] on our behalf so that we may not perish.'

7 And they said to one another, 'Come! Let's cast lots so that we might know on whose account this evil has come to us.' Then they cast the lots and the lot fell on Jonah. 8 Then they said to Jonah, 'Tell us, you on whose account this evil has come to us: What is your mission[13] and where are you coming from? What is your homeland and from what people do you come?' 9 And he said to them, 'I am a Hebrew, and the Lord, the God of Heaven, I worship—he who made the sea and the dry land.' 10 Then the men were filled with the most dreadful fear and they said to him, 'What is this that you have done!?' for the men now knew[14] that he was fleeing from the Lord, because he had told them.

11 And they said to him, 'What must we do to you for the sea to calm down for us?' for the sea was becoming increasingly violent.[15] 12 And he said to them, 'Pick me up and cast me into the sea. Then the sea will calm down for you for I know that it is on my own account that this mighty storm rages against you.' 13 Nonetheless, the men rowed hard in order to reach dry land. But they were unable to, for the sea became increasingly violent against them. 14 Then they called out to the Lord, 'Please, O Lord, do not let us perish because of the life of this man, and do not hold us accountable for innocent blood, for you are the Lord and whatever pleases you, you do.' 15 Then they picked up Jonah and cast him into the sea and the sea ceased its raging.

16 Then the men were filled with the most dreadful fear of the Lord and they offered sacrifices to the Lord and made vows.

2.1 Then the Lord appointed a large fish to swallow Jonah. And Jonah was in the belly of the fish for three days and three nights.

2 And Jonah prayed to the Lord, his God, from the belly of the fish,

> 3 'I call out, in my trouble, to the Lord
>   and he answers me.
> From the belly of Sheol I plead;
>   you hear my voice.

---

12. See Sasson, *Jonah*, pp. 89, 104.

13. Or 'occupation'. See Sasson, *Jonah*, p. 114.

14. See Hope, 'Pragmatics, Exegesis and Translation', p. 126.

15. Sasson includes the phrase 'for the sea…violent' as part of the sailors' speech (*Jonah*, p. 108, 123-24). Wolff excludes this phrase from the sailors' speech (*Obadiah and Jonah*, p. 11). Although the Hebrew allows equally for both readings, I have chosen to exclude the phrase to emphasize the urgency expressed in the sailors' comments.

[4] And you cast me into the depths, into the heart of the seas,
  and the current engulfs me;
  all of your billows and waves sweep over me.
[5] So I say, "I am driven from your sight,
  may I yet continue to gaze toward your holy sanctuary?"
[6] Waters envelop me up to my neck,
  the abyss engulfs me;
  kelp clings to my head.
[7] To the base of the mountains, I sink.
The netherworld, its bars, about me are there forever;
  but you lift me up from the Pit alive, O Lord, my God.
[8] Even as my life ebbs away,
  the Lord, I remember.
Then my prayer reaches you at your holy sanctuary.
[9] Those who hold to empty faiths, their hope for mercy[16] they
      give up.
[10] But, I, with a grateful voice, sacrifice to you;
  that which I vow, I shall fulfill.
  Deliverance belongs to the Lord.'

[11] Then the Lord spoke to the fish and it vomited Jonah upon dry land.

[3.1] Now it happened that the word of the Lord came to Jonah a second time, [2] 'Get up. Go to Nineveh, that large city, and call out to it whatever I command you.' [3] Then Jonah got up and went to Nineveh just as the Lord had commanded. And Nineveh was a large city, belonging to God,[17] a three days' walk across. [4] After Jonah had hardly[18] gone into the city a day's journey, he called out, 'Forty days more, and Nineveh will overturn.'

[5] Then the people of Nineveh believed in God; they called for a fast; and they put on sackcloth, from the greatest to the least. [6] When word reached the king of Nineveh, he got up from his throne and stripped off his royal mantle[19] and put on sackcloth and sat down in ashes. [7] Then he proclaimed, 'In Nineveh; on the authority of the king and his counselors: People and beasts—herds and flocks—must not taste anything, must

16. On the difficulties associated with translating חסדם see Sasson, *Jonah*, pp. 197-99. Sasson's translation is followed here.

17. On the difficulty of translating לאלהים in this phrase, see Sasson, *Jonah*, pp. 227-30.

18. See Sasson, *Jonah*, pp. 231-32, 236.

19. See Sasson, *Jonah*, pp. 240, 250.

not graze, and even water, they must not drink. [8] Rather, they must wrap themselves in sackcloth—people and beasts alike—and must call out to God with fervor. Each person must turn from his evil way and from the violence which is in their hands. [9] Who knows? Perhaps that god[20] will change his mind and turn away from his anger, so that we may not perish.'

[10] When God saw their deeds, that they had turned away from their evil ways, God changed his mind concerning the evil which he had commanded against them and did not do it.

[4.1] But this[21] was terribly upsetting to Jonah and he was angry. [2] And he interjected[22] to the Lord, 'Oh Lord![23] Is this not what I said while I was still in my homeland? Therefore, I hastened to flee to Tarshish for I knew that you are a gracious and compassionate God, slow to anger and extremely benevolent, who would change his mind concerning the evil. [3] Now, O Lord, take my life from me, for it is better that I die than live.' [4] Then the Lord said, 'Is it good for you to be so angry?' [5] But Jonah went from the city and sat down east of the city. And there he made for himself a booth and he sat down under its shade until he could see what would happen in the city.

[6] And the Lord God appointed a *qiqayon* plant[24] to grow up over Jonah so that there would be shade over his head in order to deliver him from his distress. And Jonah rejoiced exceedingly over the *qiqayon* plant. [7] Then God appointed a worm, at daybreak of the next day. It

---

20. Reading האלהים with the article functioning like a demonstrative pronoun. See also 1.6.

21. The insertion of 'this' as the implied subject reflects Sasson's translation (*Jonah*, p. 273); however, Sasson understands the antecedent to be the Ninevites' repentance and the Lord's changing his mind whereas I understand it to be the Lord's coercion of Jonah to fulfill his mission.

22. Rather than translating ויתפלל as 'prayed', the more basic meaning of the root—'intercede, interpose'—is maintained in my translation. Contra Sasson, who does not see Jonah as angry and protesting to God, but rather as 'dejected' and pleading to God in prayer (*Jonah*, pp. 270, 274-86).

23. אנא/אנה can be used in a petition meaning 'please' or in a complaint meaning 'oh, alas' (see Exod. 32.31). Jonah's use of אנה here contrasts with its earlier use in the sailors' prayer in 1.14.

24. The Hebrew has only the noun *qiqayon* which probably refers to a particular plant species. Having no way to identify this species (see Sasson, *Jonah*, pp. 291-92), I have chosen to follow Sasson's translation *'qiqayon* plant', which unfortunately might imply that *qiqayon* is an adjective. However, a generic translation of 'plant' would not represent the specificity of the Hebrew noun.

attacked the *qiqayon* plant so that it withered. [8] At sunrise, God appointed a fierce[25] east wind. Then the sun attacked Jonah's head and he swooned. And he asked that he might die, 'It is better that I die than live.'

[9] Then God said to Jonah, 'Is it good for you to be so angry on account of the *qiqayon* plant?' Then he said, 'It is good that I am angry enough to die.' [10] Then the Lord said, 'You yourself were fretting over the *qiqayon* plant, for which you neither toiled nor cultivated, which came up one night and perished the next night. [11] Yet I should not have compassion on Nineveh, that large city, which has in it more than one hundred and twenty thousand people, who do not know their right hand from their left hand, and many cattle as well?'

2. *Commentary*

[1.1] Now it once happened that the word of the Lord came to Jonah, son of Amittai: [2] 'Get up. Go to Nineveh, that large city, and call out against it, for their wickedness is obvious to me.'

The book of Jonah begins in a similar way to other prophetic books: a superscription is given, containing the prophet's name and patronym[26] and lending authority to the following material.[27] Here, the superscription introduces the Lord's commission to Jonah to go to Nineveh, the capital of Israel's enemies, the Assyrians, and to prophesy doom and destruction. This request is the first part of an adjacency pair, which would normally be followed by Jonah's verbal acceptance or refusal.

[3] Jonah, instead, got up to escape to Tarshish from the Lord; and he went down to Jaffa and found a ship which had just come from Tarshish. He paid its hire and sailed in it to accompany them towards Tarshish away from the Lord.

Here the narrator does not refer to any verbal response of Jonah in either direct or indirect speech. Rather, the narrator simply reports the

25. Sasson, *Jonah*, pp. 300, 303-304. Since the narrative clearly implies that God is seeking to punish Jonah with the sun, and since the plant has already withered, Sasson interprets the *fierce east wind* as God's effort to destroy Jonah's booth, thereby removing the only remaining shade from Jonah.

26. See Hos. 1.1; Joel 1.1; Zeph. 1.1. Without the patronym, see Jer. 1.4; Mic. 1.1; Hag. 1.1; Mal. 1.1.

27. See G.M. Tucker, 'Prophetic Superscriptions and the Growth of the Canon', in G.W. Coats and B.O. Long (eds.), *Canon and Authority* (Philadelphia: Fortress Press, 1977), pp. 56-70.

consequences of the request: Jonah refuses and seeks to escape from the Lord by traveling in the opposite direction, to Tarshish. Because no speech is reported, the reader wonders if Jonah responded verbally and, if so, what his refusal was. In other words, what kind of delay, preface, account and declination component did Jonah use in his refusal? Later in the narrative (4.2) we learn from Jonah himself that he 'said' something at this time, but at this point the first-time reader can only guess. We may also wonder what the conversation was between Jonah and the sailors in their effort to reach an agreeable business deal, but whatever happened it eventually involved the sailors' acceptance of Jonah's request for passage.

> [4] The Lord, however, cast mighty winds towards the sea so that a mighty storm raged upon it.

When a request is refused, the refusal itself may elicit a response such as betrayal or anger. Jonah's refusal elicits such a response from the Lord.[28] The Lord, the Creator, controls nature so as to express his rage against Jonah, as if he were saying, 'I am angry with your disobedience, Jonah.'

> When the ship threatened to break up, [5] the sailors became afraid and each prayed to his own gods. Then they cast the cargo which was on the ship into the sea in order to lighten it. Meanwhile, Jonah went down into the vessel's hold, laid down, and went to sleep.

The Lord's anger in the form of a mighty storm elicits responses from all of those on the ship. The ship's crew fear for their lives, pray for (request) deliverance, and start dumping the cargo overboard; they act as if they understand that a god or the gods are angry at them. (The reader 'knows' that the sailors' prayers to their *own gods* will meet with the dispreferred response of refusal by non-action because the Lord, not some other gods, was responsible for the storm [1.4].) Jonah, in contrast, seems to ignore the storm and its message by going to sleep—that is, he is still trying to flee from the Lord's power.

> [6] Then the helmsman approached him to ask, 'How could you sleep? Get up! Call out to your god! Perhaps that god will intercede on our behalf so that we may not perish.'

28. A.B.M. Tsui ('Beyond the Adjacency Pair', *Language in Society* 18 [1989], pp. 545-64) calls the structure for such sequences a 'three-part exchange' with the third part called the 'follow-up move'. I continue to use the terminology associated with 'adjacency pairs' and call such third parts 'consequences'.

Jonah's bizarre behavior provokes the helmsman to confront him and issue urgent requests for Jonah to get up and to pray to his god as the others are doing. As a good polytheist, the helmsman is covering his bets by insuring that all on board are praying to their own gods in hopes to appease whichever god is causing the storm. Jonah's response is once again not explicitly given. However, the narrative provides some clues to how Jonah responded to the helmsman's requests. First, the next verse presupposes that Jonah has gathered with the sailors, so he must have gotten up from his sleep. Second, since the prayers of the sailors are reported (1.5, 14-16), the absence of a report concerning Jonah's praying on board the ship probably indicates that the reader is expected to assume that he did not pray. This is especially the case since a prayer attributed to him occurs later, from the belly of the fish (2.3-10). Thus, Jonah probably responded differently to the two requests. To the first request, his getting up was itself a preferred response (acceptance). To the second request, he passively gave a dispreferred response (refusal). The helmsman's two requests are followed by an assessment, which ironically suggests that Jonah's god has the power to save them.

> [7] And they said to one another, 'Come! Let's cast lots so that we might know on whose account this evil has come to us.' Then they cast the lots and the lot fell on Jonah.

In this dense verse, two adjacency pairs are evident. First, the sailors say to one another, in choral speech,[29] *'Come! Let's cast lots'*. This request is accepted, as is reported in the narrated action: *Then they cast the lots*. Second, the casting of lots itself is, from the pagans' point of view, an adjacency pair. That is, when they cast the lots, they are questioning the gods and the gods answer the question by how the lots fall.[30] Whether or not the reader believes in the practice of lot-casting, its outcome, in this case at least, is validated, for the lot properly falls on Jonah.

> [8] Then they said to Jonah, 'Tell us, you on whose account this evil has come to us: What is your mission and where are you coming from? What is your homeland and from what people do you come?' [9] And he said to them, 'I am a Hebrew, and the Lord, the God of Heaven, I worship—he who made the sea and the dry land.' [10] Then the men were filled with the most dreadful fear and they said to him, 'What is this that you have

---

29. Note that all of the sailors' dialogue is in the form of choral speech.

30. For an excellent discussion of lot-casting in the Hebrew Bible, see Sasson, *Jonah*, pp. 108-110.

done!?', for the men now knew that he was fleeing from the Lord, because he had told them.

The answer given by the gods through the lot-casting is the first part of an adjacency pair awaiting a response by the sailors. The sailors agree with the answer/assessment given, as is evident in their address to Jonah: '...*you on whose account this evil has come to us*'. Hence, they ask Jonah for more information, posing four questions: (1) '*What is your mission?*' (2) '*Where are you coming from?*' (3) '*What is your homeland?*' (4) '*From what people do you come?*' Jonah's response as it is given in his own words—'*I am a Hebrew, and the Lord, the God of Heaven, I worship*'—only explicitly answers the fourth question concerning ethnicity. However, the phrase *for the men now knew that he was fleeing from the Lord, because he had told them* implies that Jonah answered their questions more fully, but the narrator chose to omit his fuller response.[31] This phrase also implies that Jonah admitted his guilt. The sailors' response to Jonah's full answer/admission is one of shock and horror.

> **11** And they said to him, 'What must we do to you for the sea to calm down for us?' for the sea was becoming increasingly violent.

Out of their fear, the sailors question the prophet Jonah as to what they must do to satisfy the Lord's anger and save themselves.

> **12** And he said to them, 'Pick me up and cast me into the sea. Then the sea will calm down for you for I know that it is on my own account that this mighty storm rages against you.'

Jonah responds to their question with an answer, which can be understood as one element of three different adjacency pairs. (1) The answer is a request (the first part of an adjacency pair)—'*Pick me up and cast me into the sea.*' (2) It is also an assessment (first part) of what the consequences of carrying out his request would be—'*Then the sea will calm down for you.*' (3) It is also a repetition of his admission of guilt (dispreferred second)—'*...it is on my own account...*' (see 1.10).

> **13** Nonetheless, the men rowed hard in order to reach dry land. But they were unable to, for the sea became increasingly violent against them.

Here, we have the same reported reaction by the sailors to Jonah's request as we had in 1.3 by Jonah to the Lord's request. That is, the

31. For similar interpretations of the dialogue in 1.9-11, see Sasson, *Jonah*, pp. 119-22, 126; Wolff, *Obadiah and Jonah*, pp. 115-17.

request is not followed with the dispreferred second of the adjacency pair in the characters' own words; rather, the narrator simply reports the refusal in the characters' actions. The sailors do not throw Jonah overboard, but instead row harder, trying to fight the storm and, for that matter, the Lord's will. The question now arises as to why the sailors refused Jonah's request. In contrast to Jonah's earlier refusal (1.3) and his own account (which we still have not reached [4.2]), the narrator implicitly gives the sailors' account for their refusal in the following words.

> [14] Then they called out to the Lord, 'Please, O Lord, do not let us perish because of the life of this man, and do not hold us accountable for innocent blood, for you are the Lord and whatever pleases you, you do.'

The sailors' prayer contains two different appeals to the Lord. They request that the Lord not punish them further, firstly, because of Jonah's disobedient flight (*'do not let us perish because...of this man'*) and, secondly, for their forthcoming casting of Jonah overboard (*'do not hold us accountable... '*).[32] The second appeal in this prayer implies that they did not immediately accept Jonah's request to be thrown overboard, out of their fear that the Lord might punish them further. In other words, the sailors' refusal was, from their perspective, a pious response to their uncertainty about the Lord's will. Also, their implied account is itself a pious request to the Lord—*'do not hold us accountable...'*

> [15] Then they picked up Jonah and cast him into the sea and the sea ceased its raging.

The action narrated in this verse completes various adjacency pairs, all with preferred seconds. (1) The sailors accept Jonah's request and (2) they agree with his assessment that this acceptance will save them. (3) The sea's ceasing also implies that the Lord accepted the sailors' requests not to punish them further for Jonah's disobedience or their casting him overboard.

> [16] Then the men were filled with the most dreadful fear of the Lord and they offered sacrifices to the Lord and made vows.

In response to all they had learned from Jonah and from seeing the Lord's control of nature with their own eyes, the sailors now implicitly agree with Jonah's assessment that the Lord is *'the God of Heaven... who made the sea and the dry land'* (1.9) and offer sacrifices to the

---

32   Sasson, *Jonah*, p. 132.

Lord and make vows to offer sacrifices later.[33] (Since this is the last we hear of the sailors, we can only guess what happened to them. My guess is that the Lord accepted their offering and they reached their destination safely.)

> [2.1] Then the Lord appointed a large fish to swallow Jonah. And Jonah was in the belly of the fish for three days and three nights.

Continuing the theme of divine control over nature, the Lord appoints a large fish. The word 'appoint' is sometimes used within the context of God or a ruler appointing a servant for a specific mission (for example, Ezra 7.25; Dan. 1.10, 11; 2.24, 49). The use of 'appoint' with nature (see also 4.6, 7, 8) continues the narrative's conversational theme—that is, the Lord's control over nature is expressed within adjacency pairs.[34] The 'appointing' of the fish is similar to the Lord's request of Jonah; however, here the fish obeys by accepting the request as is indicated in the reported consequences—'*And Jonah was in the belly of the fish*'.

> [2] And Jonah prayed to the Lord, his God, from the belly of the fish.

Assuming that the fish was his divinely-appointed refuge (an assessment), Jonah offers a prayer of thanksgiving. (The following remarks on the prayer only highlight those elements of the prayer that suggest conversation.)

> [3] 'I call out, in my trouble, to the Lord / and he answers me. From the belly of Sheol I plead / you hear my voice.

In these parallel lines, Jonah asserts that prayerful requests are accepted by the Lord.

> [5] So I say, "I am driven from your sight, may I yet continue to gaze toward your holy sanctuary?"...Then my prayer reaches you at your holy sanctuary. [9] Those who hold to empty faiths, their hope for mercy they give up. [10] But, I, with a grateful voice, sacrifice to you; that which I vow, I shall fulfill. Deliverance belongs to the Lord.'

Based upon Jonah's previous faith that the Lord answers prayers, this question (*'may I yet...?'*) can be understood as a prayerful request or even a rhetorical question. (Since the book closes with Jonah still in

---

33. Pope concludes that, having thrown so much of the cargo overboard, the sailors also 'vow to make further sacrifices on reaching land' ('Notes on Selected Exegetical Issues', p. 46).

34. See 2.11, where this theme is more explicit in the use of the verb רבד, 'spoke'.

Nineveh, this request/question remains as an uncompleted adjacency pair. However, Jonah's faith seems to suggests that this request will eventually be accepted.)

> [11] Then the Lord spoke to the fish and it vomited Jonah upon dry land.

Jonah's assessment that the fish was his divinely appointed refuge proves true; the Lord requests that the fish vomit Jonah onto shore and the fish obediently accepts.

> [3.1] Now it happened that the word of the Lord came to Jonah a second time, [2] 'Get up. Go to Nineveh, that large city, and call out to it whatever I command you.'

Having controlled nature so that Jonah is once again on dry land, the Lord repeats his request. (The latter part of the request differs from that in 1.2—'... *call out against it for their wickedness is obvious to me*'. Some commentators have incorrectly interpreted this difference and the ambiguity of *'whatever I command you'* to imply that the Lord is already moderating his desire to punish Nineveh. However, the narrative context denies this possibility.[35])

> [3] Then Jonah got up and went to Nineveh just as the Lord had commanded. And Nineveh was a large city, belonging to God, a three days' walk across. [4] After Jonah had hardly gone into the city a day's journey, he called out, 'Forty days more, and Nineveh will overturn.'

As before (1.3), Jonah response to the Lord's request is not given in the character's own words, but in a narrated report of his actions. However, this time Jonah accepts the request, even if under coercion, and prophesies Nineveh's destruction—'*Forty days more, and Nineveh will overturn.*' Implicit in this prophecy is a call to repentance, a request for the Ninevites to forsake their wicked ways.

> [5] Then the people of Nineveh believed in God; they called for a fast; and they put on sackcloth, from the greatest to the least. [6] When word reached the king of Nineveh, he got up from his throne and stripped off his royal mantle and put on sackcloth and sat down in ashes. [7] Then he proclaimed, 'In Nineveh, on the authority of the king and his counselors: People and beasts—herds and flocks—must not taste anything, must not graze, and even water, they must not drink. [8] Rather, they must wrap themselves in sackcloth—people and beasts alike—and must call out to God with fervor.

---

35. For the full discussion of this issue, see 'Omitted Dialogue' in Chapter 3 and the commentary in Chapter 4.

Each person must turn from his evil way and from the violence which is in their hands. [9] Who knows? Perhaps that god will change his mind and turn away from his anger, so that we may not perish.'

The Lord's implicit request (through Jonah) is accepted. From a conversation analytic viewpoint, this is nothing unusual—the Ninevites simply gave the preferred response. However, from the cultural viewpoint of the original Jewish readers, this is amazing. Never had a Hebrew prophet been so successful! The prophets often had been persecuted by their own royal and priestly leaders. When it was the most important time for repentance, the Israelite kings ignored the Lord's repeated warnings through his servants the prophets and Israel was eventually punished severely by the destruction of Jerusalem and its temple and by being taken captive into exile.[36] But Jonah speaks to heathen foreigners and they immediately repent! Even their animals! Within their repentance is an implied request for divine mercy— *'Perhaps that god will change his mind and turn away from his anger'*.

[10] When God saw their deeds, that they had turned away from their evil ways, God changed his mind concerning the evil which he had commanded against them and did not do it.

Just as the Ninevites' response is multi-layered—that is, it is an acceptance of the implied request in Jonah's prophecy and an implied request for divine mercy—God's response is likewise multi-layered: God responds favorably to the Ninevites' acceptance of the implied request and accepts the implied request of the Ninevites for his mercy. This verse possibly also suggests that the unreported conversation between the Lord and Jonah not only included Jonah's omitted dispreferred response, but also included more information *concerning the evil which* the Lord *had commanded against* the Ninevites.[37]

The following verse (4.1) returns chronologically to the time immediately following Jonah's oracle (3.4). That is, after Jonah proclaimed his oracle, the narrative describes two events that began at about the same time: (1) the Ninevites' response and the Lord's corresponding change of mind (3.5-10) and (2) Jonah's expression of anger and the Lord's corresponding lesson (4.1-11).[38]

36. This is the theological perspective of the Deuteronomic school (see 2 Kgs 24.1-17) which dominated Jewish thought during the exilic and post-exilic periods.
37. See 'Omitted Dialogue' in Chapter 3.
38. See further the section 'Flashback' in Chapter 5 §4.

Nothing in the narrative necessarily suggests that Jonah gave his oracle and waited around in the city in order to see the Ninevites' response. Had he waited around for their response, he would have had to have been in Nineveh for an extended period of time, for the ensuing events would have necessarily taken some time—a fast, word reaching the king, the king issuing a decree, the changing of everybody's clothes to sackcloth, the dressing of all the beasts in sackcloth, and the Lord's having seen all of these events. In fact, if his oracle can be taken literally, then the Ninevites had *forty days* in which to make such changes before their threatened destruction. But Jonah did not wait around to see their response; rather *Jonah went from the city...to see what would happen in the city* (4.5). That is, Jonah's waiting outside of Nineveh should not be understood as his waiting to see if the Ninevites backslide and then are divinely punished; rather the Ninevite's repentance and the Lord's changing his mind are events that Jonah had not yet seen, even though he is certain that the Lord is *'a gracious and compassionate God'*, who will *'change his mind'* (4.2).

Where the following conversation between Jonah and the Lord occurred is not clear. It could have been immediately after the oracle, as Jonah was walking out of the city, or possibly even in Jonah's booth.

> **4.1** But this was terribly upsetting to Jonah and he was angry. **2** And he interjected to the Lord, 'Oh Lord! Is this not what I said while I was still in my homeland? Therefore, I hastened to flee to Tarshish for I knew that you are a gracious and compassionate God, slow to anger and extremely benevolent, who would change his mind concerning the evil.

What is *'this'* that was so upsetting to Jonah? *This* is everything that has happened to Jonah, coercing him into a mission that he strove to avoid. *This* coercion has made Jonah upset and so he angrily questions the Lord. Interestingly, this rhetorical question now tells the reader for the first time why Jonah fled to Tarshish. After three chapters of intervening material, the reader is allowed to listen in, even if only faintly, to the conversation that took place at the beginning of the book. Jonah now provides us with his account for his dispreferred response of refusing the Lord's initial request. He knew even then that the Lord would not follow through with the destruction of Nineveh and now he is angry that he has been coerced into *this,* his present situation.

> **3** 'Now, O Lord, take my life from me, for it is better that I die than live.'

After having fulfilled the bare minimum required of him, Jonah has finished his business with the Lord. He now angrily requests that the Lord take his life. But the Lord is not yet finished with him.

⁴ Then the Lord said, 'Is it good for you to be so angry?'

The Lord does not directly refuse Jonah's request. Rather, the Lord delays with a clarifying question, 'Is your request legitimate?'

⁵ But Jonah went from the city and sat down east of the city. And there he made for himself a booth and he sat down under its shade until he could see what would happen in the city.

Jonah now gives a dispreferred response to the Lord's question (a non-answer) by going outside of Nineveh to wait and see what will happen. What is he waiting for? He is probably waiting to see if he was right when he first refused the Lord's request—that is, the Lord will not destroy the Ninevites. (Note that the Ninevites' repentance and the Lord's changing his mind have not yet occurred within the timeframe of the story.)

⁶ And the Lord appointed a *qiqayon* plant to grow up over Jonah so that there would be shade over his head in order to deliver him from his distress. And Jonah rejoiced exceedingly over the *qiqayon* plant.

While Jonah angrily waits, the Lord requests that a plant grow to provide shade for Jonah and the plant obediently accepts. Jonah, assuming the miraculous plant is divine refuge from the sun, rejoices.

⁷ Then God appointed a worm, at daybreak of the next day. It attacked the *qiqayon* plant so that it withered. ⁸ At sunrise, God appointed a fierce east wind. Then the sun attacked Jonah's head and he swooned. And he asked that he might die, 'It is better that I die than live.'

Having first provided shade, God now takes Jonah's comforts away. God explicitly requests that a worm attack the shade-producing plant and that a wind destroy Jonah's protective booth;[39] both the worm and wind obediently accept the requests. Hence, the sun beats down upon Jonah's head and, assuming that these strange occurrences were divinely wrought, Jonah once again requests that the Lord take his life. (Interestingly, the narrative does not portray God as 'appointing' the sun to act, even though it performs the same action that the worm does—that is, attacking.)

39. Sasson, *Jonah*, p. 304.

[9] Then God said to Jonah, 'Is it good for you to be so angry on account of the *qiqayon* plant?'

Again, God does not directly refuse Jonah's death-request. Rather, he begins with another question about the legitimacy of the request.

Then he said, 'It is good that I am angry enough to die.'

Jonah now angrily answers this question with a straight-forward answer that grammatically turns the Lord's question into a statement, an assessment of Jonah's situation.

[10] Then the Lord said, 'You yourself were fretting over the *qiqayon* plant, for which you neither toiled nor cultivated, which came up one night and perished the next night. [11] Yet I should not have compassion on Nineveh, that large city, which has in it more than one hundred and twenty thousand people, who do not know their right hand from their left hand, and many cattle as well?'

The book concludes with the Lord's disagreement with Jonah's assessment of the legitimacy of his request (already suggested in the Lord's questions), which is also a refusal of Jonah's death-request (4.3, 8). This dispreferred response is mitigated in two ways: (1) It does not directly follow Jonah's death-request; rather, it is delayed by intervening questions (4.4, 9). (2) It does not directly respond to Jonah's death-request; rather, the Lord shows how pettily Jonah was acting in relation to both the plant and the Ninevites. In other words, the Lord's account for refusing the death-request is a disagreement with Jonah's assessment that his situation is so bad that it calls for a death-wish. (Note that the Lord's speech does not necessarily imply that he has already changed his mind; rather, his *'compassion on Nineveh'* can be understood as his sending Jonah to Nineveh, causing Jonah's anguish.) The Lord's disagreement, however, is not necessarily the last word *in* the story, even though it is the last word *of* the story *as presented by the narrator*. The Lord's disagreement is in the form of a question, demanding some response from Jonah. The reader is left having to make guesses as to what Jonah's response may have been and what happened beyond the selected timeframe of the narrative.

3. Conclusion: The Use of Adjacency Pairs in the Jonah Narrative

In the preceding commentary, we have seen that the Jonah narrative is primarily made up of adjacency pairs, which intertwine around each other in their complexity. We have also glimpsed how the delay of dispreferred seconds can occur over an extended period of the reader's time and how such delays can influence the reading of the narrative. In the following chapters, these observations are expanded. In the next chapter, I examine more closely the use of adjacency pairs in the Jonah story in relation to the different elements of narrative—plot, character, atmosphere and tone. The last two chapters further explicate my understanding of the influence of adjacency pairs upon the process of reading the Jonah narrative.

Outlines of the Book of Jonah Based upon Adjacency Pairs
The following outlines serve as a summary for the adjacency pairs that constitute the Jonah narrative. Direct speech is simply given. Indirect speech and reported consequences are given in square brackets. Omitted dialogue is referred to in double square brackets with the reference to where the narrative suggests that dialogue was omitted. Also, other comments are given in double square brackets. The following abbreviations are used in these outlines for adjacency pairs:

First Parts	*Preferred Seconds*	*Dispreferred Seconds*
Req for Request	Acc for Acceptance	Ref for Refusal
Off for Offer	Acc for Acceptance	Ref for Refusal
Ass for Assessment	Agr for Agreement	Dis for Disagreement
Q for Question	Ans for Expected Answer	Un for Unexpected Answer
		Non for Non-Answer
B for Blame	[Den for Denial]	Adm for Admission

Only when a second part comes after intervening material will the verse in which the first part is found be given.

General Outline of the Book of Jonah

1.2	God:	Get up. Go to Nineveh... [[God's elaboration on Nineveh's destruction is omitted—see 3.10]]	Req
1.3	Jonah:	[Jonah, instead, sought to escape] [[Jonah's account is omitted—see 4.2]]	Ref

1.4–2.1	God:	[The Lord, however, hurled winds... Then the Lord appointed a large fish...] [[see below]]	Consequences of Ref
2.2-10	Jonah:	I call out, in my trouble, to the Lord...	Req and response to consequences
3.2	God:	Get up. Go to Nineveh... [[God's elaboration on Nineveh's destruction is omitted—see 3.10]]	Req repeated
3.3	Jonah:	[Then Jonah got up and went to Nineveh...]	Acc
3.4	Jonah (God):	Forty days more, and Nineveh will overturn	Implied Req
3.5-8	Ninevites:	[Then the people of Nineveh believed in God...]	Acc
3.9	king:	Perhaps that god will change his mind...	Implied Req Ass of God's response to Acc of implied Req in 3.4
3.10	God:	[God changed his mind...]	Acc of implied Req Agr to Ass
4.2	Jonah:	O Lord! Is not this what I said...	Account of Ref in 1.3
4.3 4.4-10	Jonah:	...take my life from me... [[insertion sequence—see below]]	Req
4.10-11	God:	You yourself were fretting over the plant	Ref of Req in 4.3 and Q

Outline of the Consequences of Jonah's Refusal (1.4–2.1)

1.3	Jonah:	[Jonah, instead, sought to escape...]	Ref
1.4	God:	[The Lord, however, cast mighty winds...]	Consequences
1.5	sailors:	[each prayed to his own gods]	Req
	gods:	[[The sailors' prayerful requests elicit no response from their gods]]	Ref
	Jonah:	[Jonah...went to sleep]	Impious response to consequences
1.6	helmsman:	Get up!	Req

	Jonah:	[[Jonah's presence at the lot-casting in 1.7 suggests acceptance]]	Implied Acc
	helmsman:	Call out to your god!	Req
	Jonah:	[[No reported action suggests refusal]]	Implied Ref
1.7	sailors:	Come! Let's cast lots...	Req
	sailors:	[Then they cast the lots]	Acc and Req
	lots:	[the lot fell on Jonah]	Acc and Ass
1.8	sailors:	you on whose account this evil has come to us	Agr
	sailors:	What is your mission?	Q
	sailors:	Where are you coming from?	Q
	sailors:	What is your homeland?	Q
	sailors:	From what people do you come?	Q
1.9	Jonah:	I am a Hebrew... [[1.10 implies that Jonah gave fuller answers]]	Ans
1.10	sailors:	What is this that you have done!?	Q and B
	Jonah:	[...the men now knew that he was fleeing from the Lord, because he had told them]	Ans and Adm
1.11	sailors:	What must we do to you...?	Q
1.12	Jonah:	Pick me up and cast me into the sea...	Ans and Req
	Jonah:	it is on my account [[The sailors' account is omitted—see 1.14]]	Repeated Adm to B in 1.10
1.13	sailors:	[Nonetheless, the men rowed hard...]	Ref
1.14	sailors:	...do not let us perish because of innocent blood	Implied account of Ref and Req
1.15	sailors:	[Then they picked up Jonah and cast him...]	Acc of Req in 1.12
	God:	[the sea ceased its raging]	Acc of Req in 1.14
1.16	sailors:	[they offered sacrifices...and made vows]	Off
	God:	[[implied]]	Acc
2.1	God:	[Then the Lord appointed a large fish...]	Req

	Fish:	[And Jonah was in the...fish]	Acc
2.2-10	Jonah:	I call out, in my trouble, to the Lord...	Pious response to consequences
2.11	God:	[Then the Lord spoke to the fish...]	Req
	Fish	[...and it vomited Jonah upon dry land]	Acc and Final result of consequences

Outline of Insertion Sequence (4.4-10)

4.3	Jonah:	...take my life from me...	Req
4.4	God:	Is it good for you to be so angry?	Delay of Ref, and Q
4.5	Jonah:	[But Jonah went from the city...]	Non
4.6	God:	[the Lord God appointed a plant...]	Req
	Plant:	[Jonah rejoiced...over the plant]	Acc
4.7	God:	[God appointed a worm...]	Req
	Worm:	[it attacked the plant]	Acc
4.8	God:	[God appointed a fierce east wind]	Req
	wind:	[[implied]]	Acc
	Jonah:	[he asked that he might die...]	Req
4.9	God:	Is it good for you to be so angry...?	Delay of Ref and Q
	Jonah:	It is good that I am angry enough to die	Ans
4.10-11	God	You yourself were fretting over the plant	Ref of Req in 4.3 and 4.8
		Yet I should have not have compassion on Nineveh?	Q

Chapter 3

NARRATIVE IN THE BOOK OF JONAH

As shown in the previous chapter, adjacency pairs play an important role in the Jonah narrative; however, it remains to be shown more explicitly how they relate to the various elements of narrative—plot, character, atmosphere and tone. This chapter attempts this explication.

Before beginning specifically with the Jonah narrative, some brief remarks are in order as to what is meant by plot, character, atmosphere and tone.[1] Plot is the element that focuses on the temporal processes involved in narrative. Character refers to the actors within the narrative, possibly including humans, animals, plants and even inanimate objects. Atmosphere[2] concerns any given narrative's world. It describes the boundary between the possible and the impossible in the narrative world as well as the conditions affecting this world. Thus, it is related to setting, but is more inclusive, for setting only establishes narrative boundaries in relation to time and place whereas atmosphere may allow, for example, animals to speak. Tone is the element that refers to the narrator's stance toward the narrative and contains three components: 'material selection, voice, and an attitude toward the material'.[3] Of these three components, the narrator's attitude includes both point of view and judgment. Based upon these four elements, Wesley Kort gives the following definition

---

1.   This understanding of narrative and its elements is taken from W.A. Kort, *Story, Text, and Scripture: Literary Interests in Biblical Narrative* (University Park: Pennsylvania State University Press, 1988), pp. 14-17. In this work, Kort analyses these elements in biblical narrative—plot in Exodus, character in Judges, atmosphere in Jonah and tone in Mark—and how different schools of literary theory emphasize different elements—plot and myth criticism, character and structuralism, atmosphere and critical hermeneutics, and tone and composition criticism. See also W.A. Kort, *Narrative Elements and Religious Meanings* (Philadelphia: Fortress Press, 1975), in which he analyses modern narratives in relation to each element.

2.   See Kort, *Story, Text, and Scripture*, p. 17.

3.   See Kort, *Story, Text, and Scripture*, pp. 16-17.

of narrative, which provides the structure for my following remarks concerning the Jonah narrative:[4]

> Narrative draws attention to four kinds of force or meaning in discourse: subjects (characters) involved in processes (plot) under certain limits and conditions (atmosphere) and in relation to a teller (tone).

Each element of any narrative can only be completely discerned after a careful reading of the entire narrative and is best understood after numerous careful readings. Various possibilities in how any one particular narrative develops each element can 'trick' the reader into believing one thing and then later 'correct' the reader's 'mistake'. For example, the narrator omits Jonah's account from the reader where it would naturally occur (1.3), thereby possibly tricking the reader into believing that Jonah said nothing. But later, the narrator gives the reader enough information to reconstruct Jonah's account (4.2). Hence, the reader has to skip backwards in the story line in order to fill this gap. Thus, the following discussion of the narrative elements is a synchronic approach and assumes a complete reading of the narrative.[5]

As suggested in the above definition of narrative, the four narrative elements overlap and intermingle. This creates some difficulty in discussing them in abstraction. As a result, some repetition occurs in the following discussions. The order in which the elements are discussed below—plot, character, atmosphere, tone—does not necessarily rank them according to importance in narrative in general or even specifically in the Jonah narrative. The order simply provides the best organization for discussing the roles that adjacency pairs play in relation to each element in the book of Jonah.

1. *Plot in the Jonah Narrative*

The creation of meaning can only take place in the interaction of text and reader.[6] As a reader approaches a text, he or she must take the information in the order that it is given by the text (what W. Brewer calls the 'discourse structure') and make meaning out of it as she or he reconstructs the narrative's world (what Brewer calls the 'event

---

4.   *Story, Text, and Scripture*, p. 17.

5.   In the discussion of tone, sometimes I necessarily have to change to a diachronic approach. These occasions are noted in the footnotes. For my diachronic reading of the Jonah narrative, see Chapter 4.

6.   For a full discussion of this, see Chapter 4.

structure').[7] Thus, reading involves a constant process of retrospective revisions of meaning as the reader gathers more information from the text. Two devices found in texts that demand such revision are flash-backs and prolepses. That is, the discourse structure manipulates the event structure by either jumping backwards into the past (flashback) or forward into the future (prolepsis) and describing events that happened or will happen. When narrative contains these devices, the reader must reconstruct the event structure from the discourse structure, thereby creating the plot. The Jonah narrative includes a flashback;[8] therefore, the following discussion of plot does not follow the order of events as given to the reader (the discourse structure), but rather places the events in the order in which they 'happened' in the presence of the characters (the event structure).

Jonah's story is bigger than the actual text of the book of Jonah gives us. For example, we are told nothing of his birth, childhood, or what happened to him after the Lord strongly questioned his pettiness (4.10-11). However, in the following summary the present text is followed closely (note how the plot is structured by the use of adjacency pairs): The Lord requests Jonah to go to Nineveh and prophesy its destruction. Jonah refuses and flees to Tarshish on a hired ship, because he knows that the Lord will not destroy the Ninevites. The Lord responds by throwing a mighty storm at the ship, threatening to break it up. The sailors try praying to their own gods and lightening the load as a means to avert being shipwrecked. When these methods do not work, they question the gods by means of casting lots and the lot falls on Jonah. After questioning Jonah, the sailors inquire as to what they must do to save themselves. Jonah tells them to throw him overboard. After initially refusing, the sailors throw Jonah overboard and the sea stops its raging. The sailors sacrifice and make vows to the Lord. The Lord now sends a fish to swallow Jonah and deliver him back to dry land. After the fish vomited Jonah up onto the shore, the Lord again requests that he go to Nineveh and prophesy doom. This time Jonah grudgingly accepts. After barely entering the city, Jonah gives a brief oracle. (At this time the narrative describes two events that begin simultaneously: the Ninevites

---

7.   W.F. Brewer, 'The Story Schema: Universal and Culture-Specific Properties', in D.R. Olson, N. Torrence and A. Hildyard (eds.), *Literacy, Language, and Learning: The Nature and Consequences of Reading and Writing* (Cambridge: Cambridge University Press, 1985), pp. 167-94.

8.   See the discussion in Chapter 2 in the commentary on Jon. 4.1-11.

repent and Jonah angrily leaves. In the following, the order is reversed in order to remind my readers that the description of these events could have been reversed by the narrator, but was not for specific purposes.[9]) In his anger, Jonah requests death from the Lord. The Lord questions his motives for this death-wish. He waits outside the city to see what will happen. For his own comfort, Jonah builds a booth for shade. Then the Lord commands a plant to grow and provide more shade, which pleases Jonah. The next day the Lord commands a worm to kill the plant and a wind to destroy the booth, thereby causing Jonah to sit in the heat of the sun. Jonah's anger concerning the destruction of the plant and booth causes him once again to request death. The Lord once again questions Jonah about his anger, contrasting Jonah's petty concern for the plant and booth and his own compassion for the many Ninevites and their cattle. (Jonah's answer is withheld from the reader.) Meanwhile, immediately upon hearing Jonah's brief oracle, the Ninevites repent. They fast, put on sackcloth, sit in ashes, and even force their beasts to do likewise. Seeing their humility and repentance, the Lord changes his mind and does not destroy the Ninevites.

The plot can be summarized by defining the adjacency pairs involved. The Jonah narrative begins with the Lord's request followed by Jonah's refusal followed by the Lord's response to the refusal, and so on.[10] In fact, very few of the events (words and actions) cannot be understood as part of an adjacency pair.[11] Thus, the narrative plot in Jonah, like conversation, is structured by the use of adjacency pairs, even though the parts may be 'hidden' in reported consequences and other omitted dialogue.

2. Character in the Jonah Narrative

In the Jonah narrative, there are few details concerning the characters' appearance, everyday routines, or the like. Rather, characterization in

---

9. For my discussion of the narrator's tone expressed in his chosen order for describing these two events, see the section 'Flashback' below in §4.

10. See the outlines given at the end of Chapter 2. None of these outlines, however, represents the plot directly, because they follow the order of events as given in the narrative. Therefore, the Ninevites' repentant response would need to be placed after the interaction between the Lord and Jonah concerning the plant.

11. See those narrative elements in the outlines given at the end of Chapter 2 that are denoted by 'consequences'. These 'consequences' are called 'follow-up moves' by Tsui in her discussion of 'three-part exchanges' ('Beyond the Adjacency Pair').

the book of Jonah is achieved primarily through the conversations that occur between the characters and the actions these conversations elicit. This has generally been noted in previous discussions of characterization in the Jonah narrative; however, these discussions have focused primarily upon the characters' actions and the *content* of the conversations.[12] Although the portrayals given below begin with discussions of the content of the conversations as well as the resulting actions, they also include a discussion of the linguistic *structure* of the conversations and how this structure contributes to the characters' development. This discussion of the structure will proceed by a review of the adjacency pairs initiated by, as well as those closed by, each character.

The Sailors, Including the Helmsman (1.4-16)
Although Jonah's hiring a ship implies some interaction with the sailors, the sailors make their first appearance in the narrative only after the Lord has hurled a storm at the ship. They are portrayed as pious polytheists who strive to converse with their gods as they pragmatically lighten their load (1.5). In fact, their leader, the helmsman, ensures that everyone on board is in prayer and thus rouses Jonah and demands that he pray too (1.6). The sailors inquire of their gods once again; this time by means of casting lots (1.7). Once they learn from the lot-casting that Jonah is the cause of the trouble, they accept this answer and ask him what they must do to save themselves (1.11). When Jonah instructs them to throw him overboard, they initially refuse, fearing divine punishment for Jonah's possibly innocent blood (1.13-14). Being flustered by Jonah's request to be thrown overboard, they loose their wits and strive to defy navigational common sense by trying to row ashore during such a fierce storm in order to put Jonah off (1.13).[13] After their fruitless attempt to control the ship, these pagans throw Jonah overboard, leading to the sea's calming (1.15) and their conversion: 'Then the men were filled with the most dreadful fear of the Lord and they offered sacrifices to the Lord and made vows' (1.16).

The overall picture of the sailors' piety from their actions and the content of their conversations is reinforced by the structure of their conversations, as we will see in the following two discussions of adjacency pairs. The first discussion concerns those initiated by the sailors and

---

12. For two good discussions of characterization in Jonah, see Craig, *A Poetics of Jonah*, pp. 45-72; Sasson, *Jonah*, pp. 340-51.
13. Sasson, *Jonah*, pp. 141-42, 341.

completed by the Lord/the gods; the second, those completed by the sailors.

Of the adjacency pairs begun by the sailors, four lead to a divine response: (1) Initially the sailors prayerfully request assistance from their own gods, which is refused in the form of divine inaction (1.5). (2) Having not received divine assistance, the sailors seek an answer to the question concerning the cause of their trouble through lot-casting. The lots answer by correctly identifying Jonah. Irony is involved here in that lot-casting was considered a pagan practice and, thus, forbidden to Jews; however, the lots fall truly. Does this suggest that the sailors' own gods, whom the narrator and reader deny exist, spoke through the lots? Or, does this imply that the Lord may choose to communicate even through such a pagan practice? If the implication is the latter, as I think it is, this would not be the first time that the Lord used false practices to speak his true word.[14] (3) The sailors request that the Lord not punish them further for Jonah's possibly 'innocent blood' as they throw him overboard; their request is more than accepted, in that the sea ceased its raging (1.14-15). (4) As they exit the narrative, the sailors offer to the Lord sacrifices and vows which, as is suggested by the narrative theme of the Lord accepting prayers (1.14-15; 2.3; 3.10), the Lord probably accepts.

These four adjacency pairs (sailors' first part–divinity's second part) fall into the following categories: (1) request–refusal; (2) request–acceptance; (3) request–acceptance and (4) offer–acceptance. Note that all but one include preferred seconds. The one exception—request–refusal—is set off in three other ways as well. First, it is the only adjacency pair in the entire narrative that explicitly elicits a second from the sailors' pagan gods *and* the response elicited is itself a dispreferred second in the form of a non-response. Secondly, it precedes the others, coming before the sailors' conversion to the Lord which undermines their earlier pagan commitments. Thirdly, of these four adjacency pairs, it is the least developed in the narrative. That is, while the others include more elaborate description, including direct speech, this adjacency pair is in the form of reported consequences.[15] Thus, the sailors learn to initiate conversations

14. See J.L. Crenshaw, *Prophetic Conflict: Its Effect Upon Israelite Religion* (BZAW, 124; Berlin: de Gruyter, 1971), pp. 77-88. Crenshaw discusses various passages in which the Lord uses false prophets to his own ends.

15. The fourth adjacency pair, of offer–acceptance, is also undeveloped in comparison to the second and third, including no direct speech; however, it can be under-

with the Lord not only with properly pious content, but also in ways that elicit linguistically preferred responses.

All three of the adjacency pairs that are begun by others and completed by the sailors include preferred seconds: (1) Jonah's request to hire a ship is accepted (1.3); (2) The assessment of the ship's trouble by the casting of lots (and, by inference, the Lord's answer) is accepted (1.7-8); (3) Jonah's request to be thrown overboard, although initially refused due to pious intentions, is accepted. Although these interactions with Jonah and the lots do not necessarily imply piety, they nevertheless suggest that, as we have just seen with those adjacency pairs initiated by them, the sailors are proficient in minimizing conflict through their participation in adjacency pairs with preferred seconds.

In summary, the sailors are portrayed as pious polytheists who eventually convert to worship of the Lord. They are typified not only by pious actions and words, but also in their linguistic competence to minimize conflict through the initiation of adjacency pairs that receive a preferred response from the Lord and by their proclivity towards producing preferred seconds.

The Ninevites, Including the Ninevite King and Their Animals (3.5-9)
The reader first encounters the Ninevites in a reference in the Lord's commission to Jonah, which characterizes them as wicked (1.2). This characterization finds much support in other biblical material (for example, 2 Kgs 15.19-20), for Nineveh was the capital of one of Israel's chief enemies, the Assyrians. The first appearance of the Ninevites in the narrative is after they hear Jonah's brief prophecy, and immediately 'the people of Nineveh believed in God; they called for a fast; and they put on sackcloth, from the greatest to the least' (3.5). Like the sailors before them, the Ninevites recognize the Lord's power and piously turn to him. Once again, the pagans' piety is demonstrated in the actions and words of their leader—the king of Nineveh commanded 'people and beasts alike' (!) to repent and humble themselves in sackcloth.

The Ninevites' pious attitude is found not only in their words and actions, but also in the very organization of their words. The Ninevites participate in only two adjacency pairs. The first is that begun by the Lord's word through the prophet Jonah: 'Forty days more, and Nineveh

stood as a continuation of the action and dialogue in the third, which does include direct speech. That is, in the narrator's words, 'they called out to the Lord...and they offered sacrifices to the Lord and made vows' (1.14, 16).

will overturn' (3.4). Whether or not the Lord and Jonah intended this pronouncement as a call to repentance, and whether or not the Ninevites understood it as such a call, the Ninevites respond as if it is a divine request for repentance and humility with acceptance. In the process of repenting, the Ninevites save face by not directly making a request of the Lord, but implying it indirectly: 'Who knows? Perhaps that god will change his mind and turn away from his anger, so that we may not perish' (3.9). Implied is, 'Please, oh god, have mercy on us.' Understanding their implied request, the Lord accepted and 'changed his mind' (3.10). Thus, the adjacency pairs, in which the Ninevites participate, not only incorporate pious words, but also exhibit a linguistic competence in that the two adjacency pairs are characterized by preferred seconds, which minimize conflict.

Nature

Other discussions of character in the Jonah narrative do not include a discussion of nature's role as character. However, elements within nature are presented within adjacency pairs that are begun by a divine request and followed by their acceptance (the winds in 1.4; the fish in 2.1, 11; the plant in 4.6; the worm in 4.7; the wind in 4.8). In other words, their characterization is apparent in their communicative interaction with the Lord, even though these characters do not speak. In much the same way that Jonah's refusal to the Lord's initial request (1.2-3) is depicted only in reported consequences, these natural characters are shown to respond to the Lord who, in most cases, is depicted as addressing them with the same words used with human characters in biblical stories—the Lord 'speaks' to the fish (אמר in 2.11;[16] see 3.3; 4.2) and 'appoints' the fish, the plant, the worm and the wind (ימן in 2.1; 4.6, 7, 8; see Ezra 7.25; Dan. 1.10, 11; 2.24, 49). Another aspect of their characterization, in contrast to the human characters, is in the more specific manner in which they are described. Whereas the human characters are, for example, merely 'sailors' and 'Ninevites', these characters

---

16. This is the only case in the Jonah narrative in which אמר does not precede direct speech. See S.A. Meier, *Speaking of Speaking: Marking Direct Discourse in the Hebrew Bible* (VTSup, 46; Leiden: Brill, 1992), pp. 60-61. Meier's analysis demonstrates that אמר rarely occurs without introducing direct speech—in only 103 of 3,877 occurrences, or 2.7%. This observation certainly supports the contention that the Lord's request of the fish initiates an adjacency pair which the fish then completes by accepting the request.

of nature are portrayed with descriptive adjectives (the 'mighty winds' in 1.4; the 'large fish' in 2.1, 11; 'a fierce east wind' in 4.8) or, in the case of the plant, with a noun that probably denotes its specific species (*qiqayon*). Thus, the Lord's control over nature is expressed in characters of nature piously obeying the Lord's request.

Probably related to these characters' obedience is the repentance of the Ninevites' animals. They also accept the Lord's request (implied in Jonah's oracle) and repent, putting on sackcloth and fasting (3.7-8).

The Sailors' Own Gods

The other minor characters often overlooked in discussions of the Jonah narrative are the sailors' own gods (1.5). These characters are the least developed—they are briefly mentioned without adjectives and are not given an opportunity to speak. The only adjacency pair in which they participate is a questionable one at that. 'The sailors...each prayed to his own gods' (1.5), but they received a refusal by means of no response. Thus, even in this adjacency pair, these gods are passive, thereby calling their very existence into question.

The Lord[17]

The Lord starts the narrative by commanding Jonah to go to Nineveh and declare doom[18] against the Ninevites because of 'their wickedness' (1.2). When Jonah refuses and strives to flee to Tarshish (1.3), the Lord

---

17. Although the name for the divinity in the Jonah narrative changes (the Lord, God, the Lord God), I consistently use the most prominent name—the Lord—in the following remarks. A. Lacocque and P.-E. Lacocque discern an interesting pattern in the various divine names:

> In association with Jonah, God always appears as YHWH (with the exception of 4.6-9; see below). In relation to the sailors, God is Elohim (1.6), but after being presented to them by Jonah, he becomes YHWH (1.14-15). In relation to Nineveh he is, of course, Elohim (3.5-10), and the condemnation is made on the basis of general ethical crimes, that is, wicked relations between people and their neighbor—4.6-9 constitute an exception; there God appears to Jonah as Elohim. It is noteworthy, however, that the context is one of nature. As god of nature, God is Elohim (as in the book of Job, chaps. 38–42, for instance). He becomes YHWH again when nature is replaced by history and when God's mercy is again emphasized (*Jonah: A Psycho-Religious Approach to the Prophet* [Columbia: University of South Carolina Press, 1990], p. 13).

In addition, following the Jonah narrative itself, I use masculine pronouns in reference to the character of the Lord.

18. '[D]eclare doom upon it' is Sasson's well-nuanced translation of קרא עליה in 1.2. See Sasson, *Jonah*, pp. 71-75.

begins his coercion of Jonah by throwing a mighty storm at the ship
(1.4). After Jonah is thrown overboard, the threat to the ship ceases and
the Lord spares the newly-converted sailors (1.15). But now the problem of saving Jonah must be addressed, so that he can go to Nineveh
and proclaim the Lord's message. As a solution to this problem, the
Lord appoints a fish to swallow Jonah, take him back to the dry land,
and vomit him up onto the shore (2.1, 11). Once Jonah is again on dry
land, the Lord commands him a second time, 'Go to Nineveh…and call
out to it that which I command you' (3.2). Having been coerced by the
Lord, Jonah goes to Nineveh and gives a brief oracle. Jonah remains
angry at the Lord for his coercion and issues a death-wish (4.1-3). The
Lord responds to Jonah's death-wish by manipulating him once again
through his control of nature (the plant, the worm, the wind, the sun) in
order to illustrate Jonah's lack of compassion (4.6-11). Upon hearing
Jonah's oracle, the Ninevites repent. Therefore, the Lord changes his
mind and does not punish the now humble Ninevites. Thus, the Lord
controls nature and coerces Jonah so that his message of doom can
reach Nineveh. However, as Jonah knew from the beginning, the Lord
changes his mind and spared the Ninevites. Put simply, the Lord is
omnipotent, yet compassionate.

As with the previous characters, the description just given depends
only upon the action and words of the Lord in relation to other
characters; however, in contrast to the characters discussed above, the
character of the Lord is given more elaboration through the words of
other characters. Ironically, the descriptions of the Lord given by Jonah
agree with those given by the pagan characters. Jonah and the sailors
both implicitly assert that the Lord controls nature and human events:

Jonah:	'the God of Heaven…who made the sea and the dry land' (1.9)
the sailors:	'whatever pleases you, you do' (1.14)

Jonah, the helmsman, and the king of Nineveh all suggest (at least
implicitly) that the Lord is compassionate:

the helmsman:	'Perhaps that god will intercede on our behalf so that we may not perish' (1.6)
Jonah:	'Deliverance belongs to the Lord' (2.10; this phrase sums up Jonah's prayer of thanksgiving in 2.3-10)
the king:	'Perhaps that god will change his mind and turn away from his anger, so that we may not perish' (3.9)
Jonah:	'gracious and compassionate God, slow to anger and extremely benevolent' (4.2)

Thus, descriptions of the Lord by other characters augment the characterization of the Lord in his own actions and words as one who is omnipotent but compassionate.

These two aspects of the Lord—his omnipotence and his compassion—are also evident in the structure of the conversations the Lord participates in. His omnipotence is evident in that every adjacency pair initiated by the Lord eventually[19] elicits a preferred response whether the requests are made of humans or nature (all are in the pattern of request–acceptance: 1.2 = 3.2–3.3; 2.1a–2.1b; 2.11a–2.11b; 3.4–3.5-9; 4.6a–4.6b; 4.7a–4.7b; 4.8a–4.8b).[20] His compassion is evident in that every request made by the other characters receives the preferred response of acceptance (1.7a–1.7b; 1.14–1.15; 1.16a–[implied]; 2.2-10–[implied]; 3.9–3.10), with one important exception. This exception is Jonah's death-wish, which occurs twice (4.3, 8). Jonah's death-request is refused because the Lord disagrees with Jonah's assessment of his situation: the Lord's dispreferred response (refusal) to the request is based on his dispreferred response (disagreement) to Jonah's assessment. Jonah believes that he has been unjustly treated by the Lord's change of mind concerning the destruction of Ninevites; the Lord disagrees and accuses Jonah of being petty with the following rhetorical question:

> You yourself were fretting over the plant, for which you neither toiled nor cultivated... Yet should I not have compassion on Nineveh, that great city, which has in it more than one hundred and twenty thousand people, who do not know their right hand from their left hand, and many cattle as well? (4.10-11)

Thus, the content within the Lord's only refusal of a request suggests that Jonah should not expect the Lord to respond as pettily as humans, but rather, in Jonah's own words, as 'a gracious and compassionate God' (4.2).

---

19. Of course, the Lord's request of Jonah initially receives a refusal (1.2-3). However, through his omnipotence, the Lord coerces Jonah into accepting the request the second time around (3.2-3).

20. Two adjacency pairs can be seen as an exception to this pattern. The rhetorical question—'Is it good for you to be so angry?' (4.4, 9)—occurs twice and can be interpreted as receiving a dispreferred second. In the first instance Jonah does not answer at all and in the second instance Jonah's answer is basically a grammatical change of the question into a declarative sentence—'It is good that I am angry enough to die' (4.9). However, since these questions may be rhetorical questions, such answers may be the expected answers and, therefore, preferred seconds.

In summary, the Lord's characterization occurs through three strategies: (1) his own words and actions; (2) the speech of other characters, and (3) the structures of his conversations. These three strategies combine to define the Lord as omnipotent, controlling humans and nature, but nevertheless compassionate towards all, including pagans and their beasts.

Jonah

When commanded to go to Nineveh and prophesy doom, Jonah refuses because he does not believe that the compassionate Lord will destroy the Ninevites (4.2) despite the Lord's assurance that he will (implied in 1.2; 3.10). Not wanting to participate in this charade, he disobediently hires a ship for Tarshish, which is in the opposite direction to Nineveh. His disobedience leads to the Lord's intervention by throwing a powerful storm against the ship. 'When the ship threatened to break up' (1.4), Jonah nonchalantly went to sleep, again showing disdain for pagans, in this case, in the form of the sailors' safety. At the helmsman's request, Jonah reluctantly gets up and, unfortunately for him, the sailors' lot-casting betrays his responsibility. Responding to the sailors' request for help, he suggests that they throw him overboard in order to save themselves. Once he is in the water, he is saved by a divinely appointed fish. He then prays to the Lord, thanking him for deliverance. The Lord commands the fish to vomit him up onto dry land, thereby forcing Jonah back to where the Lord wanted him. Having been so coerced, he reluctantly[21] accepts the Lord's second issuance of the command and goes to Nineveh. Even though Nineveh was an extremely large city ('a three days' walk across'), Jonah gives his brief message after he 'had hardly gone into the city' (3.3-4). After having done the minimum required, he does not wait around, but angrily leaves the city in order to 'see what would happen in the city' (4.5).[22] He builds a booth for shade and, as he waits, a divinely appointed plant miraculously grows to provide him shade. At this, he rejoices. But, when the Lord destroys the plant and booth through the appointments of a worm and wind, Jonah once again angrily requests death. This death-wish is the last thing we

---

21. A.J. Hauser also understands Jonah as giving 'the appearance of reluctance and hesitation' here ('Jonah', p. 32). See also J.C. Holbert, '"Deliverance Belongs to Yahweh": Satire in the Book of Jonah', *JSOT* 21 (1981), pp. 59-81 (74).

22. For my discussion of the narrative timeframe of the story, which is broken by 3.5-10, see the commentaries in Chapter 2 and in Chapter 4.

hear from Jonah. The narrative last portrays Jonah as sulking at the juxtaposition of his faith in the 'gracious and compassionate' Lord and his parochial disdain for non-Israelites.[23] However, Jonah's story certainly continues after the Lord's speech in 4.10-11; only the narrative stops here.

This juxtaposition is also evident in the characterization of Jonah through his name and patronym. Jonah first appears in the book's introductory superscription where he is referred to as 'Jonah, son of Amittai'. His name and patronym brings a dimension of intertextuality to the characterization of Jonah, for it is taken from a reference to 'Jonah, son of Amittai' in 2 Kgs 14.25. The Jonah of 2 Kings includes some details that are not mentioned in the book of Jonah. In 2 Kings, Jonah is a northern prophet who was active in the eighth century during the reign of Jeroboam II.[24] Even though he is only briefly mentioned, this Jonah stands out among other prophets for he has the unusual (some might say, blasphemous) task of proclaiming Jeroboam's reign as glorious and prosperous *even though* Jeroboam 'did what was evil in the sight of the Lord' (2 Kgs 14.24). That is, the Jonah of 2 Kings is portrayed as a prophet of salvation whose message is for Israel and its evil king and, by implication, uncritically against Israel's enemies. And who was Israel's chief enemy during Jeroboam's reign? Assyria, whose capital was Nineveh![25] Thus, by an inferred reference to the book of 2 Kings, the

23. Sasson reaches the opposite conclusion with Jonah's story ending on a 'happy note' (*Jonah*, p. 298)!

24. In rabbinic tradition, Jonah was understood as an active prophet during the time of the dynasty of Jehu, who even anointed Jehu as king. See L. Ginzberg, *Legends of the Jews* (Philadelphia: Jewish Publication Society of America, 1946–47), IV, pp. 246-47 and VI, p. 348 and M. Zlotowitz and N. Scherman, *Jonah* (Brooklyn: Mesorah Publications, 1988), p. xxv.

25. See Wolff, *Obadiah and Jonah*, p. 98. Contra Sasson, *Jonah*, pp. 342-44. Sasson rejects the notion of Jonah as a nationalistic prophet. Thus, he must see some other parallels between the characters of the same name in 2 Kings and the book of Jonah. Sasson argues that the parallels between these two narratives concern not the prophets' missions, but rather God's unsatisfying reasons for his mercy. In 2 Kings, Sasson correctly understands that God gave an unsatisfactory reason for his mercy: 'the Lord observed how very bitter was Israel's plight, with absolutely no ruler, no one to rescue Israel' (2 Kgs 14.27; Sasson's translation). However, Sasson incorrectly understands Jon. 4.11 as God's reason for not destroying the Ninevites: 'twelve myriads of human beings, who cannot discern between their right and left hands, and animals galore' (Sasson's translation). If this were God's reason for saving the Ninevites, then Sasson would have an interesting and convincing

character Jonah in the book of his name is portrayed as a nationalistic prophet.[26]

His name and patronym also contribute to his characterization in that these two names have underlying meanings which would have been familiar to an ancient reader of Hebrew. Jonah, son of Amittai means 'Dove, son of The Lord-Is-Steadfast' and neither name would have been considered unusual.[27] 'Dove' in today's jargon connotes someone who is peaceful in contrast to warlike 'hawks', but what did 'dove' connote in biblical times? According to James Ackerman,

> the dove has two major characteristics in the Hebrew Bible: [1] it is easily put to flight and seeks secure refuge in the mountains (Ezek. 7.16, Ps. 55.6-8), and [2] it moans and laments when in distress (Nah. 2.7; Isa. 38.14, 59.11).[28]

Both characteristics of 'dove' apply to Jonah, for he flees to Tarshish and he laments over the wilting of the plant. Similarly, Hans Walter Wolff noted that Hosea compared Israel with a dove in ways suggestive for the Jonah narrative: 'Ephraim is like a dove, silly and without sense, calling to Egypt, going to Assyria' (Hos. 7.11).[29] Since the Jonah narrative also makes use of the east–west tension (Nineveh–Tarshish), Wolff concludes concerning Jonah's name and patronym, 'Dove, son of The Lord-Is-Steadfast':

argument. But Jon. 4.11 is the Lord's account to Jonah for why he is refusing Jonah's death-wish, drawing a distinction between Jonah's petty concern for the plant and the Lord's concern for 'myriads of human beings'. The reason for the Lord's sparing the Ninevites is given in 3.10: 'When God himself examined their deeds—for they forsook their evil conduct—he renounced plans for the disaster...' (Sasson's translation). This reason is certainly satisfactory, for repentance is what the Lord wants any time judgment is proclaimed on any people. Thus, Sasson's attempt to establish a similarity between the 'unsatisfactory' reasons given by the Lord for not punishing Jeroboam and Israel in 2 Kings and the Ninevites in the book of Jonah fails.

26. Sasson also posits that the use of the phrase, 'as the Lord had commanded', in 3.3, 'may be purposefully placed here to sharpen recall of that other narrative about Jonah in 2 Kgs 14.25', which also contains this phrase (*Jonah*, p. 227).

27. See Sasson, *Jonah*, pp. 68-69; Wolff, *Obadiah and Jonah*, pp. 98-99; J.S. Ackerman, 'Jonah', in R. Alter and F. Kermode (eds.), *The Literary Guide to the Bible* (Cambridge: The Belknap Press, 1987), pp. 234-43 (234); T.S. Warshaw, 'The Book of Jonah', in K.R.R. Gros Louis (ed.), *Literary Interpretations of Biblical Narratives* (Nashville: Abingdon Press, 1974), II, pp. 191-207 (196).

28. Ackerman, 'Jonah', p. 234. See also Hauser, 'Jonah', p. 22.

29. Wolff, *Obadiah and Jonah*, p. 99. The translation is taken from Wolff.

Our didactic writer would like the name itself to hint that his 'hero' is fickle and capricious (like the dove Israel in Hos. 7.11), but that he is nonetheless a son of Yahweh's faithfulness.[30]

Thus, the use of 'Jonah, son of Amittai' itself brings certain implications to the character of Jonah. It literally means 'Dove, son of The Lord-Is-Steadfast', which suggests that he is fickle and capricious but nevertheless has faith in the Lord. It also alludes to Jonah's other mission (mentioned in Kings) in which he uncritically proclaimed glory and prosperity for the evildoer Jeroboam, king of Israel, whose chief enemy was the Ninevites.

The character Jonah, like that of the Lord, is also characterized in the speech of other characters and in the narrator's own words. The sailors address him as 'you on whose account this evil has come to us' (1.8), an accusation that Jonah later accepts without any apparent expression of regret (1.12). This lack of regret may also illustrate Jonah's nationalistic disdain for non-Israelites. The character Jonah also receives development from the narrator and the Lord's speech. The narrator states that the Lord's compassion for the Ninevites 'was terribly upsetting to Jonah and he was angry' (4.1) and, thereafter, the Lord dwells on this anger. Twice the Lord asks, 'Is it good for you to be so angry?' (4.4, 9); he describes Jonah's response to the plant episode as petty 'fretting over the plant' (4.10) and his response to the sparing of Nineveh as uncompassionate (4.11). The Lord's damning contrast between Jonah's concern for the plant and his disdain for the Ninevites highlights Jonah's petty selfishness and nationalistic lack of compassion for non-Israelites. Another character whose speech characterizes Jonah is Jonah himself: 'Those who hold to empty faiths, their hope for mercy they give up. But, I, with a grateful voice, sacrifice to you; that which I vow, I shall fulfill' (2.9-10). Here Jonah ironically contrasts his supposed obedience with the pagans' 'empty faith'; however, the pagans have been the faithful and Jonah the disobedient. Thus, Jonah is characterized in speeches of the sailors, the Lord, the narrator and Jonah himself as one who lacks compassion for non-Israelites and is thus angered easily for petty reasons.

Jonah's negative qualities are also presented in his linguistic competence. In contrast to all of the other characters, Jonah's participation in conversation is characterized by adjacency pairs with *dispreferred* seconds. He initially refuses the Lord's request (1.2–1.3; see the account in 4.2) and only accepts it, in the end, under duress (3.2–3.3). He refuses the

30. Wolff, *Obadiah and Jonah*, p. 99.

helmsman's request for prayer (1.6–implied). At first, he does not answer the Lord's question (4.4–4.5) and when he does, he angrily answers it by rewording the question into an answer (4.9a–4.9b). He initiates an adjacency pair that he knows requires the Lord to produce a dispreferred second according to his divine character—that is, he twice requests that the 'gracious and compassionate' Lord will take his life, and, naturally, the Lord refuses (4.3–4.4; 4.8–4.9-11). Even his admission of guilt to the sailors' blaming (1.8–1.10, 12) is a dispreferred second because, as is evident in various studies,[31] an admission is generally mitigated and often includes delay, a preface, an account and a declination component. Jonah's admission is mitigated in two ways: (1) Jonah chooses to take the easier path of answering the questions concerning his identity first, thereby delaying his admission, and (2) the narrator mitigates Jonah's admission by omitting Jonah's full speech when he first admits his guilt (1.10) and then, when he places the admission in Jonah's own words (1.12), by imbedding the admission within his preferred response (answer) to the sailors' question, 'What must we do?'

In summary, the characterization of Jonah occurs by means of four strategies: (1) his own words and actions, (2) his name and patronym, with their metaphorical and intertextual meanings, (3) descriptions by characters (including Jonah himself) and the narrator, and (4) his predisposition to conflict in a conversational style dominated by dispreferred seconds. Together, these strategies characterize Jonah as a nationalistic Israelite prophet who has great difficulties getting along with others when the topic of non-Israelites comes up. His disobedient behavior, his petty complaints and his nationalism all characterize him as a false prophet.[32]

---

31. For example, Atkinson and Drew, *Order in Court*, pp. 105-133; A. Pomerantz, 'Attributions of Responsibility', *Sociology* 12 (1978), pp. 115-21.

32. The most definitive study on false prophecy is Crenshaw, *Prophetic Conflict*. In this study, Crenshaw discusses three categories of criteria which have been proposed as a basis of distinguishing true from false prophecy: 'message-centered criteria', 'criteria focusing upon the man', and 'chronological criteria' (pp. 49-61). He concludes that none of these criteria could have been applied by any prophet's contemporary audience with any degree of satisfaction (p. 61). Although this is certainly the case, prophets in biblical narratives are still portrayed as either true or false and one can see these various criteria functioning at the narrative level, whether or not they could have ever functioned at the historical level behind the texts. *In the narrative itself*, Jonah is satirically judged as a false prophet by means of a message-centered criterion (his overt nationalism) and a criterion focusing upon the man's behavior (refusals and pettiness). However, it is possible, although there is no explicit

Character as Expressed through Conversation[33]

As is generally recognized, characters can be developed through the content of their conversations with other characters. Above, another aspect of narrated conversation has been used to illuminate further character development—that is, the structure of their conversations suggests something about their linguistic competence to avoid conflict. Most of the characters in the Jonah narrative—the sailors, the Ninevites, nature and the Lord—demonstrate an excellent control of language in their predisposition to participate in adjacency pairs with preferred seconds. In contrast, only one character, Jonah, is predisposed to participate in adjacency pairs with dispreferred seconds. Not only does he give dispreferred seconds to adjacency pairs initiated by other characters (for example, his initial refusal of the Lord's command) but he also initiates adjacency pairs that necessarily elicit dispreferred seconds from other characters (for example, his death-request which the compassionate Lord must refuse). In fact, all of the dispreferred seconds performed in the narrative by other characters can be theologically rationalized from the perspective of the narrator and/or characters producing the dispreferred second. The sailor's pagan gods, which from the narrator's perspective do not exist, refuse the sailors' request for help in the midst of the storm (1.5). The sailors initially refuse Jonah's request to be thrown overboard because they are piously concerned about shedding 'innocent blood' (1.12-15). And the Lord refuses Jonah's death-request, because the Lord is 'gracious and compassionate' towards Jonah and disagrees with Jonah's petty assessment of his situation. In contrast, Jonah's dispreferred seconds can not be theologically defended from the standpoint of the narrator and the Lord, especially his refusal to serve the Lord (1.3) and his death-request (4.3, 8). To these, the Lord concludes with a rhetorical question, 'You yourself were fretting over the plant, for which you neither toiled nor cultivated, which came up one night and perished the next night. Yet I should not have compassion on

---

evidence in the text itself, that the readers are expected to assume Jonah repented in response to the Lord's final speech (4.10-11) and, therefore, became (again?) a true prophet. For a fuller discussion of the reception of the Jonah narrative, see Chapter 5 §3. For an extended discussion of my own understanding of false prophecy in narratives, see R.F. Person, Jr, *Second Zechariah and the Deuteronomic School* (JSOTSup, 167; Sheffield: Sheffield Academic Press, 1993), pp. 182-93.

33. Craig also discusses characterisation as expressed through the narrator's manipulation of dialogue (*A Poetics of Jonah*, pp. 45-72).

Nineveh, that great city, which has in it more than one hundred and twenty-thousand people, who do not know their right hand from their left hand, and many cattle as well?' (4.10-11). Even Jonah himself contradicts his actions when he says, 'for I knew that you were a gracious and compassionate God, slow to anger and extremely benevolent, who would change his mind concerning the evil' (4.2). Thus, the recognition of the structure *and* content of the characters' speech has led to a clearer contrast between Jonah and the other characters. Jonah places himself in conflict (in the form of dispreferred seconds) with everyone with whom he comes in contact, whereas the other characters (except the non-existent pagan gods) characteristically use preferred seconds.

3. *Atmosphere in the Jonah Narrative*[34]

When discussing atmosphere in the Jonah narrative, one must take two different perspectives, the first concerning the conditions and boundaries upon the Lord and the second concerning those upon the other characters, especially Jonah. In the Jonah narrative, the Lord seems to have no boundaries whatsoever. Everything that the Lord requests eventually is accepted (the preferred second) and even his own previous decisions do not bound him, for he can change his mind (3.10). He controls nature (wind, fish, plant, worm) and manipulates humans' destiny, for he is the Creator (1.9). Thus, it first appears that the Lord has no limits; *however,* it is quite possible that the Lord is limited by his own compassionate nature. This limitation is suggested in (and protested by) Jonah's account for his refusal—that is, Jonah complains that the Lord is so gracious and compassionate that he absolutely could not destroy the Ninevites (4.2). Since there is nothing in the narrative that would necessarily refute Jonah's view, and since this is a view that Jonah himself strongly protests, the Lord's omnipotence probably should be understood as qualified by his own divine nature of mercy and compassion.

In contrast, the other characters have many limitations, for they are bound by the Lord's intentions. The sailors have no control over their ship during the divinely controlled storm. The characters of nature must obediently accept all of the Lord's requests. And even hard-headed Jonah must in the end accept the Lord's request to go to Nineveh and prophesy doom, even though he knows that his mission is supposed to

---

34. See Kort's discussion of atmosphere in the Jonah narrative in *Story, Text, and Scripture*, pp. 35-40.

lead to something that the Lord himself cannot follow through, Nineveh's destruction. This determination upon the other characters is represented in the narrative by the Lord speaking at the beginning (1.2) and the end (4.10-11) of the book—that is, the Lord gets the first and last word.[35]

Although the human and natural characters are bound by the Lord's intentions, the atmosphere is not necessarily as oppressive as it may appear. Although Jonah certainly does not get his way, the Lord himself is limited to mercy and compassion; therefore, the Lord's intentions may control human and natural events, but this control is itself a means for divine mercy and compassion.

4. *Tone in the Jonah Narrative*

As the element that refers to the narrator's stance toward the narrative, tone involves material selection, voice and an attitude toward the material. The narrator's attitude toward the material includes both point of view and judgment. Below, tone in the Jonah narrative is discussed in relation to all of its aspects.

Material Selection and Arrangement

Below are discussions of how the narrator selected and arranged material in four specific manners: (1) in the choice and repetition of certain key words (paronomasia); (2) in the omission of dialogue; (3) in the choice of forms of constructed dialogue (direct speech, indirect speech, reported consequences), and (4) in the use of a flashback.

Paronomasia. In their work 'Composition and Paronomasia in the Book of Jonah', Baruch Halpern and Richard Friedman discuss the paronomastic techniques used in the Jonah narrative and conclude that their prevalence indicates 'that the undercurrent of verbal frolic is not fortuitous'.[36] These techniques guide the reader, highlighting two important themes: (1) the Lord's omnipotence and (2) Jonah's disobedience and its consequences. Below, the paronomastic techniques which they identify are discussed.

The antonyms 'go down' (ירד) and 'go up' (עלה) are played against

---

35. Kort, *Story, Text, and Scripture*, p. 37.

36. B. Halpern and R.E. Friedman, 'Composition and Paronomasia in the Book of Jonah', *HAR* 4 (1980), pp. 79-92 (84).

one another in the Jonah narrative.[37] Jonah's attempt to flee the Lord is portrayed as a 'going down'. Jonah 'went down to Jaffa' (1.3) to hire a ship to Tarshish. When the storm raged, he 'went down into the vessel's hold...and went to sleep (וירדם)' (1.5). He describes his plight from the fish's belly as 'to the base of the mountains, I sink (ירדתי)' (2.7), but, in the same verse, he has faith that the Lord will save him—'but you lift me up (ותעל) from the Pit alive'.[38] Thus, the antonyms 'go down' and 'go up' are used to express the contrast between Jonah's fleeing, which leads to a descent into Sheol, the Pit, (2.3-7), and Jonah's own faith in the Lord's uplifting deliverance (2.7-10).

This contrast is strengthened by other words that connote 'going up' and 'going down'. The narrative begins with the Lord commanding Jonah to, 'Get up (קום). Go to Nineveh' (1.2), a command that is repeated later (3.2). Rather than rising up and going to Nineveh, Jonah 'got up to escape (ויקם...לברח) to Tarshish from the Lord; and he went down to Jaffa' (1.3), thereby starting his 'going down' by 'getting up'. Jonah's bizarre behavior during the storm causes the helmsman to demand that Jonah 'get up (קום)' and call out to his god (1.6).[39] Thus, Jonah's disobedience to the Lord's request is expressed not only in his disobedient actions but also in the narrator's use of the contrasts between 'going up' and 'going down' in describing these actions.

The result of Jonah's disobedience is also expressed in terms similar to 'going down'. Jonah's flight by ship leads the Lord to 'cast [down] (טול) mighty winds towards the sea' (1.4). The storm leads the sailors to 'cast [down] the cargo...into the sea' (1.5). Jonah tells the sailors to pick him up (נשא) and cast him down (טול) into the sea (1.12) in order to save

---

37. Halpern and Friedman, 'Composition and Paranomasia', pp. 80-81. Also Ackerman, 'Jonah', p. 235; J.S. Ackerman, 'Satire and Symbolism in the Song of Jonah', in B. Halpern and J.D. Levensen (eds.), *Traditions in Transformation: Turning Points in Biblical Faith* (Winona Lake, IN: Eisenbrauns, 1981), pp. 213-46 (223-24).

38. Halpern and Friedman also relate the use of 'go up' in other places of the narrative ('Composition and Paranomasia', pp. 80-81):

1.2   for the wickedness is obvious to me (literally, 'for their wickedness has come up [עלתה] before my face').
4.6   the Lord God appointed a plant to grow up (ויעל) over Jonah.
4.7   Then God appointed a worm, at daybreak (literally, 'at the coming up' [בעלות] the next day.

39. Halpern and Friedman also note that the Ninevite king 'got up (יקם)' from his throne' and then 'sat down in ashes' (3.6) ('Composition and Paranomasia', p. 81).

themselves, actions that they eventually perform (1.15). Summing up the theme of 'going up' and 'going down', Halpern and Friedman conclude,

> Lexically, then, it is as though descent represents distance from [the Lord], ascent movement toward him. [The Lord]'s 'casting down', however, precipitates an involuntary 'descent', the most meaningful descent—away from [the Lord], and into the fish's gut.[40]

Jonah's disobedience is portrayed in his actions as well as the narrator's development of the 'going up'/'going down' motif to describe Jonah's disobedient actions and their consequences. These divine consequences are expressed through the Lord's omnipotent control of nature in the casting down mighty winds.

Another theme in the Jonah narrative is presented in the repeated use of the term גדל ('large', 'mighty', 'great'). This term occurs frequently and applies to Nineveh (1.2; 3.2, 3; 4.11), the wind (1.4), the storm (1.4, 12), the sailors' fear (1.10, 16), the fish (2.1), the Ninevites 'from the *greatest* (מגדולם) to the least' (3.5), Jonah's being upset at the Lord (4.1), Jonah's rejoicing over the plant (4.6), and the Lord's statement that Jonah did not cultivate (literally, 'make to grow bigger'—גדלתו) the plant. 'Everything that is "big" in the story is produced by [the Lord], or by [the Lord]'s deeds.'[41] This includes even Nineveh, as is implied in the Lord's contrast between Jonah's fretting over a plant he did not make to grow bigger and his own compassion for 'Nineveh, that large city' (4.10-11).

The repetitious use of the two verbs 'appoint' (מנה) and 'perish' (אבד) also expresses the Lord's omnipotence.[42] The Lord 'appoints' the fish (2.1), the plant (4.6), the worm (4.7) and the east wind (4.8), and all of them comply. The verb 'perish' is used to express the Lord's destructive powers in the expressions of the sailors' (1.6, 14) and the Ninevite king's (3.9) distress at their potential demise and in the destruction of the plant (4.10). The root רעה ('evil') is similarly used to describe the storm

---

40. Halpern and Friedman, 'Composition and Paranomasia', p. 81. Also Ackerman, 'Satire and Symbolism', p. 223.

41. Halpern and Friedman, 'Composition and Paranomasia', p. 81. Halpern and Friedman understand the use of 'large' in the phrase 'from the greatest to the least' (3.5) as an 'apparent exception' to this observation (p. 81 n. 6). However, since the Lord draws a strong analogy between the people of 'Nineveh, that *large* city' and his making the plant bigger, I see no reason why the usage should be seen as an exception. See also Lacocque and Lacocque, *Jonah*, p. 13.

42. See Halpern and Friedman, 'Composition and Paranomasia', p. 82.

(1.7, 8), Jonah's distress (4.1, 6) and the potential destruction of Nineveh (4.2).[43] That is, the Lord's control of nature might be used for destruction, causing things to 'perish' or, at least, to be distressed, and these actions can be characterized as 'evil'. However, these potentially destructive powers are never fully realized in the Jonah narrative because of the Lord's compassion.

Another contrast is linked by the used of the verb 'call out' (קרא).[44] The Lord requested Jonah to call out against Nineveh, but he refused (1.2-3). The helmsman commanded Jonah to call out to his god, but he refused (1.6). However, after being saved by the fish, Jonah called out to the Lord (2.3). The Lord repeated his request for Jonah to call out to Nineveh and this time Jonah reluctantly accepted (3.2-4). In contrast, the pagans in the story do not have to be coerced. The sailors called out to the Lord for deliverance (1.14). The Ninevites called for a fast (3.6) and then called out to the Lord for their deliverance (3.8). Thus, Jonah's disobedience to call out, despite his intimate knowledge of the Lord's omnipotence, contrasts with the pagans' obedience to call out, despite their new-found knowledge of the Lord.

In summary, these paronomastic techniques are intentionally employed in order to guide the reading of the Jonah narrative, highlighting two important themes: (1) the Lord's omnipotence and (2) the contrast between Jonah's disobedience and its consequences, on the one hand, and the pagans' obedience and its consequences, on the other.

Omitted Dialogue.[45] Narrators have the power to control what the reader receives and sometimes this power is exerted through omitted dialogue. A common omission of dialogue in narrative is when the narrator simply reports the speech act. For example, the sailors are said to have prayed to their gods (1.5) and made vows to the Lord (1.16), but the narrator does not provide the reader with their words. Another common form of omitted dialogue occurs when the narrator simply reports the consequences of a previous word or action. For example,

---

43. Of course, the narrative begins with the Lord's concern about the wickedness/ evil of the Ninevites (1.2). See Halpern and Friedman, 'Composition and Paranomasia', p. 82.

44. See Halpern and Friedman, 'Composition and Paranomasia', pp. 82-83.

45. Although the blatant omission of Jonah's account is universally noted, the other omitted dialogues have generally been overlooked. For a discussion of this contrast, see Chapter 5 §2.

immediately following the Lord's second request, 'Get up. Go to Nineveh' (3.2), the narrator reports that, 'Jonah got up and went to Nineveh just as the Lord had commanded' (3.3). Sometimes a reader may not even realize that the narrator has omitted dialogue; however, at other times the narrator's own reports will suggest to the reader that an omission has occurred. Below, some such cases in the Jonah narrative are analyzed.

The most obvious case of omitted dialogue in the Jonah narrative concerns Jonah's refusal of the Lord's initial request. Although it is a convention to pietistically refuse one's prophetic call (see Exod. 3.11, 13; 4.1, 10, 13; Jer. 1.6), Jonah's refusal stand outs in two remarkable ways: (1) His own speech is not given, rather he is simply reported as fleeing from the Lord. (2) His refusal is not immediately changed into acceptance by the Lord's reassurance, rather he must be coerced into acceptance.[46] These remarkable differences force upon the reader the question as to why Jonah refused. The reader continues to read, seeking an answer, and does not find one until near the end of the narrative:

> Oh Lord! Is this not what I said while I was still in my homeland? Therefore, I hastened to flee to Tarshish for I knew that you are a gracious and compassionate God, slow to anger and extremely benevolent, who would change his mind concerning the evil (4.2).

Here the narrator explicitly refers to the omitted dialogue in 1.3 ('what I said'), thereby allowing the reader to reconstruct Jonah's account of his refusal as it may have occurred in 1.3 as something like the following:

> Well Lord, I really strive to obey your will, but I know that, 'you are a gracious and compassionate God, slow to anger and extremely benevolent', and I am certain that you will 'change [your] mind concerning this evil'.

Another instance of omitted dialogue concerns Jonah's answer to the four questions posed by the sailors: 'What is your mission and where are you coming from? What is your homeland and from what people do you come?' The narrator presents Jonah as answering in his own words only the last question: 'I am a Hebrew...' (1.9). However, the narrator implies that Jonah answered all of the questions (and possibly some others), when he[47] describes the sailors' response:

---

46. See N.C. Habel, 'The Form and Significance of Call Narratives', *ZAW* 77 (1965), pp. 297-323.

47. I try to avoid the use of any pronoun to refer to the narrator; however, occasionally I find it stylistically better to use a pronoun to avoid too much repetition.

> Then the men were filled with the most dreadful fear and they said to him, 'What is this that you have done!?' for the men now knew that he was fleeing from the Lord *because he had told them* (1.10).

Even though some of Jonah's answers are omitted, readers can reconstruct them, if desired, with some degree of success, from their knowledge of Jonah from 2 Kgs 14.25 and earlier verses in the Jonah narrative as something like the following:

> My mission is to 'go to Nineveh and call out against it' [1.2]; I am coming from Jeroboam's court in Samaria [2 Kgs 14.23-27]. My hometown is Gath-hepher in Israel [2 Kgs 14.25] and 'I am a Hebrew, and the Lord, the God of heaven, I worship—he who made the sea and the dry land.'

Since these answers would not explicitly account for 'the evil' that the sailors are suffering, they might have also asked, 'Why is the Lord, your God, trying to destroy us?' Jonah may have then answered, as suggested in 1.10, 'Because I am "fleeing from the Lord".'

Another case of omitted dialogue, which is less obvious, concerns the Lord's elaboration concerning Nineveh's destruction in his requests to Jonah (1.2; 3.2). The different wording of the two requests and the supposed ambiguity of the second request has led some commentators to suggest that in the second request the Lord is already moderating his judgment for punishment.[48] However, this interpretation is to be rejected for two reasons. (1) The two requests are both constructed speech in that they are much too vague.[49] They are vague as to the indictment brought against the Ninevites. The first simply refers to 'their wickedness' and the second gives no indictment. They are also vague as to what words Jonah must use. The first requires Jonah to declare doom,[50] the second, 'whatever I command you'. Even if Jonah's oracle as presented in the narrative (3.4) is given 'just as the Lord had commanded' (3.3), neither of the Lord's requests say that these are the exact words that Jonah was to prophesy.[51] (2) The narrator suggests that the Lord may have specified

---

I have chosen to consistently use the masculine forms of pronouns for the narrator because of the predominately male-oriented viewpoint of the narrative.

48. For example, Sasson, *Jonah*, p. 226.

49. On vague references in constructed dialogue, see Tannen, 'Constructed Dialogue', p. 314.

50. As I mentioned earlier, 'declare doom upon it' is Sasson's well-nuanced translation of קְרָא עָלֶיהָ in 1.2. See Sasson, *Jonah*, pp. 71-75.

51. See P.L. Trible, *Rhetorical Criticism: Context, Method, and the Book of Jonah* (Minneapolis: Fortress Press, 1994), p. 180.

more to Jonah about Nineveh's destruction—'God changed his mind concerning the evil *which he had commanded against them'*. Therefore, the different wording of the two requests does not suggest that in the second one the Lord was already moderating his request. In addition, the supposed ambiguity of the second request concerning the destruction of Nineveh is only ambiguous if it is abstracted from its narrative context. Rather, the narrative context implies that the conversation between the Lord and Jonah included much more dialogue than given in the form of direct speech in 1.2 and 3.2, including not only Jonah's account but also the Lord's elaboration upon the indictment of the Ninevites and the resulting destruction.

The last case of omitted dialogue that is nevertheless referred to later in the narrative concerns the sailors' initial refusal of Jonah's request to throw him overboard. After Jonah makes his request (1.12), the narrator simply reports, 'Nonetheless, the men rowed hard in order to reach dry land' (1.13). However, when their rowing fails, the sailors pray, 'Please, O Lord, do not let us perish because of the life of this man, and do not hold us accountable for innocent blood' (1.14). Now the reader can reconstruct the sailors' account for their refusal as follows: 'Well, thank you for the offer, but we could not possibly allow ourselves to be held "accountable for [your] innocent blood".'

(The omission of Jonah's answer to the Lord's final question [4.10-11] is immediately obvious to the reader; however, it is not discussed here because the narrative itself provides nothing that enables the reader to reconstruct this answer. Rather, the reader has to make guesses.)

These cases of omitted dialogue—the sailors' prayers to their own gods and their vows to the Lord, Jonah's account, Jonah's answers to the sailors, the Lord's elaboration on his indictment of the Ninevites and resulting punishment, and the sailors' account—are those to which the narrator later refers. Since the narrator seems to omit dialogue freely, other conversations may be understood as omitted or abbreviated. I suggest that the following two cases of omitted dialogue can also be made with some degree of support from the text.

First, Jonah's brief oracle—'Forty days more, and Nineveh will overturn' (3.4)—is also vague,[52] containing neither an indictment nor a specific means of destruction. The Ninevites' manner of repenting may suggest that the indictment had nothing to do with theological matters, for they still do not seem to know who Jonah's god is ('that god', 3.9).

52. See n. 49.

Rather, it concerned only their morality, as suggested in the king's demand, 'Each person must turn from his evil ways and from the violence which is in their hands' (3.8). Therefore, the reader may infer that the omitted indictment of Nineveh by the Lord (through Jonah) may have only dealt with Nineveh's transgressions, much like the indictments made by Amos (who also prophesied during the reign of Jeroboam II) against the foreign nations, including the Assyrians (Amos 1.3-5).

Second, Jonah's response to the second instance of the Lord's command (3.3) has a striking parallel to his response to the first instance (1.3)—that is, neither is given in Jonah's own words but is simply reported by the narrator. As we have seen, his initial refusal is the strongest case of omitted dialogue that can be reconstructed from the following narrative. Since his coerced acceptance is also given only in the narrator's report, it may be that Jonah's own words have been once again 'suppressed' from the reader. If this is the case, what might they have been? I suggest that his actions betray something of what his verbal response may have been. He fulfills only the bare minimum required of him—he 'hardly' enters Nineveh, quickly gives his brief oracle (3.4), immediately leaves the city (4.5), and does all of this in anger (4.1). These actions suggest that if Jonah verbalized his acceptance of the Lord's request it may have been something like this: 'OK, Lord, I will go, even though I really don't want to, because I am certain that you will change your mind concerning this evil.' The omission of Jonah's verbal acceptance (3.3) and Jonah's abbreviated oracle (3.4) are just two examples of the narrator possibly omitting or abbreviating characters' speeches and not explicitly referring to the omission as in the cases above.

Constructed Dialogue and Adjacency Pairs. As was suggested in Chapter 1, preferred seconds gravitate towards reported consequences for purposes of brevity (for example, 'The child went.'). Dispreferred seconds, however, have two gravitational poles. They gravitate towards reported consequences for purposes of mitigation (for example, 'But the child went outside to play') or towards direct speech for purposes of elaboration (for example, 'The child said, "Oh Dad, I want to go outside to play." So she went outside and played.'). If this is the case, then an analysis of a narrator's predilection for certain placements of the parts of adjacency pairs in direct speech, indirect speech, or reported consequences may inform us as to the narrator's style. In other words, the way in which the narrator arranges the parts of adjacency pairs in the various forms of constructed dialogue affects the tone of the narrative.

The constructed dialogue in the Jonah narrative consists almost exclusively of direct speech and reported consequences. Only one instance of indirect speech occurs in the narrative and it transforms itself into direct speech—'And [Jonah] asked that he might die, "It is better that I die than live"' (4.8). Note that this one occurrence of indirect speech is a repetition of his previous death-request, which is given in direct speech—'Now, O Lord, take my life from me, for it is better that I die than live' (4.3). In the following discussion, this one instance of indirect speech will be considered as direct speech, since it transforms itself into direct speech and is a repetition of previous direct speech.

An analysis of the narrator's arrangement of adjacency pairs within the various forms of constructed dialogue reveals some interesting conclusions concerning tone (see Tables 1–3 below).[53] First, the first parts of adjacency pairs are found predominantly in direct speech (see Table 3). In fact, the seven first parts which are found in reported consequences can easily be explained as exceptions to the narrator's predilection to placing first parts in direct speech. Two of the seven concern the religiosity of the sailors and do not directly affect the plot in any way (1.5, 16; see Table 2). The other five concern the Lord's control of nature presented in the form of adjacency pairs with both first and second (preferred) parts hidden in reported consequences (2.1, 11; 4.6, 7, 8; see Table 2).

Secondly, both preferred and dispreferred seconds are found predominately in reported consequences (see Table 3). Again, the three exceptions are noteworthy. The two preferred seconds (1.9; 4.9) concern Jonah's answers to questions that both contain implicit accusations. In 1.9, Jonah appears to answer only one of the sailors' four questions, which are preceded by the accusation, 'you on whose account this evil has come to us'; however, this instance of direct speech can be misleading

53. In Chapter 2 we saw how particular utterances in the Jonah narrative can have a multiplicity of functions within the structure of adjacency pairs. For example, Jonah's answer to the sailor's question, 'What must we do?' is itself a request, 'Pick me up' (1.11-12). For the sake of simple categorization, however, the following analysis assumes just one function for each utterance and this function is decided on a semantic basis. For example, Jonah's answer, 'Pick me up' (1.12), is considered a request.

because Jonah's full answer as been omitted or, at least, abbreviated by
the narrator. In this sense, Jonah's answer, 'I am a Hebrew...', is not so
much direct speech as a marker for Jonah's full answer which is lacking.
In 4.9, Jonah angrily answers the Lord's question, 'Is it good for you to
be so angry...?', which when it was first asked in 4.4 he refused to
answer. His answer, however, provides no new information, because the
words he uses are simply a rewording of the question into a declarative
sentence with his previous request in 4.3 implied: 'It is good that I am
angry enough to die'. Rather, his answer in the form of direct speech is
important in that the narrator here places Jonah's last speech act in his
own words. In the remaining exception, the dispreferred second in 4.10-
11, we see a similar strategy at work. Here the narrator places the
Lord's last speech act in his own words. The Lord's disagreement with
Jonah's assessment of his supposed sad situation ends the narrative and
sums up the theological theme of the Lord's compassion for all creation.

Thirdly, when the previous two observations are taken together in
relation to the dialogue of the two main characters, Jonah and the Lord,
an interesting pattern emerges. Every instance of dialogue between
Jonah and the Lord in the first three chapters is incomplete in that the
narrator omits the second part of the adjacency pair and only reports the
consequences.[54] When the Lord initiates the adjacency pairs, begun with
his request (1.2; 3.2), Jonah's refusal is not given in direct speech (1.3;
3.3). Likewise, when Jonah initiates an adjacency pair with the Lord
(2.3-10), the Lord's response is not given in direct speech (2.11). This
pattern, however, is broken in the fourth chapter. In 4.2-4, Jonah's
complaint provides the reader with enough information to reconstruct
Jonah's earlier omitted refusal in 1.3, and the Lord, for the first time,
responds to Jonah in direct speech ('Is it good...?'). The narrative closes
with a dialogue between the Lord and Jonah in which they both use
direct speech (4.8-11). Jonah repeats his death-request; the Lord questions the validity of this request again; Jonah answers this question; and,
finally, the Lord gives his account for why he is refusing Jonah's death-
request. Thus, the narrator not only exerts his power in his selective
choice of 'quoting' the characters' direct speech or omitting their
dialogue, but also arranges his choices in such a way as to create a
contrasting pattern between, on the one hand, the Lord's dialogue with
Jonah in the first three chapters (omitted second parts) and, on the other

54. K.M. Craig, Jr, 'Jonah and the Reading Process', *JSOT* 47 (1990), pp. 103-
14 (110); Craig, *A Poetics of Jonah*, pp. 68-69; Hauser, 'Jonah', pp. 25-27.

hand, their dialogue in the fourth chapter (second parts in direct speech). As we will see below,[55] this pattern is used in the presentation of the narrator's satirical attitude toward the material.

This intentional pattern further qualifies the exceptions to the second observation given above. That is, two of the three instances of dis-preferred seconds in the form of direct speech occur in the fourth chapter. In 4.9 Jonah angrily answers the Lord's question and in 4.10-11 the Lord explicitly disagrees with Jonah's assessment of his situation, thereby providing his account for the refusal of Jonah's death-request. The only exception remaining concerns Jonah's incomplete answer to the sailors' questions (1.9), which is information that the reader already knew anyway. In other words, the narrator's tendency in Jonah 1–3 to place dispreferred seconds in reported consequences, thereby mitigating them further, changes so that in Jonah 4 he places dispreferred seconds in direct speech, thereby allowing for more elaboration (see Table 4). This change is significant in that the gaps that are opened in his use of reported consequences in chs. 1–3 are closed by the elaboration possible in his use of direct speech in ch. 4. This is illustrated best by the gap created by Jonah's refusal in 1.3 (i.e., Why did he refuse?), which is closed by his own direct speech in 4.2. This manipulation of the reader through gaps and their filling reflects the narrator's satirical attitude in the narrative.[56]

Table 1: Direct Speech in the Jonah Narrative

First Parts

1.2:	Lord's request of Jonah: 'Get up. Go…'
1.6:	helmsman's request of Jonah: 'How could you sleep? Get up!…'
1.7:	sailors' request of one another: 'Come! Let's cast lots…'
1.8:	sailors' request of Jonah: 'Tell us…'
1.10:	sailors' question to Jonah: 'What is this that you have done!?'
1.11:	sailors' question to Jonah: 'What must we do…?'
1.12:	Jonah's request of sailors: 'Pick me up…'
1.14:	sailors' request of Lord: 'Please, O Lord, do not…'
2.3-10	Jonah's request of Lord: 'I call out, in my trouble, to the Lord…'

55. See 'The Narrator's Attitude toward the Material' below.

56. For more on the narrator's satirical attitude, see 'The Narrator's Judgment' below.

3.2:	Lord's request of Jonah: 'Get up...'
3.4:	Lord's implied request of Ninevites: 'Forty days more, and Nineveh will overturn.'
3.7-9	king's request of Ninevites: 'People and beasts...must not taste...'
4.2-3:	Jonah's question/request of Lord: 'Oh Lord! Is this not...?...take my life...'
4.4:	Lord's question to Jonah: 'Is it good for you to be so angry?'
4.8:	Jonah's request of Lord: And he asked that he might die, 'It is better that I die than live.'
4.9:	Lord's question to Jonah: 'Is it good for you to be so angry...?'

Second Parts
Preferreds

| 1.9: | Jonah's answer to sailors: 'I am a Hebrew...' |
| 4.9: | Jonah's answer to Lord: 'It is good...' |

Dispreferreds

| 4.10-11 | Lord's disagreement with Jonah: 'You yourself were fretting...' |

Table 2: Reported Consequences

First Parts

1.5:	sailors' request of their gods: each prayed to his own gods
1.16:	sailors' offers to Lord: they offered sacrifices...and made vows
2.1:	Lord's request of fish: Then the Lord appointed a fish
2.11:	Lord's request of fish: Then the Lord spoke to the fish
4.6:	Lord's request of plant: The Lord God appointed a plant
4.7:	Lord's request of worm: God appointed a worm
4.8:	Lord's request of wind: God appointed a fierce east wind

Second Parts
Preferreds

1.10:	Jonah's answer to sailors: the men now knew that he was fleeing from the Lord, because he had told them
1.15:	sailors' acceptance of Jonah's request: Then they picked up Jonah and cast him...
1.16:	Lord's acceptance of sailors' offer: (implied acceptance of sacrifices and vows)
2.1:	fish's acceptance of Lord's request: And Jonah was in the...fish

2.11:	fish's acceptance of Lord's request: it vomited Jonah upon dry land
3.3:	Jonah's acceptance of Lord's request: Then Jonah got up and went...
3.5:	Ninevites' acceptance of Lord's request: Then the people of Nineveh believed in God...
3.10:	Lord's acceptance of Ninevites' request: God changed his mind...
4.6:	plant's acceptance of Lord's request: Jonah rejoiced over the plant
4.7:	worm's acceptance of Lord's request: It attacked the plant
4.8:	wind's acceptance of Lord's request: (implied acceptance)

Dispreferreds

1.3: b	Jonah's refusal of Lord's request: Jonah, instead, sought to escape
1.5: b¹	god's refusal of sailors' request: (no response to sailors' request implies refusal)
1.13: b²	sailors' refusal of Jonah's request: Nonetheless the men rowed hard...
4.5:	Jonah's non-answer to Lord: But Jonah went from the city

Table 3: Comparison of Direct Speech and Reported Consequences

	Direct speech	Reported consequences
First parts:	16	7
Second parts (total):	3	15
Preferred seconds:	2	11
Dispreferred seconds:	1	4

Table 4: Comparison of Direct Speech and Reported Consequences in Jonah 1–3 and Jonah 4

	Direct speech	Reported consequences
Jonah 1–3		
First parts:	12	4
Second parts (total):	1	11
Preferred seconds:	1	8
Dispreferred seconds:	0	3
Jonah 4		
First parts:	4	3
Second parts (total):	2	4
Preferred seconds:	1	3
Dispreferred seconds:	1	1

Flashback. As noted in the above section on plot, the narrator describes
two roughly simultaneous events: the Ninevites' repentance and Jonah's
anger. Although the narrator would necessarily be required to describe
one of these events first, the narrator did not have to choose to describe
the Ninevites' repentance first. In fact, it is probable that the action described in 4.1-11 (Jonah's anger and the Lord's lesson) ended before that
described in 3.5-10 (the Ninevites' repentance and the Lord's changing
his mind); therefore, one could argue that the most 'natural' chronological order would be the reverse. So why might the narrator describe
the Ninevites' response before the account of Jonah leaving the city and
his interaction with the Lord concerning the plant? This question can be
addressed in at least two ways: from the perspective of first, the account
of the Ninevites' repentance and secondly, the plant episode. Jonah's
oracle requires some kind of response—whether passive or active, negative or positive—because it contains an implied request. Therefore, the
placing of the account of the Ninevites' repentance is explained by preference organization. That is, the implied request in Jonah's oracle begins
an adjacency pair, which elicits a preferred or dispreferred response,
and the narrative presents the Ninevites' response. Secondly, this order
allows the plant episode to end the entire narrative, thereby placing
emphasis on the Lord's words to Jonah, 'You yourself were fretting
over the plant, for which you neither toiled nor cultivated...Yet I should
not have compassion on Nineveh...?' (4.10-11). Thus, the narrative ends
with a universal theological statement (in the form of a rhetorical
question) about the Lord's compassion, which is the basis for the Lord's
changing 'his mind concerning the evil which he had commanded'
against the Ninevites (3.10).

Summary: Material Selection and Arrangement. The selection and
arrangement of material in the Jonah narrative informs us about the
narrator's stance.[57] (1) The use of paronomastic techniques suggests an

57. Another possible indication of tone concerning the selection of material is the
evidence that parts of the Jonah narrative seem to parody (or at least draw from) earlier
biblical texts. On Jon. 3.1–4.11 and Joel 2.1-17, see T.B. Dozeman, 'Inner-Biblical
Interpretation of Yahweh's Gracious and Compassionate Character', *JBL* 108 (1989),
pp. 207-223. On Jon. 2.3-10 and Psalms, see Ackerman, 'Satire and Symbolism',
pp. 221-22; Magonet, *Form and Meaning*, pp. 44-49; Miles, 'Laughing at the Bible,'
pp. 174-75. On Jon. 4.5-11 and 1 Kgs 19, see A.J. Band, 'Swallowing Jonah: The
Eclipse of Parody', *Prooftexts* 10 (1990), pp. 177-95 (187); Magonet, *Form and
Meaning*, p. 69; Miles, 'Laughing at the Bible', pp. 177, 180; F. Zimmerman,

intentional shaping of the material to highlight the themes of the Lord's omnipotence and the contrast between Jonah and the pagan characters. (2) The narrator not only withholds material, but flaunts this power by explicitly referring to omitted dialogue. (3) The narrator tends to place first parts of adjacency pairs in direct speech and second parts in reported consequences. (4) The narrator demonstrates control of the narrative by re-ordering the plot by using a flashback. Taken together, these observations suggest that the narrator not only utilizes the power to select and arrange the material, but seems to enjoy his manipulation of the reader.

The Narrator's Voice
As is typical in biblical narrative, the narrator only describes the plot and characters in the third person. The more modern techniques of addressing characters or the reader in the second person are not found in biblical narratives, including the story of Jonah.

The Narrator's Attitude toward the Material
The Narrator's Point of View. The narrator in the book of Jonah is clearly omniscient. He overhears private conversations between the characters and senses their innermost emotions and motives. He not only knows these things, but also manipulates them in his selection and arrangement of the material as presented to the reader. In fact, his explicit references to omitted dialogue suggests that this narrator even likes to flaunt his power and control over the material.

The Narrator's Judgment. The narrator's judgment has often been characterized as satirical.[58] Since the secondary literature on Jonah contains

'Problems and Solutions in the Book of Jonah', *Judaism* 40 (1991), pp. 580-89 (585). On Jonah and Isa. 60, see Lacocque and Lacocque, *Jonah*, pp. 18-19.

58. The following works refer to the genre or the tone of the book of Jonah as either 'parable', 'irony' or 'satire'. All of these works were consulted; therefore, my characterization of the tone of Jonah as satirical draws from many of them.

A group from Renne, France (trans. J.C. Kirby), 'An Approach to the Book of Jonah: Suggestions and Questions', *Semeia* 15 (1979), pp. 85-96; Ackerman, 'Jonah'; *idem*, 'Satire and Symbolism'; Band, 'Swallowing Jonah'; M. Burrows, 'The Literary Category of the Book of Jonah', in H.T. Frank and W.L. Reed (eds.), *Translating and Understanding the Old Testament: Essays in Honor of Herbert Gordon May* (Nashville: Abingdon Press, 1970), pp. 80-107; B.S. Childs, 'The Canonical Shape of the Book of Jonah', in G.A. Tuttle (ed.), *Biblical and Near*

some confusion concerning what 'satire' (as well as 'parody' and 'irony')
is, Abrams's definition is used here:

> Satire is the literary art of diminishing a subject by making it ridiculous
> and evoking toward it attitudes of amusement, contempt, indignation, or
> scorn. It differs from the comic in that comedy evokes laughter mainly as
> an end in itself, while satire 'derides'; that is, it uses laughter as a weapon,
> and against a butt existing outside the work itself. That butt may be an
> individual (in 'personal satire'), or a type of person, a class, an institution,
> a nation, or even...the whole race of man.[59]

Abrams continues by describing the most common form of satire, what
he calls 'indirect satire':

> The most common form is that of a fictional narrative, in which the
> objects of the satire are characters who make themselves and their opinions

Eastern Studies: Essays in Honor of William Sanford LaSor (Grand Rapids:
Eerdmans, 1978), pp. 122-28; J.D. Crossan, *The Dark Interval: Towards a Theology
of Story* (Niles: Argus, 1975); Dozeman, 'Inner-Biblical Interpretation'; Halpern and
Friedman, 'Composition and Paranomasia'; Holbert, '"Deliverance Belongs to
Yahweh"'; Hope, 'Pragmatics, Exegesis and Translation'; Lacocque and Lacocque,
Jonah; D. Marcus, *From Balaam to Jonah: Anti-prophetic Satire in the Hebrew
Bible* (Brown Judaic Studies, 301; Atlanta: Scholars Press, 1995), pp. 93-170; J.
Mather, 'The Comic Art of the Book of Jonah', *Soundings* 65 (1982), pp. 280-91;
Miles, 'Laughing at the Bible'; M. Orth, 'Genre in Jonah: The Effects of Parody in
the Book of Jonah', in W.W. Hallo, B.W. Jones and G.L. Mattingly (eds.), *The
Bible in the Light of Cuneiform Literature: Scripture in Context III* (Lewiston, NY:
Edwin Mellen, 1990), pp. 257-81; Payne, 'Jonah from the Perspective of Its
Audience'; P. Trudinger, 'Jonah: A Post-Exilic Verbal Cartoon?', *Downside Review*
107 (1989), pp. 142-43; Warshaw, 'The Book of Jonah'; M. West, 'Irony in the
Book of Jonah: Audience Identification with the Hero', *Perspectives in Religious
Studies* 11 (1984), pp. 233-42; Wolff, *Obadiah and Jonah*, pp. 80-85.

    Contra, A. Berlin, 'A Rejoinder to John A. Miles, Jr., with Some Observations
on the Nature of Prophecy', *JQR* 66 (1976), pp. 227-35; R.E. Clements, 'The
Purpose of the Book of Jonah', in *Congress Volume, Edinburgh 1974* (VTSup, 28;
Leiden: Brill, 1975), p. 16-28; J. Day, 'Problems in the Interpretation of the Book of
Jonah', in A.S. van der Woude (ed.), *In Quest of the Past: Studies on Israelite
Religion, Literature and Prophetism* (OTS, 26; Leiden: Brill, 1990), pp. 32-47; E.
Levine, 'Jonah as a Philosophical Book', *ZAW* 96 (1984), pp. 235-45; J.W. Roffey,
'God's Truth, Jonah's Fish: Structure and Existence in the Book of Jonah',
Australian Biblical Review 36 (1988), pp. 1-18; Sasson, *Jonah*, pp. 331-34; P.L.
Trible, *Studies in the Book of Jonah* (PhD dissertation; Columbia University, 1963).

    59. M.H. Abrams, *A Glossary of Literary Terms* (New York: Holt, Rinehart &
Winston, 1981), pp. 167-68.

ridiculous by what they think, say, and do, and are sometimes made even more ridiculous by the author's comments and narrative style.[60]

Abrams's definition applies well to the Jonah narrative in that Jonah makes himself look ridiculous and the narrator's selection and arrangement of material makes him look even more ridiculous.

From the first verse of the book, the reader understands that Jonah is a prophet of the Lord. This verse itself is a prophetic superscription, which ascribes authority to the prophetic career of Jonah. In addition, Jonah's name and patronymic identifies him with 'Jonah, son of Amittai' of 2 Kgs 14.25. In the second verse, the Lord requests Jonah to get up and go to Nineveh to proclaim judgment.

Thus far, nothing is out of the ordinary. A standard prophetic superscription refers to a known prophet, and then the Lord commands him to speak judgment against one of Israel's chief enemies during the prophet's time, the Assyrians whose capital was Nineveh.[61] However, Jonah's response (1.3) begins to call into question his character in a number of ways: (1) Although reluctance towards a prophetic call is conventional (see Exod. 3.11, 13; 4.1, 10, 13; Jer. 1.6), it is generally followed by the Lord's reassurance which convinces the prophet to accept his call. In the Jonah narrative, however, Jonah is not only reluctant but disobedient, and he appears to give the Lord no opportunity for reassurance. (2) Prophetic call narratives include the prophets' reluctance in their own words, but Jonah does not (appear to)[62] verbalize his refusal in 1.3 at all. (3) The narrator's choice of words plays on the contrast between the Lord's request and Jonah's refusal. The Lord tells Jonah to 'get up' and go to Nineveh, but Jonah 'gets up' and 'goes down' to Jaffa. (4) Rather than going to Nineveh under the Lord's guidance, Jonah ironically chooses to go to sea. Irony occurs here because '[i]n the Bible the sea is almost invariably hostile, but Jonah assumes that it will be the helpful means of escape to a haven'.[63]

Once again, Jonah calls in question his own character in his response

60. Abrams, *A Glossary of Literary Terms*, p. 169.
61. For an excellent discussion of the traditional language in 1.1-2, see Trible, *Rhetorical Criticism*, p. 124-27.
62. From a diachronic viewpoint, Jonah does not verbalize his refusal in 1.3. From a synchronic viewpoint, he does.
63. Warshaw, 'The Book of Jonah', p. 196. See also K. Almbladh, 'The Israelites and the Sea', in *Studies in the Book of Jonah* (Studia Semitica Upsaliensis, 7; Stockholm: Almqvist & Wiksell, 1986).

to the storm that the Lord casts down upon the ship. 'Jonah went down into the vessel's hold, laid down, and went to sleep' (1.5). Jonah's actions are in sharp contrast to the seriousness demonstrated by the sailors' actions. While the pagan sailors pray and lighten the ship's load, Jonah goes to sleep! Jonah's bizarre behavior even provokes the helmsman to reprimand him, 'Get up! Call out to your god!' (1.6). Again the narrator plays with the contrasts of 'going up' and 'going down'. Jonah's refusal leads to the Lord's casting down the winds, creating a mighty storm. In response, the sailors pray (up) to their gods and pick up cargo to cast it down into the sea. But Jonah continues to 'go down'—down into the ship's hold and down to sleep. Thus, in 1.4-6 Jonah's actions of 'going down' contrast not only with the Lord's request to 'go up', but also with the pagans' pious actions implying 'going up'.

Although the reader and Jonah know what the cause of the storm is, the sailors do not, so they resort to the abominable practice (see Deut. 18.9-14; Jer. 14.13-16; Zech. 10.2) of casting (down) lots. Ironically, this pagan practice works. Once again the sailors seem to get closer to the truth than Jonah, even in spite of Jonah's revealed knowledge and their own paganism.

The sailors' sudden conversion to the Lord also contrasts with Jonah's refusal and flight. The sailors ask Jonah for more information concerning the cause of the evil they suffer. When Jonah tells them he is fleeing from the Lord, they immediately want to know what they must do. Before they accept Jonah's advice to cast him down into the sea, they pray to the Lord. When the storm ceases, they offer sacrifices and make vows. Their piety makes Jonah's disobedience look ridiculous.

Soon Jonah is in the belly of a fish, who obediently accepted the Lord's request to rescue Jonah. Now that he has been 'cast into the depths' (2.4), Jonah offers a prayer of thanksgiving?[64] This prayer with the theme of 'Deliverance belongs to the Lord' (2.10) comes from the same Jonah who has been fleeing from the Lord! And Jonah continues to be cocky in that he still thinks himself better than pagans: 'Those who hold to empty faiths, their hope for mercy they give up. But, I, with a grateful voice, sacrifice to you; that which I vow, I shall fulfill' (2.9-10). The fish obediently vomits Jonah upon dry land.

This is certainly not a typical prophetic book. But the conventional prophetic superscription does occur again (3.1) and the Lord repeats his

---

64. On the shift from individual lament to prayer of thanksgiving, see Ackerman, 'Satire and Symbolism', pp. 221-22.

request for Jonah to go to Nineveh and prophesy against it. This time Jonah obeys, but *how* does he obey? Not surprisingly, Jonah performs the bare minimum required: 'After Jonah had *hardly* gone into the city...he called out, "Forty days more, and Nineveh will overturn."' (3.4). The narrator suggests that he just makes it inside the city and utters the briefest oracle of all biblical prophets.

Jonah's earlier disobedience is once again contrasted with the sudden response of pagans in the form of the Ninevites' repentance.

> The response of the Ninevites is unprecedented in the prophetic tradition: Jonah barely enters the city and speaks five Hebrew words (not even introduced by 'thus says the Lord'), and thereby instigates the most frantic reform ever heard of.[65]

This reform not only includes the people of Nineveh fasting, putting on sackcloth and praying, but even the animals are expected to do likewise! Such repentance leads the Lord to change his mind and not punish the Ninevites.

What is Jonah's response to what appears to be his incomparable success?[66] He becomes so terribly upset and angry that he twice says, 'it is better that I die than live' (4.3, 8). The reasons he gives for this death-wish are petty: (1) because the Lord is compassionate toward the Ninevites and (2) because his shade was destroyed.

Clearly, Jonah's actions and words make him look ridiculous and the narrator selects and arranges material to emphasize his ridiculousness in three ways: (1) The narrator uses word-play to highlight the Lord's omnipotence and Jonah's disobedience. Jonah's refusal to 'go up' to Nineveh leads him to 'go down' until eventually the Lord casts him down 'into the heart of the seas' (2.3). In contrast to Jonah's refusal, even nature—the fish, the plant, the worm, the east wind—obediently accepts the Lord's 'appointing'. Whereas Jonah must be coerced into his 'calling out' to the Lord, the pagan sailors and Ninevites are quick to 'call out' even when it is only suggested. (2) The narrator omits dialogue that could lessen Jonah's ridiculous behavior. Jonah's account of his refusal is omitted, thereby allowing the Ninevites' repentance, the Lord's changing his mind, and Jonah's anger to be more surprising. The Lord's elaboration on the destruction of Nineveh is omitted, thereby

---

65. Ackerman, 'Jonah, pp. 238-39.

66. From a diachronic viewpoint, Jonah's response in 4.1-3 seems to occur after the Ninevites' repentance. From a synchronic viewpoint, it does not; however, Jonah is still angry about effecting Nineveh's deliverance.

making Jonah's anger appear more out of proportion. (3) The narrator's tendency to place dispreferred seconds within the form of reported consequences increases their indirectness, thereby creating gaps in the narrative. With the creation of these gaps, the narrator withholds information from the reader, thereby allowing himself to play on the possibilities for filling these gaps that the reader creates before he reveals enough information to guide the reader to the filling of the gaps. This is especially the case with Jonah's initial refusal (1.3) which raises the question, 'Why?', with its various possible answers (for example, inadequacy, fear), a question that is not answered until the reader overhears Jonah's account implied in his complaint—'Is this not what I said...that you are a gracious and compassionate God?' (4.2). (4) The narrator uses flashback in order to describe first Jonah's success and, therefore, make his anger look even more ridiculous. Thus, the narrator uses his omniscience and omnipotence over the narrative in order to present Jonah as a petty character, most worthy of our ridicule, and the Lord as gracious and compassionate, most worthy of our praise. In other words, the tone of the Jonah narrative is satirical in its characterization of the prophet Jonah.

5. *Conclusion: The Jonah Narrative*

Above, analyses of the various elements of the Jonah narrative have been given with special attention to the contributions of the conversations in the narrative. The plot of the Jonah narrative can be understood as consisting of adjacency pairs—that is, the Lord's request is refused by Jonah, and so on. The development of the various characters includes the contrasts not only between the different contents of the characters' speeches but also their structures. The disobedient Jonah is predisposed to participating in adjacency pairs with dispreferred seconds (for example, his initial refusal) whereas the other characters—the pagan, yet obedient, sailors and Ninevites as well as nature—are generally obedient to the Lord and tend to participate in adjacency pairs with preferred seconds. The narrative's atmosphere is developed by the portrayal of the omnipotent Lord controlling humans and nature in the universal (even if delayed and coerced) acceptance of all his requests; however, the Lord is not unlimited for, as is expressed in Jonah's protest (4.2), he is limited by his divine nature of mercy and compassion. The narrator's satirical tone is produced in three ways: (1) the use of paronomasia that highlight the themes of the Lord's omnipotence (for example, 'appointing') and Jonah's disobedience and its consequences (for example, 'going up'/ 'going down'); (2) the omission of dialogue that could lessen Jonah's ridiculous behavior (for example, his account for his refusal); and (3) the use of a flashback to emphasize Jonah's 'success', thereby highlighting the ridiculousness of his anger.

In summary, the author of the Jonah narrative has crafted a text which utilizes various strategies in the development of the different narrative elements. Recalling the definition of narrative given above, we can summarize the Jonah narrative as follows: The prophet Jonah (the main character) unsuccessfully strives to avoid his divinely ordained mission (plot). In the process, he learns about the limitations that can be placed upon him (atmosphere) by the omnipotent Lord (the other major character). Throughout the narrative, the omniscient narrator ridicules Jonah and praises the Lord by means of exerting control over the selection and arrangement of the material (tone).

Chapter 4

READING THE JONAH NARRATIVE: THE IMPLIED READER

It has only been within the last couple of decades that literary critics have been paying more attention to the role of the reader in the creation of meaning; that is, serious consideration is now being given to the interplay between text and reader.[1] This reader-response approach in literary criticism has affected biblical studies, including recent studies on the book of Jonah.[2] This chapter also pays close attention to the interaction between text and reader in the Jonah narrative. In order to do this

---

1. Two anthologies contain excellent introductory articles and present various approaches to reader-response criticism: S.R. Suleiman and I. Crosman (eds.), *The Reader in the Text: Essays on Audience and Interpretation* (Princeton, NJ: Princeton University Press, 1980); J.P. Tompkins (ed.), *Reader-Response Criticism: From Formalism to Post-Structuralism* (Baltimore: The Johns Hopkins University Press, 1980).

2. For example, R.M. Fowler, *Let the Reader Understand: Reader-Response Criticism and the Gospel of Mark* (Minneapolis: Fortress Press, 1991); R. Detweiler (ed.), *Reader Response Approaches to Biblical and Secular Texts* (*Semeia* 31; Atlanta: Scholars Press, 1985); M. Sternberg, *The Poetics of Biblical Narrative* (Bloomington: Indiana University Press, 1985).

On Jonah, e.g., Band, 'Swallowing Jonah'; Craig, 'Jonah and the Reading Process'; *idem*, *A Poetics of Jonah*; Hauser, 'Jonah'; Hope, 'Pragmatics, Exegesis and Translation'; Mather, 'The Comic Art of the Book of Jonah'; Payne, 'Jonah from the Perspective of Its Audience'; Sasson, *Jonah*, pp. 334-40. In contrast to this study, most of these studies seem to understand the reader as either a contemporary or intended reader or any actual reader, all of whom are reading the narrative for the first time. However, in some cases this can only be inferred from the discussion of the reader, because, unfortunately, some of these commentators do not explicitly state what 'reader' they refer to or, when they do, their terms still do not communicate much. For example, Band refers to the 'acute reader' or 'competent reader' ('Swallowing Jonah', p. 189); however, neither of these terms unambiguously relates well to those of other reader-response critics and, thus, they do not clarify the use of 'reader'.

most effectively, some theoretical groundwork must first be laid. Hence, the particular theoretical understanding of 'reader' used below is explicated, as well as some of the principles that guide this reader in the interpretive process. Then a profile of the implied reader of the Jonah narrative is given before the commentary describes the reading process associated with the Jonah narrative.

1. *The Implied Reader: Interaction between Text and Reader*

The terminologies for various theoretical readers vary greatly from one reader-response critic to another, but they can generally be understood in a continuum from the reader whom the author had in mind (the 'intended reader') to actual readers.[3] Thus, if one wants to participate in conversations concerning reader-response criticism, one must be very explicit about which understanding one thinks most effectively describes the reading process. In my opinion, this is the 'implied reader' as formulated by Wolfgang Iser.[4]

Iser's implied reader can not be located within the text or even outside of the text in actual readers, but must be found only in the 'interaction between text and reader'.[5] In this interaction, 'text' and 'reader' must not be thought of as independent subjects or objects, but rather as representing two interrelated poles—the 'artistic pole', which consists of the influence of author's text upon the reader, and the 'aesthetic pole', which consists of the realization accomplished by the reader. In other

---

3.   For fuller discussion of this variety and complexity, see S.R. Suleiman 'Introduction: Varieties of Audience-Oriented Criticism', in Suleiman and Crosman (eds.), *The Reader in the Text*, pp. 3-45 and J.P. Tompkins, 'An Introduction to Reader-Response Criticism', in *idem* (ed.), *Reader-Response Criticism*, pp. ix-xvi.

4.   Wolfgang Iser's major works are *Act of Reading*; *The Implied Reader: Patterns of Communication in Prose Fiction from Bunyan to Beckett* (Baltimore: The Johns Hopkins University Press, 1974); and *Prospecting: From Reader Response to Literary Anthropology* (Baltimore: The Johns Hopkins University Press, 1989). In order to place Iser within the cacophony of voices, one can turn to the two introductory essays mentioned in the previous note and to Iser's own work and interviews with him. See Bloom, 'In Defense of Authors and Readers'; Iser, *Act of Reading*, pp. 27-50; Iser, *Prospecting*, pp. 42-69. Iser also explicitly relates his work to the speech-act theory of Austin and Searle in *Prospecting*, pp. 54-62, and responds to the 'traditional objections' to reader-response criticism in *Act of Reading*, pp. 20-27.

5.   This phrase occurs frequently in Iser's writings, including headings. See *Prospecting*, pp. 31-41; *Act of Reading*, pp. 161-231.

words, the 'text' is that which guides the reader by use of different narrative strategies; the 'reader', that which produces a particular meaning from his or her interaction with a particular text within the context of his or her own literary and historical tradition. At the woven intersection of these two poles lies the implied reader, who immerses himself or herself (with all of his or her preconceptions) in the text in order to fully realize the work.

The question remains, however, as to what the text, which can be read by numerous actual readers, and the implied reader, whose actual reader probably has already read various texts, brings to any particular interaction. Although the specific answer to this question will vary according to each particular text and each unique reader, all actual texts and all actual readers bring to such interactions certain common elements, as is evident in the discussions below.[6]

What Texts Bring to Interactions

For Iser, a literary text is a collection of signals that guide readers in their decoding. What are these signals? Iser has been very forthright in his discussion of the signals that he calls 'gaps of indeterminacy'.[7] These

---

6.   In his theoretical writings, Iser is not as explicit about what actual texts and actual readers bring to the reading process as he could be, especially as concerns readers. That is, rather than emphasizing what each participant in the interaction brings to it, he emphasizes the interaction itself. However, when he applies his method to actual texts, Iser necessarily changes this emphasis somewhat. For example, although his discussion of the reader's knowledge of history is quite brief (*Act of Reading*, pp. 27-28, 74-75), he nevertheless discusses Lockean empiricism as it relates to Sterne's *Tristan Shandy* (*Act of Reading*, pp. 74-76), eighteenth-century thought as it relates to Fielding's *Tom Jones* (*Act of Reading*, pp. 76-77), the Calvinist doctrine of predestination as it relates to Bunyan's *Pilgrim's Progress* (*Implied Reader*, pp. 1-28) and the political situation of the 'briefly considered' marriage between Elizabeth and the Duc d'Alençon as it relates to Spenser's *Shepheards Calendar* (*Prospecting*, pp. 73-97). Therefore, the following draws conclusions not only from the implications of Iser's theoretical writings but also from his own application of this theory to actual texts. This shift of emphasis has not gone unnoticed by other readers of Iser. For example, J.M. Foley, *Immanent Art: From Structure to Meaning in Traditional Oral Epic* (Bloomington: Indiana University Press, 1991), pp. 39-60; Suleiman, 'Introduction', pp. 21-27.

7.   See especially, 'Indeterminacy and the Reader's Response in Prose Fiction', in *Prospecting*, pp. 3-30. For discussions of analogous 'gaps' in conversation, see the essays in D. Tannen (ed.), *Coherence in Spoken and Written Discourse* (Advances in Discourse Processes, 12; Norwood: ABLEX, 1984).

gaps of indeterminacy occur in the text in places where either the author omitted information assumed to be already known by its readers (its presuppositions) *or* information about the narrative world that its readers cannot know and may or may not learn from the text itself. In other words, what is often missing in the text creates a gap of indeterminate knowledge which the readers themselves must fill from information found elsewhere in the text or from their knowledge of the world. This notion is important to Iser's understanding of reading literary texts, for he clearly distinguishes literary texts (which produce meaning primarily through their indeterminacy) from expository texts (which produce their meaning through their determinacy):

> [Literary texts] must...be still further differentiated...for there are texts that constitute something without being literary. For instance, all texts that present claims, state aims, define purposes, and formulate rules likewise produce new objects, but these objects achieve their existence only through the determinacy brought about by the text.[8]

Thus, indeterminacy has a particular role to play in the interaction between literary text and reader.

Iser distinguishes two basic types of indeterminacy: blanks and negations. In both types, the reader is induced to fill in the indeterminacy; however, they differ as to the status of this filling in at the end of the reading of the text.[9] In other words, when readers encounter an indeterminacy, they are spurred to fill it with reference to their knowledge of literature and tradition. In the case of blanks, readers have the last word, so to speak, in filling in the indeterminacy. In contrast, with negations readers are initially induced to fill in the indeterminacy only to have the text counteract this filling later by overtly providing information as to how the indeterminacy should have been filled. Because of the possibility of negation, the readers' experience of filling in indeterminacies is precarious, for as they continue in the interactive process of reading they never know until the reading of the text is completed

---

8.   *Prospecting*, p. 6. Iser's understanding of literary texts is remarkably similar to that of Tannen, who says,

> If expository prose is minimally dependent on immediate context and maximally dependent on lexicalization . . . then literary discourse is also maximally contextualized, not in the sense of depending on immediate context but by requiring the reader (or hearer) to fill in maximal background and other elided information ('Relative Focus on Involvement in Oral and Written Discourse', p. 137).

9.   See *Prospecting*, p. 34.

whether or not the indeterminacy is, on the one hand, a blank and, therefore, their filling in will go unquestioned or, on the other hand, a negation, and, therefore their filling in may be refuted.

Different narrative strategies actually guide the reader into filling the indeterminacies.[10] Concerning the process of filling in indeterminacy, Iser writes:

> This process is steered by two main structural components within the text: first, a repertoire of familiar literary patterns and recurrent literary themes, together with allusions to familiar social and historical contexts; second, techniques or strategies used to set the familiar against the unfamiliar.[11]

Elsewhere, Iser explicates the relationship between the narrative strategies in the text and the systems outside the text.

> To put it briefly, a literary text draws from two different systems which exist outside the text itself: the system of its historical situation and social norms and the system of previous literatures and literary norms.[12]

Hence, the text embodies extratextual referents including, but not necessarily limited to, prevalent theological–philosophical systems, traditional customs, literary genres, and previous uses of the narrative elements of plot, character, atmosphere and tone.

Given the various possibilities open to an author in crafting a literary work in the selection of these extratextual referents and the location of indeterminacies in the text, an author, who writes within a particular literary tradition, crafts the text according to some generic standards with a particular range of readers in mind.[13] Because of this selective

10. See especially, W. Iser, 'Narrative Strategies as a Means of Communication', in M.J. Valdés and O.J. Miller (eds.), *Interpretation of Narrative* (Toronto: University of Toronto Press, 1978), pp. 100-117 and *Act of Reading*, pp. 86-104.

11. *Implied Reader*, p. 288.

12. 'Narrative Strategies as a Means of Communication', p. 100.

13. Iser does not completely reject the validity of such a reader as Wolff's 'intended reader'; rather, he argues that such an understanding of an intended reader does not in any way do justice to the reading process, the interaction between text and reader:

> There can be no doubting the usefulness, and indeed necessity, of ascertaining this figure, and equally certain is the fact that there is a reciprocity between the form of presentation and the type of reader intended; but the question remains open as to why, generations later, a reader can still grasp the meaning (perhaps we should say a meaning) of the text, even though he cannot be the intended reader (*Act of Reading*, p. 33).

crafting of the text, various presuppositions are assumed in the text in reference to these extratextual realities, and these presuppositions are made with certain readers in mind. The most obvious example of intended readers in a text is the use of a particular language—for example, a contemporary author in New York City who publishes a short story in Spanish certainly has a Spanish-speaking audience in mind. Thus, authors' texts presuppose a certain range of readers.

What Readers Bring to Interactions
What readers bring to interactions between texts and themselves can be understood as simply the other side of the interaction. That is, if authors draw from literary traditions and history in their construction of texts, then readers bring their particular knowledge of their tradition (and possibly others) based upon their own experiences.

This knowledge pertains to literary traditions and their standard narrative strategies (for example, genre) as well as the history of the ideas and events of their own culture and, possibly, other cultures.[14] In other words, readers bring to the interaction between texts and themselves the knowledge they have previously gained from their interactions with texts (whether an earlier reading of the same text or readings of different texts) and reality. As they bring this knowledge to the interactions, readers thus have certain presuppositions about texts. For example, they presuppose certain things based upon their previous experience of other texts of the same genre[15]—so a biography is presumed to tell the reader something about someone's life story, and so on. They also assume specific behaviors and attitudes from particular character types—for example, that a detective will generally use his or her inductive skill to solve crimes. Thus, readers presuppose certain narrative strategies and themes within certain genres.

The Implied Reader: Beyond Objectivity and Relativity
Both texts and readers bring their own unique contributions to every interaction. Given this reality, what is one to make of the variety that

14. See the above discussion of Iser's use of history with his implied reader, p. 92 n. 6.

15. For the implied reader's knowledge of genre, see Iser's discussions of Spenser's *Shepheardes Calendar* (*Prospecting*, pp. 73-97) and Smollett's *Humphry Clinker* (*Implied Reader*, pp. 57-80). See also his related discussion of the intertextuality of Joyce's *Ulysses* (*Implied Reader*, pp. 179-233; *Prospecting*, pp. 131-39).

exists among both groups of participants, texts and readers? In other words, is it appropriate to discuss competency in relationship to both texts and readers? Before directly addressing this question, it might be helpful to place Iser's theory of the implied reader within its broader philosophical tradition.

In *Beyond Objectivism and Relativism*, Richard Bernstein discusses modern theorists in various areas including natural science, social science and the humanities. Among the theorists he discusses are Hannah Arendt, Hans-Georg Gadamer, Jürgen Habermas, Richard Rorty, Mary Hesse, Thomas Kuhn and Clifford Geertz. The thrust of his own work is to show that 'the spirit of our time is characterized by a movement beyond objectivism and relativism'.[16] This movement recognizes that when one approaches the tasks of understanding, interpretation and application nothing in this process can be characterized as purely 'objective' or 'relative'; rather, there is always a degree of objectivity and a degree of relativity involved. In other words, the conception of 'objectivity' and 'relativity' as polar opposites does not adequately describe the herme-neutical process, for this process is 'beyond objectivism and relativism'.

Iser draws from this 'spirit of our time', especially in his dependence upon the phenomenologists, Gadamer, Cassier and Husserl. Even his terminology ('horizon', 'play', 'passive syntheses') betrays this philo-sophical dependence.[17] The following quote can easily be translated into the terminology used by Bernstein:

> [The interaction between text and reader] cannot be reduced to the reality of the text or to the subjectivity of the reader.[18]

A Bernsteinian translation might be as follows: The interaction between the text and the reader cannot be reduced to the objectivity of the text or to the relativity of the reader. In fact, although Iser does not explicitly say so, the converse is also true: The interaction between the text and the reader cannot be reduced to the objectivity of the reader or to the relativity of the text. Neither the text nor the reader is wholly objective or subjective because both are mutually influencing each other in a

16. R.J. Bernstein, *Beyond Objectivism and Relativism: Science, Hermeneutics, and Praxis* (Philadelphia: University of Pennsylvania Press, 1983), p. xiv.

17. Iser specifically refers to the following as the source for the first two terms: 'horizon' from Gadamer (see *Act of Reading*, p. 97) and Cassier (see *Act of Reading*, pp. 63-64) and 'passive syntheses' from Husserl (see *Act of Reading*, pp. 135-59).

18. W. Iser, 'Interaction between Text and Reader', in Suleiman and Crosman (eds.), *The Reader in the Text*, p. 106.

dynamic process that involves both objectivity and relativity, or put even better, their interaction transcends the concepts of objectivity and relativity.[19]

Competence and the Implied Reader[20]

After reviewing the various positions that move beyond objectivity and relativity, Bernstein addresses the question concerning the practical tasks that confront critics. Although there is certainly no one objective inter-pretation, the plurality of interpretations all have some common ground:

> [P]lurality does not mean that we are limited to being separate individuals with irreducible subjective interests. Rather it means that we seek to dis-cover some common ground to reconcile difference through debate, conversation, and dialogue.[21]

In other words, when a reader interacts with a text, the reading falls within a range of readings, each of which draw from those aspects that the reader and text share with other readers and texts (the 'objective') as well as those aspects which are particular to the reader and text (the 'relative').

Like those theorists Bernstein discusses and Bernstein himself, Iser shies away from any explicit theoretical discussion of competence. However, during a panel discussion he once responded to the issue as to whether or not there can be such a thing as a 'wrong' reading with the following brief answer: 'It is a question of competence.'[22] Although this

19. M. Toolan (*Stylistics of Fiction*, pp. 7-14) also criticizes what he calls the 'bi-planar model of language' which he finds in linguistics and literary theory for its charactcrisation of language as either objectivistic or relativistic.

20. Iser's implicit understanding of competence is quite similar to Jonathan Culler's explicit understanding (found, for example, in 'Literary Competence', in Tompkins (ed.), *Reader-Response Criticism*, pp. 101-117). Both Iser and Culler demand that the 'act of reading' itself be taken seriously (Culler, 'Literary Competence', p. 102) and argue that competence depends upon one's knowledge of the text's literary tradition ('a repertoire of familiar literary patterns and recurrent literary themes' in Iser, *Implied Reader*, p. 288; 'the "grammar" of literature' in Culler, 'Literary Competence', p. 102). For an excellent discussion comparing Iser, (the early) Fish and Culler, see Tompkins, 'An Introduction to Reader-Response Criticism', pp. xiv-xviii. For Iser's discussion of the 'literary competence' of Fish's 'informed reader', see Iser, *Act of Reading*, p. 31.

21. Bernstein, *Beyond Objectivism and Relativism*, p. 223.

22. Bloom, 'In Defense of Authors and Readers', p. 25.

seems to be his most explicit statement on this issue, the following quotes show that he distinguishes between successful and unsuccessful literary communication:

> Now, if communication between text and reader is to be successful, clearly the reader's activity must also be controlled in some way by the text.[23]

> If literary communication is to be successful, it must bring with it all the components necessary for the construction of the situation, since this has no existence outside the literary work.[24]

Although he generally avoids explicit discussions of competence, '[Iser's] own readings of specific works', notes Suleiman, 'leave no doubt that he considers some realizations more correct, more true to the intentions of the text, than others'.[25]

Since literary meaning is produced in the interaction between text and reader, and since texts and readers both bring certain elements that influence such interactions, when we discuss competence in the reading process we must discuss both texts and readers. In other words, competence must concern two interrelated questions: How effective is a particular text's manipulation of its readers as it opens and closes gaps? And how effective is a particular reader in the recognition of gaps and in the use of textual and extratextual referents in closing those gaps?

Above, we saw that texts bring various extratextual referents to their interaction with readers—that is, they may refer to, for example, literary genres, theological systems, and traditional customs. This variety of possible extratextual referents presents itself to potential authors and readers, who must create their literary works from this repertoire. Some authors have more extensive knowledge of literary traditions and are more perceptive of their own times; therefore, some texts are more successful than others in the way in which they bring various extratextual referents to interactions. In other words, some texts are crafted in such a way as to successfully guide their intended readers in the process of filling indeterminacies by appropriately locating both the indeterminacies and references to extratextual realities.

Readers, on the other hand, bring their own knowledge of literature and history to their interactions with texts. This knowledge includes, for

---

23. *Prospecting*, p. 33.
24. *Act of Reading*, pp. 68-69.
25. Suleiman, 'Introduction', pp. 23-24. See also Foley, *Immanent Art*, p. 53.

example, recognition of various literary genres and motifs, socio-political history, linguistic structures, religious and cultural traditions. Therefore, those readers who have a more nuanced knowledge of the literary tradition and the history to which particular texts are related will produce more successful readings. In fact, those readers who not only know the particular literary and historical traditions involved but have also come to know the particular text well through repeated readings will realize more successful readings.[26]

In summary, the most successful interactions between texts and readers occur whenever both texts and their readers aid each other in crossing any cultural and chronological chasms. Such chasms can be traversed when the texts are more determinate in their guiding of the readers' filling of indeterminacies *and* when the readers bring with them a heightened knowledge of the literary and historical contexts to which the texts point. The most likely situation in which these ideal circumstances can arise is when the text and readers are both contemporary and culturally related. However, a certain degree of success can also be obtained whenever later readers immerse themselves in the literary and historical world contemporary to any given text.[27]

2. *Principles Guiding the Interaction between Text and Reader*

Iser's understanding of the implied reader can be further developed and clarified by relating it to some principles that guide conversational interactions. Below, three such principles are shown to enhance Iser's theories—the Cooperative Principle, the Given-New Contract and Preference Organization. Each of these principles further develops how indeterminacies are realized and filled in the interaction between text and reader.[28]

26. See Iser, *Implied Reader*, p. 282.

27. For Iser's discussion of contemporary readers, see *Act of Reading*, pp. 27-30, 74-75.

28. This combined use of the Cooperative Principle and Preference Organization to interpret literature is quite similar to that of Toolan ('Analysing Fictional Dialogue'; *The Stylistic of Fiction*). Well into the writing of the first draft, I first came across his work; therefore, our independently developed methods are mutually complementary.

The Cooperative Principle and the Given-New Contract
In his article 'Logic and Conversation',[29] H. Paul Grice argues that conversational interaction is logically governed by what he calls the
Cooperative Principle. The Cooperative Principle is an implicit social
contract between speakers and hearers about how information is to be
given and received. The Cooperative Principle has four categories of
maxims that guide the speaker (the converse of each would then guide
the hearer):[30]

Quantity maxims:
    1.   Make your contribution as informative as is required (for
the current purposes of the exchange).
    2.   Do not make your contribution more informative than is
required.

Quality maxims:
    1.   Do not say what you believe to be false.
    2.   Do not say that for which you lack adequate evidence.

Relation maxims:
    1.   Be relevant.

Manner maxims:
    1.   Avoid obscurity of expression.
    2.   Avoid ambiguity.
    3.   Be brief (avoid unnecessary prolixity).
    4.   Be orderly.

---

    29. H.P. Grice, 'Logic and Conversation', in P. Cole and J. Morgan (eds.),
Syntax and Semantics. III. *Speech Acts* (New York: Academic Press, 1975), pp. 41-
58. Although it has received some criticism and revision, Grice's Cooperative
Principle underlies the approach which can be called 'radical pragmatics'. See the
essays in P. Cole (ed.), *Radical Pragmatics* (New York: Academic Press, 1981),
especially Cole's Preface; A.C. Graesser and L.F. Clark, *Structures and Procedures
of Implicit Knowledge* (Advances in Discourse Processes, 17; Norwood: ABLEX,
1985), pp. 27, 192; Levinson, *Pragmatics*, pp. 97-166; Toolan, 'Analysing Fictional
Dialogue'; Toolan, *Stylistics of Fiction*, pp. 289-91. A good summary of the
Cooperative Principle can be found in H.H. Clark and S.E. Haviland,
'Comprehension and the Given-New Contract', in R.D. Freedle (ed.), *Discourse
Production and Comprehension* (Norwood: ABLEX, 1977), pp. 1-40. The only other
application of Grice's theory to the Jonah narrative is, to my knowledge, that of E.R.
Hope, 'Pragmatics, Exegesis, and Translation', pp. 124-26.
    30. From Grice, 'Logic and Conversation', pp. 45-46.

Within this social contract, speakers agree to subscribe to these maxims and hearers agree to assume that speakers have adhered to them. Of course as with any social contract, either one of the participants can break it, thereby inhibiting successful communication. That is, the speaker can mislead the hearer or the hearer can misunderstand the speaker. The Cooperative Principle nevertheless provides some guidelines for establishing successful communicative interaction.

Developing one aspect of the Cooperative Principle further, Herbert Clark and Susan Haviland have described the workings of what they called the Given-New Contract.[31] This contract concerns the mechanism that regulates the interaction in relation to both the knowledge shared by the speaker and hearer (the Given) as well as that not shared by them (the New). The Given need not be explicated; the New must be. The Given-New Contract is governed by the Antecedence Maxim that instructs the speaker thusly:

> Try to construct your utterance such that the listener has one and only [sic] direct antecedent for any given information and that it is the intended antecedent.[32]

This maxim has three requirements.[33] (1) Appropriateness: the distinction a speaker makes between Given and New ought to be appropriate to the present circumstances. In other words, the speaker should extrapolate from the conversational environment and from his or her knowledge of the hearer(s) in order to determine how much information can be assumed to be common knowledge (the Given) and what must be explicated (the New). (2) Uniqueness: any shared information should have a unique antecedent that the hearer can appropriately compute. For example, ambiguous terms should be avoided so that each term has but one referent or antecedent. (3) Computability: the information must be presented in such a way that the hearer has sufficient knowledge (Given and/or New) in order to compute the intended antecedent. In other words, the speaker must accept some responsibility for guiding the hearer by providing enough information in appropriate ways so that the hearer understands what the intended antecedent is. As long as the speaker adheres to these requirements, successful communication occurs.

31. See Clark and Haviland, 'Comprehension and the Given-New Contract'. The Given-New Contract is further revised by E.F. Prince, 'Toward a Taxonomy of Given-New Information', in Cole (ed.), *Radical Pragmatics*, pp. 223-55.

32. Clark and Haviland, 'Comprehension and the Given-New Contract', p. 4.

33. Clark and Haviland, 'Comprehension and the Given-New Contract', p. 9.

If the speaker intentionally or unintentionally violates the Given-New Contract, however, the hearer must use one of three strategies to identify the antecedent: bridging, addition, or restructuring. Bridging describes the hearer's forming 'an *indirect* antecedent by building an inferential bridge from something he already knows'.[34] The following example requires bridging: 'John is a Democrat. Bill is honest too.' When a speaker hears this, there are no immediately obvious antecedents for 'Bill' or 'honest' in the second sentence; however, the speaker can infer that a bridge should be made between the two sentences. With this bridge, the hearer then assumes that the speaker believes that all Democrats, including John and Bill, are honest.[35] Addition describes the creation of a new hypothetical antecedent in the hearer's memory that does not correspond with any known information.[36] For example, if a story began, 'The old woman died', the hearer would receive the New information that there is a woman who is old; however, since the hearer does not know anything else about this particular old woman, he or she must create a special memory category for this particular, undeveloped 'old woman'.[37] Restructuring describes the process of rearranging what was Given and what was New in such a way as to posit an antecedent. The following example requires restructuring in order to make sense out of the two sentences: 'Agnes saw somebody. It was Agnes who saw Maxine'. By restructuring the second sentence so that the redundant 'it' is eliminated, the hearer can understand the information in these two sentences as, 'Agnes saw Maxine'. By any of these three strategies, a hearer may be able to compensate for the speaker's violation of the Antecedence Maxim. However, as long as the speaker adheres to the maxim, successful communication occurs.

In summary, the Cooperative Principle and its extension, the Given-New Contract, together describe the implicit social contract between speakers and hearers that must be followed for successful communication to occur. In their interaction, both speaker and hearer agree to cooperate in an economical system of communication in which quantity, quality and manner are balanced in relationship to the particular situation.

34. Clark and Haviland, 'Comprehension and the Given-New Contract', p. 6.
35. See Clark and Haviland, 'Comprehension and the Given-New Contract', pp. 6-7.
36. See Clark and Haviland, 'Comprehension and the Given-New Contract', p. 7.
37. See Clark and Haviland, 'Comprehension and the Given-New Contract', pp. 7-8.

This balance includes a determination of what can be assumed to be shared knowledge (the Given) and what must be expressly communicated (the New). When a speaker adheres to this implicit contract *and* when a hearer assumes that the speaker has adhered to it, then the speaker's message can be successfully received by the hearer.

What might be the relationship between the conversational interaction described in the Cooperative Principle (and the Given-New Contract[38]), on the one hand, and Iser's understanding of the interaction between text and reader, on the other? The Cooperative Principle can accurately be applied to the interaction between an expository text and its reader quite well, for both conversation and expository prose concern themselves with the exchange of information from speaker/author to hearer/reader. In Iser's terminology, the Cooperative Principle describes the rules governing the interactions between two related determinate modes of communication—conversation and expository prose.

Since Iser makes a distinction between (determinate) expository texts and (indeterminate) literary texts, it would at first seem that some revision of the Cooperative Principle may be required. However, upon a closer look, the Cooperative Principle, especially as it is further developed in the Given-New Contract, relates well to Iser's understanding of the role played by indeterminacy in the interaction between text and reader. On the one hand, the Cooperative Principle's description of the social contract applies very well to both expository prose and everyday conversation. For example, an article in *Language in Society* can use terms such as 'preference organization' and 'adjacency pairs' with little explanation as to what they refer to because the general audience of this sociolinguistic journal can be assumed to compute successfully their antecedents from their professional knowledge—that is, they are Given information. However, since my audience is broader, a lot of energy had to be spent on introducing my readers to their proper antecedents because they are New information. In Iserian terms, when I first used the terms 'preference organization' and 'adjacency pairs', I opened up gaps that conversation analysts could immediately fill due to their familiarity with this technical language. In contrast, the gap remained open for my other readers until they had finished my introduction and had an adequate

---

38. Since the Given-New Contract is an extension of the Cooperative Principle, I will not always repeat 'and the Given-New Contract' below but rather will assume that my comments concerning the Cooperative Principle apply equally well to the Given-New Contract.

new knowledge of these terms and their antecedents. On the other hand, the Cooperative Principle's description of various strategies for hearers to overcomeintentional or unintentional violations of this contract— especially as formulated in the Given-New Contract—accurately describes Iser's understanding of the process by which readers fill in indeterminacies in literary texts.[39] A reader who experiences an indeterminacy can use one of the same three strategies that are useful in similar situations in everyday conversation: bridging, addition or restructuring. Bridging describes the reader's use of previous knowledge to find an indirect antecedent in order to fill the indeterminacy. Addition describes the reader's formation of a new hypothetical antecedent that does not correspond to any known information. Restructuring describes the reader's rearranging of what was previously known and what is causing the indeterminacy in such a way as to posit an antecedent. By any one of these strategies, readers can fill indeterminacies by creating some antecedent and locating this antecedent somewhere within the text or within their (possibly new) understanding of history and tradition.

In summary, the Cooperative Principle and the Given-New Contract can be understood as complementary to Iser's understanding of the implied reader. Whereas the Cooperative Principle describes the interactions of speakers and hearers, Iser's theory describes the interaction between literary text and reader. However, both strive to describe the mechanisms of the process that governs both participants in these interactions and, in my opinion, both succeed in their striving, especially when taken together.

Preference Organization and Constructed Dialogue

Preference organization, especially in the structure of adjacency pairs, has been shown to be a very effective description of conversational interaction, but how does preference organization relate to the interaction between text and reader? In order to answer this question, we

39. See Iser, *Prospecting*, p. 34:

> Communication in literature, then, is a process set in motion and regulated, not by
> a given code, but by a mutually restrictive and magnifying interaction between the
> explicit and the implicit, between revelation and concealment.

Adapting Iser's language, the Cooperative Principle should be thought, 'not [as] a given code, but [as a description of] a mutually restrictive and magnifying interaction'. Also, Iser could have just as easily added the following appositive to this sentence: 'between the new and the given.'

must first address how preference organization relates to each participant in the interaction.

As demonstrated in the previous chapter, the various narrative elements are developed to some extent through the use of adjacency pairs. The plot of the Jonah narrative itself consists of a complex network of adjacency pairs. The Lord's request is refused by Jonah, which leads to the Lord's angry storm-making, which in turn leads to the sailors' pious responses and Jonah's continued disobedient responses, and so on. Adjacency pairs also contribute to characterization in the Jonah narrative. Jonah's predisposition for dispreferred seconds (for example, his initial refusal in 1.3) contrasts with all the other characters' predisposition for preferred seconds. The atmosphere, which limits all of the characters according to the Lord's compassionate nature, is developed by the use of adjacency pairs. For example, all of the Lord's requests eventually lead to the preferred seconds of acceptance. The satirical tone of the narrative is effected to a certain degree through constructed dialogue, especially including the delay of Jonah's account for his initial refusal (4.2). Thus, authors' crafting of texts can be effectively described by how they construct adjacency pairs within their narratives.

All readers, even before they could read, have acquired their language skills by overhearing and then participating in conversational interactions; therefore, all readers bring their acquired knowledge of preference organization to their experience of texts. In fact, as will be demonstrated in the following chapter, readers' competence can be evaluated on the basis of their (conscious or unconscious) knowledge of the possible complexities of adjacency pairs and constructed dialogue.

Now that we have concluded that texts consist to a large degree of a series of adjacency pairs and that readers have an acquired knowledge of preference organization, how do texts and readers interact? A difficulty in answering this question relates to the observation that no text can consist of only one character's speech. This is the case even with the genre of 'monologues', for either they have an implied dialogue between the speaking character and some assumed character(s) or they are really a dialogue between different personae within the same character's thoughts and emotions. Hence, no text provides a reader with only one perspective from which the reader can interpret the material, so the reader must shift viewpoints throughout the reading. This process Iser calls 'the wandering viewpoint':[40]

40. See *Act of Reading*, pp. 108-18.

[T]he wandering viewpoint permits the reader to travel through the text, thus unfolding the multiplicity of interconnecting perspectives which are offset whenever there is a switch from one to another.[41]

Now let us return to the question of how preference organization informs the interaction between text and reader as the reader wanders from viewpoint to viewpoint. I contend that as a reader receives what he or she perceives as the first part of an adjacency pair in the text (for example, request) the reader assumes the point of view of the character speaking the first part. The reader then assumes with this character, firstly, that the second part of the adjacency pair (for example, acceptance or refusal) will be produced by the other addressed character as is relevant to the situation and, secondly, that the second part will generally follow the structure of either preferred seconds or dispreferred seconds. In other words, rather than simply participating in the interaction from his or her own perspective as is natural in ordinary conversation, the reader will shift his or her viewpoint to that of the characters who are perceived as initiating adjacency pairs. This process of the wandering viewpoint can be as complex as the reader's own perception of the complexity of the adjacency pairs in the text.

One example of the complexity of the reader's wandering viewpoint concerns the interaction between the reader and the text's description of the relationship between the sailors and Jonah. Jonah's request (first part) for the sailors to pick him up and cast him into the sea (1.12) is also his answer (second part) to the sailors' question, 'What must we do?' (1.11). Therefore, the reader wanders to the sailors' viewpoint when they ask their question, 'What must we do?' (1.11), so that both the reader and the sailors together expect that Jonah will respond either with the preferred second of an expected answer (itself a request to 'do' something) or the dispreferred second of an unexpected answer or a non-answer. They also assume that Jonah's response will likely follow the characteristics of preferred seconds or dispreferred seconds. This expectation is affirmed when Jonah answers with the brevity and direct-ness characteristic of preferred seconds: 'Pick me up and cast me into the sea' (1.12). At this point, the sailors' and the reader's viewpoints diverge, for now the reader wanders over to Jonah's viewpoint, since the answer also begins a new adjacency pair in the form of a request. Now the reader and Jonah expect the sailors to respond either with the preferred response of acceptance or the dispreferred response of refusal

41. Iser, *Act of Reading*, p. 118.

and to likewise adhere to the basic characteristics of seconds. However, this time the expectation is violated, for the narrator has suppressed the sailors' speech and simply reported the consequences: 'Nonetheless the men rowed hard' (1.13). This violation sparks the reader's interest, raising the question as to why the sailors refused, a question that will be implicitly answered later when the sailors pray, 'do not hold us account-able for innocent blood' (1.14). Thus, as we have seen in this example, the reader's point of view wanders from that of one character to another, changing often according to the reader's perception of the beginning of another adjacency pair.

The complexity of this wandering viewpoint is augmented further in relationship to the narrator's choice of the medium of presentation for each part of the adjacency pair—that is, the narrator's choice of direct speech, indirect speech or reported consequences further influences the interaction between text and reader. As suggested above,[42] preferred seconds tend to gravitate towards the briefer medium of reported con-sequences. Dispreferred seconds, however, have opposing tendencies. On the one hand, they will gravitate towards direct speech when elabo-ration is more important. For example, in 4.2 Jonah's account is given in direct speech in order to develop fully the information readers need to fill in the gap created by his refusal in 1.3. On the other hand, they gravitate towards reported consequences when mitigation is more important to the narrative strategy. For example, the narrator mitigated Jonah's refusal by omitting Jonah's verbal response in 1.3 in order to manipulate readers' interest and to develop Jonah's character further. But what presuppositions about these narrative strategies do readers bring to the text? Here the situation is, I think, simpler than with the narrator because the reader wants to know as much of the 'necessary' or 'natural' information as possible. Hence, a preferred second in the form of reported consequences delivers all (or at least most) of the information the reader may want. To use an example from Chapter 1, the phrase, 'The child went', tells the reader clearly that the parent's request was not only accepted, but performed. In contrast, a dispreferred second in the form of reported consequences lacks much of the expected information. In other words, the dispreferred second is *so* mitigated that indeterminacies are created. To use the example again, the phrase, 'But the child went outside to play', tells the reader that the child refused to go to the store, but it does not explicitly give the child's account. The

---

42. See 'Constructed Speech and Adjacency Pairs' in Chapter 1 §2.

reader must fill in the indeterminacy concerning the account by assuming that the child's playing may have been the reason for the refusal. However, the direct speech form of the child's refusal—'The child said, "Oh Dad, I want to go outside and play." So she went outside to play.'— explicitly gives the reader all the wanted information and conforms to the characteristics of dispreferred seconds (delay, preface, account, declination component). Therefore, even though these two forms of speech are similar in relationship to preferred seconds, the attraction of dispreferred seconds to the different narrative strategies differs for the narrator and the reader. For the narrator, there are opposing tendencies at work causing gravitation towards direct speech or reported consequences given different requirements of crafting the narrative (for example, tone). For the reader, however, there is only one tendency and that is the gravitation towards the fullest, most direct presentation of all of the characteristic elements of dispreferred seconds, especially the account.

In summary, both the text and the reader bring something to their interaction in relationship to preference organization. The text brings the structures of adjacency pairs that are preserved within it as well as the narrative strategy controlling its tendency to place dispreferred seconds in either direct speech or indirect speech. The reader brings acquired knowledge of the function and characteristics of adjacency pairs and a predilection for dispreferred seconds in the form of direct speech. Thus, when text and reader interact, the reader is guided through the various adjacency pairs, wandering from viewpoint to viewpoint as each new adjacency pair is initiated and desiring to receive dispreferred seconds in the form of direct speech.

3. *Who is the Implied Reader of the Jonah Narrative?*

The theoretical groundwork has now been laid. However, before describing the reading process associated with the Jonah narrative, we first must have some background information on this particular implied reader.[43] Where do we get this information? From the extrapolation from the presuppositions drawn from the text and its historical and literary contexts (in Clark and Haviland's words, 'the Given') as sketched

---

43. As earlier with the narrator of Jonah, I have chosen to consistently use the masculine forms of pronouns for the implied reader of the Jonah narrative because of the predominantly male-oriented viewpoint of the narrative.

immediately below. These presuppositions, however, do not necessarily reflect the author's, the narrative's or even the reader's viewpoint. Rather, they define a common knowledge which author, text and reader share about the world that the narrative reflects, creates and/or critiques. For example, the sixth presupposition in the list is that Israelites are *considered to be* more righteous than pagans; however, in the interaction between the Jonah narrative and the implied reader, this presupposition, at least in the specific case of Jonah and the Ninevites, is strongly denied. The presuppositions of the Jonah narrative are as follows:[44]

(1)   The Hebrew text can be understood by both its author and its actual readers.

(2)   Nineveh is the capital of Israel's enemies, the Assyrians.

(3)   Israel's enemies, including the Ninevites, are considered to be the Lord's enemies.

(4)   Nineveh is east of Israel.

(5)   Tarshish is west of Israel.

---

44.   This list of presuppositions depends heavily on Hope, 'Pragmatics, Exegesis and Translation', p. 118. See also Payne, 'Jonah from the Perspective of Its Audience'. Hope ('Pragmatics, Exegesis and Translation', p. 118) also mentions the possibility that it is presupposed that prophets are acquainted with the Hebrew scriptures, since there are obvious parallels between sections of the Jonah narrative and other biblical books. I prefer to understand the existence of these parallels somewhat differently—that is, these parallels suggest knowledge of the biblical tradition, which does not necessarily mean knowledge of biblical texts but may mean knowledge of traditional genres and character-types. For example, in some discussions of these interbiblical references, it seems as if the commentator assumes that when the reader reads 'Jonah, son of Amittai' (1.1) he immediately recalls the chapter and verse in 2 Kings. (Indeed, readers of this work may have gotten that impression when I discussed the character of Jonah above.) However, it is best to understand that both Jon. 1.1 and 2 Kgs 14.25 refer to a character named Jonah in the tradition, whose characteristics include elements from both texts as well as other stories which may no longer exist. Therefore, rather than discussing specific 'quotations of' and 'references to' other biblical passages I will use the intertextual evidence to refer to traditional themes and character-types (for example, the prophet Jonah, which should not be necessarily equated with the character in the book of Jonah and/or 2 Kgs 14.25). Because of this understanding, I will describe in the following paragraphs the knowledge about prophets and prophetic literature which I think the implied reader 'knows'. This description, however, is certainly influenced by my own readings of the various biblical parallels which have been suggested. For bibliographic information for these various textual parallels, see above p. 82 n. 57.

(6)   The sea is a place of chaos.[45]

(7)   The Lord's chosen people, the Israelites, are considered to be more righteous than pagans, like the sailors and the Ninevites.

(8)   Sackcloth, ashes, and fasting are signs of repentance.

(9)   When delivered from peril, one utters a prayer of thanksgiving to the Lord.[46]

(10)   Jonah is a prophet and, therefore, should be loyal and obedient to the Lord.[47]

(11)   The Jonah narrative purports to be a prophetic book.

Taken together, these presuppositions assume a certain knowledge of the pertinent geo-political environment and, to some extent, help to create this knowledge for those readers who do not bring such information to their interaction with the text. They also assume that the reader shares its caricature of the typical Hebrew prophet—that is, a Hebrew prophet consistently sides with Israel against her enemies.[48]

As was stated before, these presuppositions, separately or taken together, do not necessarily reflect the author's, the narrative's or the reader's viewpoints. They simply define knowledge of the narrative world about which the author, the text and the intended readers share. Thus, by the time they reach the end of their interaction, the narrator and the reader reject the caricature as not reflecting a true prophet, because such a nationalistic and petty prophet does not completely understand the Lord's true compassionate nature. This is the essential meaning derived from the satirical portrayal of Jonah in the narrative— that is, prophets who closely resemble the narrative's caricature are false prophets, who misunderstand the Lord's universal mercy. Also, the reader's experience of other prophets may likewise suggest a rejection of this caricature of a prophet, in that other biblical prophets can have favorable views of foreign peoples and their leaders. For example, the prophet of Third Isaiah calls the pagan king of Persia, Cyrus, the Lord's anointed servant whom the Lord formed in the womb (Isa. 44.24–45.7).

The last two presuppositions require further development in order to

45. This presupposition is not given by Hope, but is taken from Almbladh, 'The Israelites and the Sea'; Warshaw, 'The Book of Jonah', p. 196.

46. This presupposition is not given by Hope, but is taken from Miles, 'Laughing at the Bible', pp. 173-75.

47. Although Jonah is not explicitly called a prophet, he certainly is to be understood as one, as the prophetic superscription to the book (1.1) makes clear.

48. See the discussion of the character of Jonah in Chapter 3 §2.

understand fully what 'prophet' and 'prophetic literature' refer to in the implied reader's interaction with the text; references which the implied reader then rejects because of their having been satirized. The best way to comprehend these terms as they are realized in this interaction is first to look at them as that which is being satirized and then to compare this satirical presentation with other prophetic literature and extrapolate their meaning.[49]

A 'prophet' is a servant of the Lord who stands in his presence (for example, 1 Kgs 17.1) and receives a message that he must then give to its intended human audience.[50] When the prophet is first called by the Lord, he first voices reluctance out of his perception of inadequacy (see Exod. 3.11, 13; 4.1, 10, 13; Jer. 1.6), but, after being reassured by the Lord, he accepts (for example, Exod. 2.23–4.17; Jer. 1.4-10). When confronted by a divine sign (often in the context of the call), a prophet expresses awe at the Lord's power and glory (see Exod. 3.1-6; Ezek. 1.4–3.27). The message that the prophet is commanded to give is very often one of judgment, including an address, an indictment and a call to repentance (for example, Amos 1.2–2.16). This damning message often brings the prophet into conflict with the king, leading to his persecution (for example, 1 Kgs 22.5-12; Jer. 37.1–38.28). The anguish caused by such persecution is expressed in the form of a lament or complaint, sometimes including a preference for death over suffering (for example, Num. 11.10-15; Jer. 20.7-8; 1 Kgs 19.4).[51]

'Prophetic literature' obviously concerns prophets, but what else can be said about it? A prophetic book will generally be introduced by a superscription like, 'Now it once happened that the word of the Lord came to [the prophet and his patronym]' (for example, Hos. 1.1; Joel 1.1; Jon. 1.1; Zeph. 1.1). Also, prophetic books may contain some narratives about the prophet's life, but are primarily collections of the prophet's sayings (for example, Isaiah, Jeremiah, Ezekiel).[52]

In summary, the notion of the implied reader of Jonah represents the

---

49. The following is particularly influenced by Miles, 'Laughing at the Bible'. See further Chapter 3 §4.

50. See Ackerman, 'Jonah', p. 235. This is consistent with anthropological models of prophecy. See T.W. Overholt, 'The Ghost Dance of 1890 and the Nature of the Prophetic Process', *Ethnohistory* 21 (1974), pp. 37-63; R.R. Wilson, *Prophecy and Society in Ancient Israel* (Philadelphia: Fortress Press, 1980).

51. See Band, 'Swallowing Jonah', p. 187.

52. See A group from Renne, France, 'An Approach to the Book of Jonah', p. 86.

careful and repeated interactions between text and reader that have produced the greatest familiarity possible with the Jonah narrative. This heightened familiarity suggests that the implied reader has completely grasped all of the presupposed knowledge (the Given), including geopolitical information as well as a full understanding of prophets and prophetic literature. This knowledge, including the implied reader's previous knowledge of literature and history as well as the new-found knowledge from repeated interactions with the text, guides the implied reader in the filling of the gaps of indeterminacies with the utmost skill.

4. *The Implied Reader of Jonah Reads his Narrative*

What follows is intended to be the implied reader's exact description of the interaction that occurs when he reads the Jonah narrative, having the most heightened familiarity with the text. But what really follows is, of course, my own best attempt to describe the interaction between text and reader of the Jonah narrative based on my careful and repeated readings of both primary and secondary texts. In this sense, the following commentary is one of many relative readings. Nevertheless, I still assert that my reading reflects a high degree of objectivity as well, and I challenge my own readers to question my competence in accordance with the method I have described above. In other words, my formulation of the implied reader must be judged on the basis of the two participants in the interaction: the text and its strategies, on the one hand, and the reader's (my) knowledge of the tradition from which the text comes and which the text creates anew, on the other. Only then can one speak of the competence of the following commentary.[53]

The following commentary describes the interaction between text and reader, especially in relationship to gaps of indeterminacy and their filling, as well as the wandering viewpoint of the reader in relationship to the text's adjacency pairs. Thus, familiarity with the previous chapters is presumed,[54] especially concerning paronomasia, the narrator's satirical tone, and the structure of adjacency pairs; however, previous observations are

---

53. In Chapter 5 I will analyze various readings of the Jonah narrative, including my own earlier readings, in accordance with the method described above. In other words, I will be more explicit in the next chapter concerning my assertion that the implied reader's reading presented here is, as of now, the best.

54. In addition, since the secondary sources are fully noted in the previous chapters, here substantially fewer notes are given.

often repeated to describe fully this interaction. The following is also more illustrative than exhaustive in that some of the minor adjacency pairs are not discussed (for example, Jonah's request to hire a ship and the sailors' acceptance). Also, not necessarily all of the multiple functions of each utterance are discussed; rather, those functions that are more important to the flow of the conversational interaction between characters are discussed in full. As in the previous commentary, the text itself is indented; however, because of the different nature of the following commentary, the units of meaning of the primary text are sometimes broken into much smaller units.

1.1 Now it once happened that the word of the Lord came to...

This superscription immediately informs the reader that what follows is generically a prophetic book or, at least, a satire of prophetic books.

Jonah, son of Amittai.

Every time the reader runs across the character's name his entire persona is recalled.[55] His patronym, found only here, strengthens this recall, especially as it relates to those elements of his persona as portrayed in 2 Kgs 14.25. Thus, the name Jonah represents a false prophet who was all of the following things: uncritically pro-Israelite and anti-Ninevite, reluctant and disobedient regarding his divinely-ordained mission to Nineveh, a very difficult conversational partner and petty about his own personal comforts (for example, the plant's wilting).[56] The implied reader also notices the irony within his name and patronym in that they mean, 'Dove, son of The Lord-Is-Steadfast'. On the one hand, both characteristic connotations of 'dove' in the Hebrew Bible equally apply to Jonah: he is easily put to flight and laments when in distress.[57]

---

55. This observation is commonly made by those who carry on the study of oral traditions as begun by the work of Milman Parray and Albert Lord. For example, see Foley, *Immanent Art*, pp. 1-37.

56. See further the discussion of the character of Jonah in Chapter 3 §2. Payne concludes that, the 'audience-reaction to the person of Jonah would have been neither hostile nor strongly sympathetic, but rather, objective and critical—a dispassionate scrutiny of a rather remote character' ('Jonah from the Perspective of Its Audience', pp. 6-7). Although this conclusion may adequately describe the reaction of the contemporary readers/hearers of the Jonah narrative when they first read/heard the narrative, it certainly does not apply to the implied reader or even to actual readers who have just finished reading the narrative for the first time.

57. See Ackerman, 'Jonah', p. 234. See also Hauser, 'Jonah', p. 22.

On the other hand, the Lord's steadfast compassion is, ironically, the very thing that Jonah protests so strongly (4.2). Thus, the name and patronym recall all of the character's persona to the mind of the implied reader, describing both Jonah's true nature (like a fleeing and moaning 'dove') and his anguish at the Lord's steadfast compassion.

> [2] 'Get up. Go to...

The Lord's word to Jonah is a request, which can be expected to be followed by either acceptance or refusal in their characteristic narrative forms. Of course, the Lord's prophets are supposed to be obedient; therefore, it is assumed that Jonah, if he is a true prophet, will accept the request even if only reluctantly. This request also initiates and recalls the theme of the contrasts between 'going up' and 'going down', which will play an important role in contrasting Jonah's disobedience with the Lord's request.

> Nineveh, that large city.

'Nineveh' recalls the following: It is the capital of Israel's traditional arch-enemies, the Assyrians. As such, it is a 'large' center of power, typified as evil from the perspective of stereotyped Israelites. However, it is also one of the many 'large' things that the Lord created, controls and cares for (the wind, the storm, the sailors' fear, the fish, Jonah's anguish at his situation, the plant, Jonah's rejoicing over the plant).

> ...and call out against it, for their wickedness is obvious to me.

The Lord's request is made more explicit. The Ninevites were guilty of a great wickedness characterized by violence (3.8). Thus, the Lord is angry with them and sends Jonah to Nineveh to preach judgment.

> [3] Jonah, instead, got up...

This translation properly reflects how the implied reader understands the verse based on previous readings of the entire narrative—that is, it introduces the reported consequences of Jonah's refusal. However, the implied reader also knows that grammatically the Hebrew phrase could also mean simply, 'And Jonah got up...', which does not yet imply that Jonah is refusing the Lord's request and could be the introduction to the reported consequences of Jonah's acceptance, as it is later (3.3). In other words, the implied reader sees through the narrator's manipulation of first-time readers in the ambiguity of the Hebrew and the phrase's form in reported consequences rather than direct speech. The repetitious use of the verb 'go up' further manipulates the reader. Jonah's 'going up' could be grammatically construed at this point as obeying the Lord's request to 'go up'; however, it introduces Jonah's disobedience in 'going up' in the opposite direction,

> ...to escape...

Now the semantic information confirms what the implied reader already knew was being introduced—Jonah's refusal. Even though reluctance is expected of a prophet, Jonah's outright refusal sets him apart.

> ...to Tarshish from the Lord; and he went down to Jaffa and found a ship which had just come from Tarshish. He paid its hire and sailed in it to accompany them towards Tarshish away from the Lord.

Jonah's plan of escape is described. He 'went down' to Jaffa and hired a ship to take him overseas in the opposite direction to Nineveh as he attempts to flee from the Lord. His plan itself is realized as ironic in two ways: (1) In a typical prophetic call narrative, the prophet stands before the Lord (for example, 1 Kgs 17.1); in contrast, Jonah is portrayed as trying to escape from the Lord (see also 1.10). (2) The specific means of his flight—that is, his decision to go overseas—contrast with what would normally be expected of any biblical character, for the sea is understood as a realm of chaos and danger.[58] Thus, his decision to go to sea foreshadows his experience of the Lord's presence in the actions of the mighty storm and the fish that cause him to 'go down' further into the depths of chaos. Since Jonah's refusal is in the form of reported consequences, his account has been withheld from the reader, thereby creating an indeterminacy which the reader now fills with information from 4.2, as follows: 'Well Lord, I really strive to obey your will, but I know that "you are a gracious and compassionate God, slow to anger and extremely benevolent", and I am certain that you will "change [your] mind concerning this evil".'

> [4] The Lord, however, cast mighty winds towards the sea so that a mighty storm raged upon it.

When a request is refused, the refusal may provoke a response such as anger or betrayal. The reader thus expects that the Lord will respond somehow to Jonah's refusal, and the Lord does. The Lord angrily responds to Jonah's disobedient 'going down' by 'casting down' mighty (literally 'large'—גדל) winds which in turn create a threatening ('large')

58. Almbladh, 'The Israelites and the Sea'; Warshaw, 'The Book of Jonah', p. 196.

storm. Here the Lord's control of nature expresses his rage, as if he were saying, 'Jonah, I am angry with your disobedience.'

> When the ship threatened to break up, [5] the sailors became afraid and each prayed to his own gods. Then they cast the cargo which was on the ship into the sea in order to lighten it.

The first-time reader wonders what Jonah's response will be to the Lord's angry storm. Will it be one of repentance for his disobedient refusal in the face of the Lord's awesome power? This is what is to be generally expected of prophets (for example, Exod. 3.1-6; Ezek. 1.4–3.27), but the implied reader knows better about Jonah. Indeed, the portrayal of the sailors' own pagan piety (prayer) and their pragmatic actions (lightening the load) is crafted so as to create a contrast with the following portrayal of Jonah's response and to foreshadow the Ninevites' response (3.5-10). Indeed, the very imagery of the sailors' actions continues the play on the 'going up'/'going down' contrast—that is, they pray up to their gods and they pick up and cast down the cargo. Even though their efforts have no immediate result, the sailors are at least doing the best they can with their limited knowledge of their sad situation, and the implied reader knows that eventually they will have their prayers answered by the Lord (1.16).

> Meanwhile, Jonah went down into the vessel's hold, laid down, and went to sleep.

In contrast to the sailors' pious efforts to save themselves and all on board, Jonah goes to sleep! His bizarre behavior is emphasized as disobeying the Lord in that Jonah 'goes down' into the ship, when he should have been praying 'up' to the Lord as the sailors' were praying to their gods and, of course, 'going up' to Nineveh rather than Tarshish. Why would Jonah act in such a bizarre manner? The implied reader and Jonah both know what the sailors and the first-time reader do not—that the Lord is 'a gracious and compassionate God...who [will] change his mind concerning this evil' (4.2). In other words, Jonah is confident that the storm will not end in disaster.

> [6] Then the helmsman approached him to ask, 'How could you sleep?

Not only does Jonah's behavior appear bizarre to the first-time reader, but the sailors, represented by their helmsman, also find it peculiar, leading him to ask his rhetorical question, 'How could you?'

> Get up!

The helmsman follows his rhetorical question with a command, using the exact same word that the Lord used earlier (1.2). Not only is Jonah's behavior contrasted with that of the sailors, but the helmsman himself ironically repeats the Lord's request of Jonah.

> Call out to your god!

Having just repeated the Lord's request, the helmsman unknowingly ties this request to a religious activity, that is, prayer. The sailors have prayed to their gods, and they believe strongly that Jonah should not be sleeping but should also be in prayer, requesting deliverance from the Lord. Therefore, the helmsman requests that Jonah pray to his god.

> Perhaps that god will intercede on our behalf so that we may not perish.'

The helmsman is making an assessment that Jonah's god, whoever that is, may have the power to save them. As the reader knows (1.16), the helmsman is right and seems, ironically, to demonstrate more faith in a god he does not even know than this same god's chosen prophet, Jonah.

> [7] And they said to one another, 'Come! Let's cast lots so that we might know on whose account this evil has come to us.'

Jonah's response to the helmsman's request is not immediately given. Instead, the sailors continue to seek the truth about their situation by means of their limited pagan ways. In the form of choral response, they request that they cast lots in order to learn the truth.

> Then they cast the lots...

As expected, they accept their own request. Jonah's response to the helmsman's requests has still not been given, contributing further to his characterization as someone who is a difficult conversational partner. The reader knows that even if or when he responds, it will not be exactly what the helmsman expected.

> ...and the lot fell on Jonah.

Jonah must have, at least, accepted the helmsman's request to get up, because he is no longer in bed and is present for the lot-casting. The sailors' questioning of the gods by means of the lots is ironically answered, in that the pagan practice correctly identified Jonah as the cause of their evil. Even the pagan practice of lot-casting is aware of Jonah's refusal!

> [8] Then they said to Jonah, 'Tell us, you on whose account this evil has come to us:

The answer given by the lots is immediately accepted by the sailors, who now accuse Jonah of being responsible for 'this evil' and request that he tell them more.

> What is your mission and where are you coming from? What is your homeland and from what people do you come?'

The sailors ask four questions, seeking more information about 'this evil'. The sailors and reader now wait for Jonah's response to their accusation and their four questions (even though the reader already knows all of the answers).

> ⁹ And he said to them, 'I am a Hebrew, and the Lord, the God of Heaven,
> I worship—he who made the sea and the dry land.'

Jonah's answer, as it is given here, only directly answers the last of the four questions, 'From what people do you come?'[59] However, the implied reader knows that this one answer is only a small part of Jonah's full answer, 'because he had told them' (1.10) more. His full answer to the questions was probably something like the following: 'My mission is to "go to Nineveh and call out against it" [1.2]; I am coming from Jeroboam's court in Samaria [2 Kgs 14.23-27]. My hometown is Gath-hepher in Israel [2 Kgs 14.25] and "I am a Hebrew, and the Lord, the God of Heaven, I worship—he who made the sea and the dry land."' But even this reconstructed speech does not explicitly respond to the accusation made by the sailors, so they may have asked, 'Why is the Lord, your God, trying to destroy us?' Jonah may have then answered, 'Because I am "fleeing from the Lord" [1.10]'. Even though the narrator did not include all of Jonah's answer in direct speech, nothing has been hidden from the reader. The reader knew the answers to all of the sailors' questions and the truth about their accusation, even before they verbalized them; the narrator has simply used direct speech sparingly, assuming that the reader already has this Given information. Of course, in this sense even Jonah's answer as explicitly given in direct speech is not New information, so the question arises as to why this

---

59. Contra Hope, 'Pragmatics, Exegesis and Translation', pp. 125-26. Hope understands Jonah as being uncooperative with the sailors here. Although Jonah's being uncooperative is consistent with his character, I reject Hope's understanding for two reasons: 1. If Jonah's answer is only that which is given, then the sailors must have the insight necessary to infer from Jonah's response 'taken at face value' that he is 'fleeing from the Lord' and is the cause of 'this evil'. 2. The narrator consistently omits and abbreviates the characters' speeches in chs. 1–3.

particular segment was chosen to represent the whole, rather than another. This particular segment of Jonah's speech emphasizes his faith as he confesses that the Lord that he is fleeing unsuccessfully is the Creator, who not only 'made the sea and the dry land' but controls them for his own purposes. In other words, this answer, more explicitly than the others, addresses the threatening situation in which the sailors and Jonah find themselves.

> [10] Then the men were filled with the most dreadful fear and they said to him, 'What is this that you have done!?' for the men now knew that he was fleeing from the Lord, because he had told them.

The sailors accept Jonah's assessment of the situation and respond to his full answer, not surprisingly, with the most dreadful fear (literally, 'the men feared a large fear'). As their rhetorical question suggests, they now fully understand what this is that Jonah has done. Ironically, Jonah said that he feared the Lord ('I worship' literally means 'I fear' in Hebrew) in his answer, but his actions suggest that he does not fear the Lord at all. In contrast, the sailors' reactions, earlier (1.4-8) as well as now, suggest that they really take the Lord's anger seriously.[60] Why is Jonah not more fearful? Because, as the implied reader knows, Jonah believes that 'deliverance belongs to the Lord' (2.10) and that the Lord is necessarily 'a gracious and compassionate God...who [will] change his mind concerning the evil' (4.2).

> [11] And they said to him, 'What must we do to you for the sea to calm down for us?' for the sea was becoming increasingly violent.

Having accepted Jonah's assessment, they now question him for information as to what they might do to save themselves. This question is urgent because the sea is 'becoming increasingly violent'.

> [12] And he said to them, 'Pick me up and cast me into the sea.

Jonah answers their question with a request, continuing the 'going up'/ 'going down' contrast—that is, 'pick me up and cast me down'. His request could be perceived as self-sacrificial concern for the sailors, especially by the sailors themselves.[61] However, as Jonah and the implied reader know, the abuse Jonah suffers is less life-threatening than

---

60. See Hauser, 'Jonah', pp. 27-28.
61. Some commentators interpret Jonah's request in this way—for example, Hauser, 'Jonah', pp. 26-27.

it may first seem,[62] for 'deliverance belongs to the Lord' (2.10), even
for Jonah.

> Then the sea will calm down for you for I know that it is on my own
> account that this mighty storm rages against you.'

Jonah properly assesses what the outcome will be if they accept his
request—that is, the mighty ('large') storm created by the Lord will
cease. The reader now awaits the sailors' responses to Jonah's request
and assessment and, since they have thus far accepted all requests and
assessments without question and they have demonstrated great piety,
one might assume they will accept Jonah's offer to save themselves.
Also, buried within this answer/request is Jonah's first admission of guilt
('on my account') given in his own words. Thus, even though the
implied reader knew that he was admitting his guilt before (1.9-10), it is
made explicit here.

> [13] Nonetheless, the men rowed hard in order to reach dry land.

As the implied reader knows, this narrator likes to omit dialogue for his
own satirical purposes, and once again the narrator plays with the reader's
expectations and reports the sailors' refusal in the same manner as
Jonah's refusal—that is, in reported consequences. What might the sailors'
verbal response to Jonah have been? 'Well, thank you for the offer, but
we could not possibly allow ourselves to be held "accountable for [your]
innocent blood" [1.14]'. Having accounted for their refusal, the sailors
try then to execute their alternative plan of escape—that is, to row ashore
during the storm, a deadly strategy as all good sailors would know.[63]

> But they were unable to, for the sea became increasingly violent against
> them.

Not surprisingly, their plan of escape is as ineffective as Jonah's. The
Lord, the Creator of sea and dry land, refuses to allow their plan to
work and makes this refusal obvious by increasing the storm's violence.

> [14] Then they called out to the Lord, 'Please, O Lord, do not let us perish
> because of the life of this man, and do not hold us accountable for
> innocent blood, for you are the Lord and whatever pleases you, you do.'

The sailors make two requests of the Lord: (1) that he not let them perish
because of Jonah's disobedience (which was never his intention) and

---

62. See Mather, 'The Comic Art of the Book of Jonah', p. 283.
63. See Sasson, *Jonah*, p. 141-42.

(2) that he not punish them for accepting Jonah's request to throw him overboard. Within these requests, the sailors state their belief that the Lord is all-powerful.

> [15] Then they picked up Jonah and cast him into the sea...

After fully realizing the futility in fleeing from the Lord and after requesting their deliverance, the sailors accept Jonah's request and throw him overboard.

> ...and the sea ceased its raging.

As expected, the compassionate Lord accepts their requests and Jonah's assessment of the sailors' acceptance of his request is confirmed.

> [16] Then the men were filled with the most dreadful fear of the Lord and they offered sacrifices to the Lord and made vows.

The sailors' piety is elevated even further to the superlative, 'most dreadful fear of the Lord' (literally, 'the men feared a large fear'), contrasting with Jonah's disobedient and nonchalant behavior. They offer sacrifices and make vows, which most likely the Lord happily accepts.

> [2.1] Then the Lord appointed a large fish to swallow Jonah.

The Lord now requests that a large fish save Jonah from drowning. The description 'large' reminds the reader that the fish is created by the Lord in that 'large' refers to only those things that have the Lord as their cause.[64]

> And Jonah was in the belly of the fish for three days and three nights.

The fish accepts the Lord's request and rescues Jonah from the raging seas. As is consistent throughout the narrative, the narrator does not allow nature (for example, the fish) to verbalize its acceptance of the Lord's request, but simply reports the consequences.

> [2] And Jonah prayed to the Lord, his God, from the belly of the fish,

For the first time in the text itself, Jonah addresses the Lord in direct speech. Jonah assumes correctly that the fish was divinely ordained to rescue him from the seas and that the Lord will somehow return him safely to dry land.

---

64. That is, Nineveh, the wind, the storm, the sailors' fear, Jonah's anguish, the plant, Jonah's rejoicing.

> [3] 'I call out, in my trouble, to the Lord and he answers me. From the belly of Sheol I plead; you hear my voice. [4] And you cast me into the depths, into the heart of the seas, and the current engulfs me; all of your billows and waves sweep over me. [5] So I say, "I am driven from your sight, may I yet continue to gaze toward your holy sanctuary?" [6] Waters envelop me up to my neck, the abyss engulfs me; kelp clings to my head. [7] To the base of the mountains, I sink. The netherworld, its bars, about me are there forever; but you lift me up from the Pit alive, O Lord, my God.'

The implied reader knows that Jonah knows that he will be saved—'deliverance belongs to the Lord' (2.10). This Given information is expressed here in Jonah's prayer—'I call out, in my trouble, to the Lord and he answers me...' (2.3). In other words, Jonah knows that the compassionate Lord will accept requests for deliverance. This tendency has already been demonstrated in the Lord's treatment of the sailors. However, even though Jonah knows all of this, he first expresses himself in the form and style most pertinent to his present situation, that of individual laments.[65] Ironically, Jonah assumes that the Lord, who in fact 'cast [him] into the depths' downward, will 'lift [him] up from the Pit', again playing on the 'going up'/'going down' contrast.[66]

> [8] Even as my life ebbs away; the Lord, I remember. Then my prayer reaches you at your holy sanctuary. [9] Those who hold to empty faiths, their hope for mercy they give up. [10] But, I, with a grateful voice, sacrifice to you; that which I vow, I shall fulfill. Deliverance belongs to the Lord'.

Now Jonah's knowledge of the Lord's compassionate nature is expressed in the form and style of a prayer of thanksgiving.[67] Jonah promises obedience, which seems to be against his own true nature, and he is already grateful for his deliverance, even though he is *still* in the depths of the seas in the belly of the fish. This knowledge, which finds expression in thanksgiving even before he is delivered from harm, is the reason Jonah was so nonchalant previously on the ship during the mighty storm. He knew even then that the Lord would not destroy him. Ironically, Jonah draws a contrast between himself and, implicitly at least, the sailors and the Ninevites, 'who hold to empty faiths'. Jonah boasts that, unlike such pagans, he is faithful to the Lord and gratefully

65. Ackerman, 'Satire and Symbolism', pp. 221-22.

66. On this contrast, see Halpern and Friedman, 'Composition and Paranomasia', pp. 80-83 and the section 'Paronomasia' in Chapter 3 §4.

67. Ackerman, 'Satire and Symbolism', p. 222.

sacrifices to him. What Jonah does not know, though, is, firstly, that the sailors also piously expressed gratitude to the Lord in the form of sacrifices and vows after they threw him overboard (1.16) and, secondly, that the Ninevites will repent piously with fasting and sackcloth (3.5-9). Therefore, the contrast that the character Jonah strives to maintain between pagan hopelessness and his own faith is known by the implied reader to be ironically false. Even though, in contrast with the pagans, Jonah knows that the Lord's truly compassionate nature (2.10; 4.2) requires the Lord to deliver all from adversity, this contrast can only be made at the level of the knowledge of the Lord's true character, for certainly the pagans in the narrative obey the Lord's will far better than Jonah.

11 Then the Lord spoke to the fish and it vomited Jonah upon dry land.

Just as Jonah suspected, the Lord delivers him from harm by requesting that the always-obedient fish vomit him up onto the shore. Thus ends Jonah's attempt to flee the Lord by 'going down', in his being 'vomited up' onto dry land.

3.1 Now it happened that the word of the Lord came to Jonah...

Once again the narrator begins with a standard prophetic superscription, informing the reader that the following is authoritative, prophetic literature. Maybe Jonah has learned his lesson and is now ready to faithfully accept his call. The implied reader, however, knows that all of this is the narrator's attempt to manipulate his readers. The use of this prophetic superscription has the semblance of introducing authoritative prophetic material but, as before (1.1), it serves a satirical function in that it introduces Jonah's continued conflict with the Lord. Even though Jonah accepts the repeated request (3.3), he only does so reluctantly and under duress.

...a second time,

This alerts the reader that the Lord is repeating his previous request.

2 'Get up. Go to Nineveh, that large city, and call out to it whatever I command you.'

Clearly, on the basis of content, the Lord's request here is not necessarily any different from his first request (1.2). The exact verbal repetition is quite remarkable, including the introductory superscription ('Now...Jonah') and the first part of the request ('Get up...call out').

Nothing in that which has been changed ('to it whatever I command you') necessarily implies that the Lord is moderating his view at all. In other words, since Jonah has already been told to call out judgment against it (1.2), the repetition of the request does not necessarily have to be as explicit as before. Also, the implied reader knows that this is not all that the Lord said to Jonah in his requests. That is, the Lord's requests as narrated are examples of constructed dialogue that only represents a full conversation between the Lord and Jonah, as is suggested to the reader in two ways. (1) The requests are vague as to what the Ninevites' wickedness is and as to what words Jonah must proclaim. (2) The narrator reports that, the Lord 'changed his mind concerning the evil he had commanded against them' (3.10), a statement that is also vague, only this time as to what the 'evil' really was supposed to be. However, even though the repeated request itself in no way suggests that the Lord is moderating his view at this time, the implied reader already knows that the Lord will, in fact, change his mind concerning the destruction of Nineveh. Therefore, this subtle change, making the Lord's continuing angry judgment of Nineveh less implicit, does not in and of itself suggest that the Lord is moderating his view, but nevertheless is understood as ironic. Once again, the reader awaits Jonah's response.

> [3] Then Jonah got up and went to Nineveh just as the Lord had commanded.

Here Jonah's acceptance is simply reported, possibly suggesting that Jonah has had a complete change of heart. However, the implied reader knows better and understands this report as once again manipulative and satirical. The implied reader imagines Jonah saying something like, 'OK, Lord, I will go, even though I really don't want to, because I am certain that you will change your mind concerning this evil.'

> And Nineveh was a large city, belonging to God, a three days' walk across. [4] After Jonah had hardly gone into the city a day's journey,

Jonah's hardly going into the large city could possibly be understood as his eagerness to obey the Lord; however, the implied reader knows that the reluctant Jonah is simply in a hurry to be done with it.

> …he called out, 'Forty days more, and Nineveh will overturn.'

He is in such a hurry that he gives one of the briefest prophetic oracles in the Hebrew Bible. Or does he? His oracle, as given to the reader in direct speech, is one sentence containing only five Hebrew words. Such a brief oracle could be expected from Jonah, who is very resistant to his mission; however, such a brief and vague oracle probably does not adequately reflect what the Lord wanted to communicate to Nineveh through his prophet Jonah. Therefore, Jonah's oracle as given in the narrative should be viewed as constructed dialogue that does not fully represent the Lord's word to Nineveh (through Jonah), which Jonah is said to have given 'just as the Lord had commanded' (3.3). In its given form, the oracle lacks an indictment and a specific means of punishment, both of which were probably part of the Lord's full message to Nineveh. Since the Ninevites' repentance concerns violence (3.8), it is likely that the indictment also concerned violence, similar to the indictments of Amos against the foreign nations (1.3–2.3) and Nahum against Nineveh (3.1). The implied reader also understands the irony in the oracle as 'quoted' in the text. Firstly, it will not take nearly forty days for the Ninevites to repent and, secondly, 'overturn' is ambiguous as to whether the overturning will be destructive (as in Nineveh's annihilation) or constructive (as in the Ninevites' repentance).[68] The Lord intends it to be destructive, even though the implied reader and Jonah know that it will be constructive.

From previous readings, the implied reader knows that the following description of the Ninevites' repentance and the Lord's change of mind overlap that of Jonah's anger and the Lord's lesson. This overlapping itself contributes to the satirical tone of the narrator. The Ninevites, whom Jonah earlier characterized as holding empty faiths with no hope for mercy in contrast to himself (2.9), immediately and piously repent in sackcloth and ashes. Jonah's brief oracle has had unprecedented success and this 'success' is described first, making Jonah's anger appear much more ironic.

> [5] Then the people of Nineveh believed in God; they called for a fast; and they put on sackcloth, from the greatest to the least.

The Ninevites' response to Jonah's oracle is immediately summed up: All of the Ninevites and their animals (3.3-8)—'from the greatest [literally, "from the largest"] to the least'—fasted and put on sackcloth. The Ninevites' belief in the Lord, which they immediately put into obedient and pious action, like the sailors' before them, contrasts strikingly with Jonah's disobedience.

> [6] When word reached the king of Nineveh, he got up from his throne and stripped off his royal mantle and put on sackcloth and sat down in ashes.

68. Sasson, *Jonah*, pp. 234-37.

> **7** Then he proclaimed, 'In Nineveh, on the authority of the king and his counselors: People and beasts—herds and flocks—must not taste anything, must not graze, and even water, they must not drink. **8** Rather, they must wrap themselves in sackcloth—people and beasts alike—and must call out to God with fervor. Each person must turn from his evil way and from the violence which is in their hands. **9** Who knows? Perhaps that god will change his mind and turn away from his anger, so that we may not perish.'

Here we have a flashback explaining exactly how the Ninevites' reaction, as summarized in 3.5, occurred.[69] Upon hearing Jonah's message, the king himself put on sackcloth, sat in ashes and began his fast. He then demanded that all of the people and beasts of Nineveh to do likewise. The Ninevite king's response defies the typical response of kings, including Israelite kings, when they hear a message of judgment from one of the Lord's prophets, thereby heightening the contrast between Jonah and the Ninevites even further. The king is also explicit about the motivation for this request; he makes the assessment that the Lord might change his mind (3.9; see also Joel 2.14[70]). The implied reader already knows that the compassionate Lord will change his mind and, therefore, reads the king's assessment as ironic. In fact, the king's unassertive manner of making this assessment in the form of a question, 'poses the key question, of the book'[71]—that is, Will the Lord's compassion be able to overcome his anger? The answer is an unqualified, 'Yes' (2.10; 4.2, 10-11).

> **10** When God saw their deeds, that they had turned away from their evil ways, God changed his mind concerning the evil which he had commanded against them and did not do it.

Now what Jonah and the implied reader knew would happen all along, and what the Ninevite king assessed, comes to be. The Lord changes his mind and repents of the evil he had commanded against Nineveh.

Next, the reader returns to the actions of Jonah immediately following his oracle. This flashback contributes to the satirical tone of the narrative in that his unprecedented success in affecting repentance has been described before Jonah's anger at his mission.

> **4.1** But this was terribly upsetting to Jonah and he was angry.

69. See Wolff, *Obadiah and Jonah*, p. 145.

70. On the relationship between Jon. 3.1–4.11 and Joel 2.1-17, see Dozeman, 'Inner-Biblical Interpretation'.

71. Hauser, 'Jonah', p. 34.

Consistent to his true nature, Jonah remains angry with the Lord for coercing him to prophesy to Nineveh. The Lord as the cause of his anger is not only suggested in the demonstrative 'this' but also in the use of 'large' in the description of his anger—'terribly upsetting' (literally, 'it was distressing to Jonah, a large distress'). The use of 'large' here suggests the Lord as the cause and object of Jonah's anger, in that in the narrative 'large' always refers to that which the Lord has affected. Of course, in the world of the narrative Jonah does not even know that the Ninevites have repented, but he knew all along that, whether or not they did, the Lord would repent and change his mind concerning the evil he had commanded against Nineveh.

> [2] And he interjected to the Lord, 'Oh Lord! Is this not what I said while I was still in my homeland? Therefore, I hastened to flee to Tarshish for I knew that you are a gracious and compassionate God, slow to anger and extremely benevolent, who would change his mind concerning the evil.

Although Jonah and the implied reader have known all along that the compassionate Lord would not destroy Nineveh, only here is this knowledge explicated in his reference to the (previously omitted) account for his refusal (1.3). As foreshadowed in his prayer (2.10: 'deliverance belongs to the Lord'), Jonah reveals his knowledge of the Lord's true nature: 'a gracious and compassionate God, slow to anger and extremely benevolent'. But Jonah does not glory in this knowledge, even though only a compassionate Lord could have put up with all of his foolishness. Rather, he curiously uses it as an accusation against the Lord because he wanted the Ninevites destroyed but knew that the Lord's compassionate nature could not allow it to happen.[72]

> [3] 'Now, O Lord, take my life from me, for it is better that I die than live.'

Not only does Jonah not fully appreciate that the only reason he is still alive is because of the Lord's compassion, but he goes so far as despising his own life and requesting from the Lord the impossible. Although other prophets have also cursed their own life (see, for example, Jer. 20.7-8), Jonah's lament differs dramatically. Other prophets lament over their ineffectiveness to change the people's ways and their resulting unjust punishment; Jonah laments over a suffering he creates for himself in his narrow nationalism vis-à-vis his prophetic success.

---

72. A similarly expanded form of this confession is found in Joel 2.13, where it functions as confession rather than as accusation. On the relationship between Jon. 3.1–4.11 and Joel 2.1-17, see Dozeman, 'Inner-Biblical Interpretation'.

Thus, he requests death, which is antithetical to the Lord's character, for a gracious and compassionate Lord could not possibly take his life! Therefore, the implied reader knows that the Lord will refuse and wonders as to what form this dispreferred second will take. If the pattern set in the previous chapters continues, the Lord's refusal will simply occur in the form of reported consequences.

> ⁴ Then the Lord said, 'Is it good for you to be so angry?'

For the first time in the entire narrative, dialogue between the Lord and Jonah is being fully given in direct speech. Previous conversations between the Lord and Jonah have been presented in only abbreviated form and/or with much omitted by placing the second part of the adjacency pairs in reported consequences.[73] However, beginning with 4.2, the Lord and Jonah's face-to-face conversation is given in full. Here the Lord has begun his dispreferred second of refusal verbally, by using a delay and preface in the form of an insertion sequence. In other words, rather than simply saying 'No, it is against my nature', the Lord mitigates his refusal by first questioning Jonah's implicit assessment of his own situation. Jonah perceives his situation as completely meaningless and conflict-ridden; the Lord sees Jonah's attitude as petty. What will Jonah's answer be to this question?

> ⁵ But Jonah went from the city and sat down east of the city. And there he made for himself a booth and he sat down under its shade until he could see what would happen in the city.

Characteristically, Jonah gives a dispreferred response to the Lord's question, a non-answer. Since he has not yet seen with his own eyes what he already knows—that is, that the Lord will not destroy Nineveh—he leaves the city to see what response his oracle will have and how soon the Lord will give in to his true, compassionate nature. Of course, this waiting is ironic in two ways: (1) the narrative has already told its readers of Jonah's 'success' in the previous account (3.5-10) and (2) Jonah himself has already said that the Lord will change his mind (4.2). Nevertheless, he builds a booth, sits in its shade, and waits.

> ⁶ And the Lord God appointed a *qiqayon* plant to grow up over Jonah so that there would be shade over his head in order to deliver him from his distress.

73. See Hauser, 'Jonah', p. 32.

The Lord continues to delay his refusal of Jonah's death-request by beginning to teach Jonah a lesson through his miraculous control of nature. Rather than taking Jonah's life as requested, he shows concern for Jonah's comfort and requests a plant to grow quickly to provide more shade than Jonah's hastily constructed booth could.

> And Jonah rejoiced exceedingly over the *qiqayon* plant.

The obedient plant accepts the request and Jonah, knowing that this miraculous plant is God-given, rejoices greatly. Just as 'large' was used previously to show the Lord as the cause of Jonah's distress (4.1), 'large' is used here to attribute to the Lord why he 'rejoiced exceedingly' (literally, 'he rejoiced a large rejoice').

> [7] Then God appointed a worm, at daybreak of the next day. It attacked the *qiqayon* plant so that it withered.

The lesson continues. The Lord requests a worm to attack the plant and it accepts. The plant withers.

> [8] At sunrise, God appointed a fierce east wind. Then the sun attacked Jonah's head...

The Lord requests that a strong wind come to destroy Jonah's booth[74] and it accepts. The booth and plant are now gone and the sun attacks Jonah's head.

> ...and he swooned. And he asked that he might die, 'It is better that I die than live.'

In the heat of the day, Jonah shows signs of heat exhaustion and swoons. The choice of this verb 'swoon' may be a subtle hint from the narrator that Jonah's following words should be viewed as coming from someone who is dizzy-headed. In other words, the narrator may be hinting at his pejorative attitude toward the character Jonah. In his light-headed state, Jonah repeats his death-request, assessing his situation as horribly pathetic. Of course, the compassionate Lord can be expected to respond as he did before.

> [9] Then God said to Jonah, 'Is it good for you to be so angry on account of the *qiqayon* plant?'

The Lord responds exactly as before, only here he adds, 'on account of the *qiqayon* plant'. That is, the Lord does not directly reject Jonah's

---

74. See Sasson, *Jonah*, p. 304.

death-request, but rather questions Jonah's underlying assessment of his situation. It is as if the Lord were saying, 'Is your life really so miserable that you want to die? I think not.' Jonah's response to this line of questioning is easy to imagine.

> Then he said, 'It is good that I am angry enough to die.'

Whereas before Jonah's response to this question was a non-answer (one type of dispreferred second), Jonah now issues another type of dispreferred second to questions, an unexpected answer. He answers by disagreeing with the Lord's disagreeable assessment, by changing the syntax of the Lord's question into his own assertion. As before, the Lord can be expected to respond.

> [10] Then the Lord said, 'You yourself were fretting over the *qiqayon* plant, for which you neither toiled nor cultivated, which came up one night and perished the next night. [11] Yet I should not have compassion on Nineveh, that large city, which has in it more than one hundred and twenty thousand people, who do not know their right hand from their left hand, and many cattle as well?'

The Lord now gives his delayed answer to Jonah's question, 'Is this not...?' (4.2), and his delayed account for his refusal of Jonah's death-requests (4.3, 8), using the plant episode as a lesson in the contrast between Jonah and himself. The force of this speech is in agreement with that which Jonah understood, at least to some extent, 'while [he] was still in [his] homeland' (4.2)—that is, the Lord's compassionate nature. However, it strongly asserts that Jonah does not fully understand the implications of the Lord's compassion, for he remains angry at the Lord's compassion towards the many Ninevites and their animals and, therefore, pettily issues a death-request which further ignores the Lord's compassionate nature. This episode, more than anywhere else in the narrative, demonstrates the Lord's compassion for Nineveh and, thus, for all of his creation.[75] The Lord draws an analogy between Nineveh and the plant. He implies that he is the one who cultivated (literally, 'made to grow larger') the plant and then contrasts Jonah's petty attitude towards the plant with his compassion towards 'Nineveh, that large city.' In other words, the paronomastic theme of 'large' representing only those things that the Lord affected is used to show the Lord's close

---

75. This repetition of the theme of compassion is similar to that in Joel 2.17. Again, on the relationship between Jon. 3.1–4.11 and Joel 2.1-17, see Dozeman, 'Inner-Biblical Interpretation'.

relationship with Nineveh, which is the motivation for his compassion. The Lord's answer and account for his refusal is itself a question, which remains unanswered by Jonah within the limits of the narrative. The Lord is allowed to have the last word.

Chapter 5

READING THE JONAH NARRATIVE: ACTUAL READERS

In the previous chapter, competence was discussed in relation to the interaction between text and reader. Since texts bring certain narrative strategies to the interaction, texts can be judged, to some extent, as successful or unsuccessful. Since readers bring their own knowledge of history and literary conventions to the interaction, they can be judged, to some extent, as successful or unsuccessful. Since each reading involves both the text's and the actual reader's competence, the success of each particular interaction must be judged within a broad survey of numerous and various actual readings in order to determine the competence of the text and its numerous readers. (No particular interaction between a text and any actual reader can be understood as *absolutely* successful or unsuccessful. 'Successful' and 'unsuccessful' are only used here in somewhat relative terms.)

In this chapter, I attempt such a judgment of the interaction between the text of the Jonah narrative and many of its actual readers. The actual readers have been sought out in various ways:[1] (1) title searches containing the word 'Jonah', 'Iona', and 'Yonah', (2) subject searches, (3) hours and hours of browsing through open stacks, (4) using the indexes in major series and encyclopedias (such as *20 Centuries of Great Preaching, The Fathers of the Church*) and (5) consulting the bibliographies in Limburg's and Sasson's commentaries. During this search, I made a conscious effort to seek out various works that exhibit a rich diversity. I was somewhat successful in that I found works diverse in terms of genre (for example, children's Bible stories, sermons, references in literature), time (first century to the present), language (for example, German, Dutch, Hebrew, French), the author's religious heritage (for

---

1.   The two institutions in which library searches took place are Duke University and the University of Missouri at Columbia. Various works were also received through inter-library loans.

example, Jewish, Lutheran, Congregational) and the author's gender.[2]

The previous chapter presented an account of the implied reader interacting with the Jonah narrative. However, this implied reader was only as competent as I, an actual reader, could make him; in other words, he was necessarily an imperfect presentation of the theoretical implied reader. My presentation of this implied reader was only the end product of a long interrelationship between the text and me. This statement indicates that I changed my mind concerning different interpretations as I interacted more and more with the text. I prefer to think that in this interactive process the text exerted its 'true self' on me, bringing me closer and closer to its true implied reader. Below, I will include my journey of being guided by the text to my final[3] reading as an example of the text's success in enabling me to fill its gaps. Unfortunately, I do not have this type of information for any other actual reader and, since my notes about my own reading are sometimes sketchy, the account of my own reading may be somewhat selective.

In the following, the only way in which I could discuss these various readings was to break the interactions up according to what I understand are some of their more indeterminate places. That is, the following discussions describe certain parts of the interaction according to the gaps of indeterminacy that the text, the most relatively constant participant,[4] brings to different stages of the interaction. The consequence of this abstraction is that, in the discussion of my own reading journey, the false impression could be given that I necessarily realized the first understanding concerning a particular segment, then the next, and so on. In other words, my expository prose seems to be describing a logical, linear process, which did not occur; rather, many of my own insights came in groups.[5] Therefore, I ask my readers to withhold judgment until all of

---

2.   Unfortunately, my sample is still heavily weighted towards white, Protestant, English-speaking, male academics, like myself. However, I think that the diversity is relatively significant.

3.   That is, at the time of the last revision of this manuscript. In other words, I reserve the right to change my mind in the future as the evidence requires.

4.   I have not attempted to come to terms with what particular text each reader read. For example, did every reader consult the original Hebrew (which is highly unlikely) and, if so, which Hebrew text? If not, did the reader consult the Greek or Latin traditions, or did he or she use a vernacular translation? I can only assume, for the purposes of this chapter, that the variety of texts which probably underlie these readings did not significantly influence what differences there are in the interpretations.

5.   This is certainly consistent with my own understanding of reading, which is

this chapter has been read in order to understand the full picture of the dynamic process I am struggling to describe in my expository prose.

I begin this discussion with the constructed dialogue in the narrative, first concerning the omission of Jonah's verbal refusal in 1.3 and his reference to this speech in 4.2. I then discuss the narrator's satirical tone and the use of flashback in the narrative. In most sections, I begin by describing my own interactions as a reader of the Jonah narrative. I then examine similar readings, before turning to those that are divergent. I then conclude each section with a brief generalization of why the 'unsuccessful' readers—that is, those who differ significantly from the implied reader of the previous chapter—may have failed due to their own limitations.

1. *The (Almost) Universal Recognition of Jonah's Omitted Refusal (1.3; 4.2)*

The text's manipulation of its readers is extremely successful in enabling them to fill the gap created by Jonah's omitted verbal refusal. This success stems from what both the text and its readers bring to the interaction. The text brings two significant elements to the interaction: (1) The omission creating the gap is blatant and is thus easily recognized as such by readers. Jonah's refusal defies the paradigm of adjacency pairs—that is, his dispreferred second is given with neither a delay, preface, account nor declination component, but is simply reported in his narrated actions. This forces the following questions: 'Why is Jonah so reluctant to go to Nineveh in the first place?',[6] 'Why does Jonah not want to carry out an assignment in Nineveh?',[7] 'Why does Jonah flee?'[8] In other words, these questions put into words what the nature of this particular gap is. (2) The information given in 4.2—which guides the reader to answering this question and, therefore, filling the gap—is also blatantly obvious, as illustrated in these examples:

based on Iser's. Gaps of indeterminacy may open up in a linear fashion, but whole groups of gaps can be closed with one small bit of information.

6.   T. Eagleton, 'J.L. Austin and the Book of Jonah', in R.M. Schwartz (ed.), *The Book and the Text: The Bible and Literary Theory* (Cambridge: Basil Blackwell, 1990), pp. 231-36 (231).

7.   J. Limburg, *Jonah: A Commentary* (OTL; Louisville: Westminster Press, 1993), p. 42.

8.   T.E. Fretheim, *The Message of Jonah* (Minneapolis: Augsburg, 1977), pp. 76-77.

We finally learn [in 4.2] why Jonah had fled his divine commission.[9]

Here Jonah openly declares why he bore so ill the deliverance of Nineveh from destruction, because he was thus found to have been false and lying.[10]

In fact, as we learn later, in Jonah 4:2, Jonah did in fact argue; he there says to the Lord, 'O Lord,...'[11]

Jonah explicitly states why he refused to participate in God's mission: 'O Lord,...'[12]

In 4.2f. he launches into a prayer, but after mention of that act the hand of the author of chs. 1–2 worked in the flashback about the supposed attempt of Jonah to evade his commission by going to sea, and giving the reason (not disclosed in 1.3) why he did so.[13]

Ja er wagt es sogar, seine Haltung Gott gegenüber mit erregten Worten zu verteidigen. Er wendet sich an Gott in einem Gebete, in dem er die Besorgnisse aber auch den Unmut seines Herzens offen zum Ausdruck bringt. Nicht erst jetzt, sondern schon früher, als ihm zum ersten Male der Auftrag Gottes erteilt wurde, hat er geahnt, daß es so kommen werde. Aus diesem Grunde hat er sich damals durch die Flucht seiner Sendung entzogen; er wollte dem Erbarmen Gottes zuvorkommen and verhindern, daß durch seine Mithilfe Gottes Gnade dieser heidnischen Stadt geschenkt werde. (Yes, he even dared to defend his attitude towards God with charged words. He turned to God in a prayer, in which he openly expresses the fear, but also the displeasure, of his heart. Not only now, but before now, when the command of God had be given to him for the first time, he had foreseen that it would happen thusly. On this basis, he took flight of his mission; he wanted to prevent and hinder the mercy of God, because with his assistance God's grace would be given to this heathen city.)[14]

9.   Ackerman, 'Jonah', p. 240.

10.   J. Calvin, *Commentaries on the Twelve Minor Prophets.* III. *Jonah, Micah, Nahum* (trans. J. Owen; Grand Rapids: Eerdmans, 1950), p. 120.

11.   D.N. Freedman, 'Did God Play a Dirty Trick on Jonah at the End?', *Bible Review* 6 (1990), pp. 26-31 (28).

12.   Levine, 'Jonah as a Philosophical Book', p. 243.

13.   E.G. Kraeling, 'The Evolution of the Story of Jonah', in *Hommages à A. Dupont-Sommer* (Paris: Libraire d'amérique et d'orient Adrien-Maisonneuve, 1971), pp. 305-18 (311). Kraeling understands that the Jonah narrative evolved as follows: From stories about the eighth-century prophet Jonah behind the present text, to Jonah 3–4, and finally to Jonah 1–4. The later author of Jonah 1–2 then tied his story to that of Jonah 3–4 by adding Jonah's account of his refusal to Jon. 4.2. Although his understanding of the text's evolution is questionable, it is nevertheless interesting that he also fills in the gap realized at 1.3 with 4.2.

14.   P.M. Schumpp, *Das Buch des zwölf Propheten* (Herders Bibelkommentar, 10.2; Freiburg: Herder, 1950), p. 179.

Hence, the text brings to its interaction with readers the blatant gap of Jonah's verbal refusal which demands to be filled (1.3), and the obvious and necessary information in order to successfully fill the gap (4.2). In other words, this indeterminacy is what Iser calls a negation—that type of gap that is opened allowing readers to reach various conclusions for filling the gap only to later explicitly contradict these conclusions. The strategy used for filling this gap is what Clark and Haviland have called 'restructuring'—that is, the phrase, 'what I said while I was still in my homeland' (4.2), has no antecedent in the text itself; therefore, the reader restructures the following information in order to create an antecedent for this phrase that then successfully fills the gap created in 1.3.

The reader brings acquired knowledge of adjacency pairs to the inter-action, which causes him or her to identify the gap in 1.3 and then fill it with 4.2. But this is not all the reader brings to the interaction. The reader's previous experience with prophetic literature plays an important role in the interaction as well. Even though prophets often express reluct-ance toward their divine mission, Jonah is the *only* prophet in biblical narrative who flatly refuses his call, who is presented as not verbalizing his reluctance and who flees from the Lord. Therefore, readers (at least, those somewhat familiar with biblical prophets) assume that the prophet in every prophetic book will accept his call, even if he is somewhat reluctant. Jonah, however, stands out as aberrant. In other words, Jonah's refusal not only defies the paradigm of adjacency pairs, but also defies the paradigm of prophets with which readers are familiar. This observa-tion of Jonah's aberrance in refusing his call is heightened in that Jonah's mission should not present any political problems for him—that is, his call is one of judgment against Israel's enemies, the Ninevites.

In summary, the interaction between the text and its actual readers is highly successful in creating and filling the gap concerning Jonah's refusal of the Lord's initial request—so successful that commentators sometimes are compelled to explicitly reconstruct what Jonah 'said' in 1.3 in his own words:

> Please, Lord, I realize that you are a gracious and compassionate God, very patient and abundantly benevolent, who will relent from bringing disaster.[15]

> So Jonah did not mind telling the people of Nineveh that God was about to destroy them! 'But God is loving', he thought, 'He forgives people and

---

15. Sasson, *Jonah*, p. 329.

lets them have a second chance. He won't destroy Nineveh. And I shall look silly'.[16]

Both of these examples are reconstructed well in relation to the characteristics of dispreferred seconds. The first begins with a delay by means of a preface in the form of interjection and address ('Please, Lord') and in the form of an appreciation ('I realize that you are...'). This appreciation itself functions as the account—that is, it implies that there is no need for Jonah to go to Nineveh since the Lord will relent. Nothing more is said; the declination component is mitigated and indirect. The second example is intriguing in that it occurs at the beginning of the retelling of the Jonah narrative in a children's storybook. This retelling reconstructs Jonah's refusal and places it where it 'belongs' in order to facilitate an easier reading for its young audience. The reconstruction here also contains the characteristic parts of an adjacency pair: delay by means of a preface in the form of the conjunction, 'But', and the following appreciation ('God is loving...He won't destroy Nineveh'), an implicit account ('I shall look silly'), and declination component, which is mitigated and indirect in that Jonah's words are presented as his inner thoughts rather than his direct speech to the Lord. Therefore, these two examples reflect not only the readers' competence at recognizing the gap, but also their competence in filling the gap with speech attributed to Jonah, which still conforms to the characteristics of dispreferred seconds.

Despite this tremendous success, some interpreters nevertheless present other explanations for Jonah's refusal, including those who successfully realize the filling of the gap in accordance with the text's guidance. In other words, the gap created is so strong that commentators are sometimes compelled to realize other accounts for Jonah's dispreferred second of refusal. For example, George Abbot, the Archbishop of Canterbury, wrote in 1845,

> We need not doubt but Satan...could yield reasons enough for the hindrance of this work...It might be, that our prophet might have a conceit, that for bringing such a message as the destruction of Nineveh, he might be murdered, or at least be much abused...Perhaps he remembered that he did no good by preaching in his own country to men of rebellious hearts: what good then should he do in preaching to infidels...Thus have I touched such causes, as sense and reason yield, and the expositions on this place. The text does not contradict these, and it is not unlikely that all, or

16. P. Alexander, *The Nelson Children's Bible: Stories from the Old and New Testaments* (Nashville: Thomas Nelson, 1981), n.p.

diverse of them, were tumbling at the time in the working head of Jonah. But there is one, which expressly is named in the body of the text, as appears in the fourth chapter.[17]

Another example comes from the contemporary French biblical scholar, Jacques Ellul:

> He has every reason to refuse from the human standpoint. It is veritable folly to go to Nineveh, that great city which was always in arms against God and his people. To begin with, he would have to make a tremendous journey across the desert: about 750 miles on foot. Then he would arrive at a very large city with far more than 120,000 inhabitants, and he would be quite alone there...[T]he Ninevites...[were] a traditional foe of Israel. The age of Jonah was the zenith of Assyrian power...The kingdom of Israel where Jonah lived was an Assyrian province. God orders Jonah to go to the very place he could not go—a light among the darkness. In sum, Nineveh is the 'world' in the theological sense.[18]

These two elaborations upon Jonah's account demonstrate how two particular readers draw upon their knowledge of the narrative's extra-textual historical and literary world to fill in the gap of Jonah's refusal, even beyond that explicitly given in the text. In the first, the commentator draws upon his knowledge of Satan in biblical material, the themes of the abuse of prophets ('he might be murdered...'; for example, 1 Kgs 22.5-12; Jer. 37.1–38.28), and the prophet Jonah of 2 Kgs 14.25 ('he did no good...'). The writer of the second quote draws upon his knowledge of geography ('750 miles') and ancient political history ('The Ninevites...traditional foe of Israel'). However, both interpreters understand that the text intends to have the gap filled with information from Jonah's speech in 4.2 ('one...expressly named'; Ellul refers to 4.2 on a different page[19]).

The tremendous success in the interaction between text and readers concerning Jonah's refusal can be supported by numerous readings (see Appendix 1). However, there are some readings that do not provide explicit support for the highly successful interaction between text and reader, thus the use of '(Almost)' in this section's title. However, these

17. G. Abbot, *An Exposition upon the Prophet Jonah* (London: Hamilton, Adams & Co., 1845), pp. 31-35.

18. J. Ellul, *The Judgment of Jonah* (trans. G.W. Bromiley; Grand Rapids: Eerdmans, 1971), pp. 26-27.

19. Ellul, *The Judgment of Jonah*, p. 73. See Appendix 1 for this quote.

exceptions[20] do not necessarily suggest that the interaction between the text and these actual readers was unsuccessful concerning Jonah's account. Rather, these exceptions are qualified in some way. Three examples will suffice here.[21] (1) Don Marquis wrote a short story,[22] using the character Jonah in conversation with Noah and Cap'n John Smith, which does not refer to Jonah's refusal. In fact, this story, in which the characters are telling their most outrageous fishing stories, does not even mention the Lord or Nineveh but rather focuses upon Jonah's story of being caught by the fish. (2) Karin Almbladh's study, 'The Israelites and the Sea', does not intend to give a full interpretation of the Jonah narrative, but rather concerns Jonah's flight at sea. She discusses the irony in Jonah's choice to flee from the Lord by going to sea, which is characteristically understood as chaos by the land-loving Israelites. (3) James Ackerman's 'Satire and Symbolism in the Song of Jonah' emphasizes the interpretation of Jonah 2 and does not, therefore, deal extensively with the other chapters. Therefore, he does not intend to give a full exposition of Jonah, but elsewhere when he does (in his commentary), he explicitly discusses 4.2 in relation to 1.3. In summary, the exceptions to the observation that the reader's interest gravitates to 1.3 and 4.2 can be explained as limited in relation to the purpose of the secondary works in which these exceptions are found. In other words, the genre and/or topic of these works does not require a discussion of all, or even the more important, elements of the Jonah narrative, but limits the writer to only those parts of the narrative that concern the topic at hand. Therefore, these exceptions are qualified in that they do not present the full picture of these reader's interaction with the text, which may have included the identification and filling of the gap of indeterminacy concerning Jonah's refusal.

2. *Omitted Dialogue other than Jonah's Account*

The interaction between text and readers has been extremely successful in relation to the gap concerning Jonah's refusal and its filling. This success, however, does not hold true for all other segments of the interaction between the text and its readers. These segments—those which

20. See the section 'Contra' in Appendix 1.

21. Similar arguments are made for each 'Contra' entry in Appendix 1.

22. *Noah an' Jonah an' Cap'n John Smith: A Book of Humorous Verse* (New York: D. Appleton, 1921).

have not been as successful across a wide spectrum of readers—are
discussed below with the hope of answering the question as to why they
have not been as successful. The previous section, including Appendix 1,
was exhaustive, whereas the following discussions are only illustrative
because there is really no way to be exhaustive in my presentation of
unsuccessful readings. If the interaction between the text and any
particular, actual reader did not succeed, then this reader would not
necessarily have anything to report concerning the matter. This reader
may provide an interpretation that illustrates a misreading, but may also
provide no information at all. Therefore, sometimes I am unfortunately
limited to presenting examples of successful interactions and discussing
the unsuccessful interactions only in abstraction.

The assumption underlying the following discussions is that my
presentation of the interaction between the text and the implied reader
of the Jonah narrative in the previous chapter was quite successful given
the particular purview of this study and that, where other readings differ,
a misreading (at least from the purview of this study) has occurred. In
other words, in my interaction with the text, both the text and I are
understood as contributing to the successful interaction from the particular perspective of this study; in other interactions, the text contributed
the same information, but all other readers, with their particular limitations and/or different approaches, caused the interaction to be less
successful. I declare this assumption here because the discourse that
follows evaluates different readings from my own viewpoint. This is the
objective aspect of my argument—that is, my own perspective provides
an objective criterion by which I can evaluate other readings. However,
relative aspects remain. First, my *own* perspective is certainly influenced
by my relative competence. Secondly, if my interaction with the text has
been unsuccessful in some segment of the process, I am, like any other
reader, necessarily unaware of this inadequacy. Otherwise, my recognition of this inadequacy would have forced me to interact with the text
further until the inadequacy was overcome. Nevertheless, I am aware of
how this corrective process did, in fact, operate at times. In other words,
I know about the inadequacies of my initial and earlier interactions with
the text that were overcome through additional interactions, and this
process is reported below. If other inadequacies exist in my interaction,
they are outside of my necessarily limited purview.

What do my first unsuccessful readings have in common with the
other unsuccessful readings? In other words, why have so many

commentators, including myself earlier, misread the text? The answers to these questions lie in the very phrase for the concept that Deborah Tannen has described as a 'misnomer'—that is, 'reported speech':

> What is commonly referred to as reported speech or direct quotation in conversation is constructed dialogue, just as surely as is the dialogue created by fiction writers and playwrights.[23]

Tannen suggests that the use of 'reported speech' as applied to conversation is really the imposition of a literate mentality carried over from familiarity with expository prose. Herein lies the answer to the questions just posed, for too often readers, including myself, assume that what purports to be 'reported speech' or 'direct quotation' in narrative is exactly what was said by the character, nothing added and nothing omitted. However, this is often not the case, as is obvious to readers of Jonah's refusal (1.3) and subsequent account (4.2). As we will see below, this common tendency to accept such constructed dialogue as 'quotation' leads to numerous misreadings.[24]

How has the text contributed to these misreadings? The text provides all the information necessary to realize a successful reading; however, the selection and arrangement of this material, which expresses the narrator's satirical tone, violates the Cooperative Principle in various ways, forcing the reader to actively compensate. In other words, readers begin with the assumption that the author's text adheres to the Cooperative Principle and, therefore, faithfully reports the character's speech. For example, if the readers assume that the author's text follows the Quantity maxim, 'Make your contribution as informative as is required', and the Manner maxim, 'Avoid obscurity of expression', then they also assume that the characters' speech is exactly reported. It is only after they realize that the text violates the Cooperative Principle for the purpose of a satirical tone that the readers begin to question the text's cooperative role. Therefore, the narrator's selection and arrangement of material contributes to these misreadings by presenting this material with a satirical tone that may not be recognized by a reader.[25]

---

23. Tannen, 'Constructed Dialogue', p. 311.

24. G.W. Savran (*Telling and Retelling: Quotation in Biblical Narrative* [Indiana Studies in Biblical Literature; Bloomington: Indiana University Press, 1988], pp. 77-78) also discusses this tendency.

25. This is always a danger with a satirical tone and does not necessarily imply that the text is unsuccessful, for even a successful text can contribute to a misreading. See Band, 'Swallowing Jonah', pp. 179-80, 182-85.

For example, the text systematically omits the second parts of the adjacency pairs between the Lord and Jonah in the first three chapters. Since the text omits so much material, readers might assume, incorrectly however, that at least what is given in the text as direct speech follows the Cooperative Principle. Therefore, although the text contributes to a successful reading after repeated interactions, it requires a high degree of patience and competence in its readers in order for them to overcome its violations of the Cooperative Principle.

The following cases of constructed dialogue will be discussed below: the Lord's requests (1.2; 3.2), Jonah's answer to the sailors' questions (1.9-10), the sailors' initial refusal to throw Jonah overboard (1.12-14), Jonah's oracle (3.4), Jonah acceptance of the Lord's repeated request (3.3), and Jonah's omitted answer to the Lord's final question (4.10-11). As I discuss my own interaction with the text, the genre of expository prose limits my description of this process. In other words, what seems to be described as a linear process—'First, I realized this and then that'—does not adequately describe what often came all at once. Hopefully, this limitation will not adversely inhibit my readers' ability to understand something of this process and possibly to experience this process themselves as they read the Jonah narrative once again.

The Lord's Requests (1.2; 3.2)

On first reading the Jonah narrative, I recognized on reading 4.2 that the narrator had omitted Jonah's verbal refusal. However, on numerous occasions I overlooked the constructed nature of the Lord's requests (1.2; 3.2). I did not realize the constructed nature of the Lord's requests until I approached the material differently than my first interactions. That is, it was not until I later de-emphasized the direct speech given in the narrative and analyzed closely the narrator's reports that I saw the Lord's requests as vague and only representing more specific and elaborate requests. This was suggested in three ways: (1) Both requests are vague as to what the Ninevites' wickedness is and as to what words of judgment Jonah must proclaim. (2) The narrator reports, again in vague language, that the Lord 'changed his mind concerning the evil he had commanded against them' (3.10), thereby suggesting that the Lord was more explicit about this evil. (3) Even if Jonah's oracle (3.4) is given 'just as the Lord had commanded' (3.3), then the words of the oracle themselves are omitted from the Lord's request as given in 1.2 and 3.2. These three observations taken together suggest that the Lord's requests as 'quoted' in the narrative are simply abbreviated markers for requests that must have been more specific and elaborate.

This observation that the Lord's requests are blatant examples of constructed dialogue not containing the exact words of the requests has been made, to my knowledge, by only five other modern commentators, Burrows, Craig, Limburg, Trible and Wolff, and they report this observation only concerning the second request in 3.2. In fact, Wolff explicitly says of the request in 1.2: 'Jonah's commission is *unambiguous*, great, and full of danger.'[26] Burrows, Craig, Limburg, Trible and Wolff, respectively, note that the exact words of Jonah are not given in the narrative's reported request in 3.2:

> After delivering him from the sea God commanded him to proclaim to Nineveh 'the message that I tell you' (3.2), but what that was or would be is not stated.[27]

> The second command redirects the prophet and reminds us, however subtly, that this message remains known only to the Lord and his spokesman for the moment.[28]

> We are to assume that the Lord's word to Jonah continues with the content of the proclamation 'that I am telling you'. The narrator does not indicate the content of the proclamation until 3:4.[29]

> Nowhere in the story has Yhwh given Jonah these exact words [3.4] to speak.[30]

> What the message is to be is not expounded. In light of the book's theme, the only important thing at this point is that Jonah's preaching should reproduce exactly what Yahweh now says to him.[31]

Similarly, three pre-twentieth-century commentators—Henry Smith, Rashi and Radak[32]—note that the exact words Jonah is commanded to prophesy are not given in the Lord's requests. Smith and Radak each

---

26. Wolff, *Obadiah and Jonah*, p. 100. Emphasis mine.

27. Burrows, 'The Literary Category of the Book of Jonah', p. 99.

28. Craig, 'Jonah and the Reading Process', p. 109; Craig, *A Poetics of Jonah*, p. 80.

29. Limburg, *Jonah*, p. 76.

30. See Trible, *Rhetorical Criticism*, p. 180.

31. Wolff, *Obadiah and Jonah*, p. 139.

32. H. Smith, *Jonah the Messenger of Ninevehs Repentance Set Forth in His Calling, Rebellion, and Punishment* (London: n.p., 1617), pp. 18-19; Rashi and Radak as cited in Zlotowitz and Scherman, *Jonah*, p. 80.

suggest that at least Jonah's oracle (3.4) would have been included in the Lord's requests.

Admittedly, there may have been other successful interactions that I have not found. However, the predominant assumption that the exact words of the Lord's requests have been faithfully preserved and presented to the reader is astounding and illustrates well the common tendency to naively accept constructed dialogue as 'quotation'.

Jonah's Answer to the Sailors' Questions (1.9-10)

The sailors ask four questions of Jonah, all of which concern information I knew, for the most part, even before the questions were raised. 'What is your mission and where are you coming from? What is your homeland and from what people do you come?' (1.8). In other words, these questions do not even momentarily create gaps of indeterminacy for most readers because most of the information needed for the answers has already been given in the narrative. Therefore, when Jonah's answer is given simply as, 'I am a Hebrew, and the Lord, the God of Heaven, I worship—he who made the sea and the dry land' (1.9), I initially did not question whether or not this was his full answer. In fact, this possibility did not occur to me for quite a few readings, until finally the sailors' response (1.10) seemed increasingly strange. What was there in Jonah's answers to create their 'most dreadful fear' of the Lord? Does, 'the God of Heaven', suggest such fear? But most importantly, how did they know, 'that he was fleeing from the Lord'? Of course, once these questions were asked the answer was obvious: 'because he had told them' (1.10). That is, he had explicitly told them what I already knew from the previous verses, that 'he was fleeing from the Lord'. This now obvious omission of dialogue had only been 'hidden' from me in that I was emphasizing the direct speech rather than paying close attention to the narrator's own report as well.

Other readers of the Jonah narrative have had a similar interaction with the text.[33] For example, both Sasson and Wolff explicitly state that the narrator has omitted dialogue:

---

33. Other modern commentators besides Sasson and Wolff (discussed below) are L.C. Allen, *The Books of Joel, Obadiah, Jonah and Micah* (Grand Rapids: Eerdmans, 1976), p. 210; Craig, *A Poetic of Jonah*, p. 65; P.C. Craige, *Twelve Prophets. I. Hosea, Joel, Amos, Obadiah, and Jonah* (Philadelphia: Westminster Press, 1984), p. 221; Fretheim, *Message*, p. 85; Limburg, *Jonah*, p. 54.

The narrator knows too that, once posed, the sailors' questions will not rate of equal importance to his audience. Much too skillful to burden the tale with unnecessary detail, the narrator does not waste ink on formal and sequential responses to the sailors' inquisition. Do Israelites need to learn what ought to be the [mission] of a prophet? Where else but from among the Hebrews could a true prophet arise? For all these reasons, Jonah's explanation of why he boarded the ship in Jaffa, as well as his reply to the sailors' remaining queries, are brusquely relegated to passages attributed to Jonah but not quoted.[34]

> Where have 'the men'...derived their 'knowledge'?...[From] information given by Jonah...Something said is not always expressed in direct speech, even in the immediate context.[35]

Sasson and Wolff both recognize the abbreviated form of Jonah's full answer as expressed in the 'quote' from the narrator. Perhaps they would generally agree with my reconstruction of what Jonah's full answer may have been:

> My mission is to 'go to Nineveh and call out against it' [1.2]; I am coming from Jeroboam's court in Samaria [2 Kgs 14.23-27]. My hometown is Gath-hepher in Israel [2 Kgs 14.25] and 'I am a Hebrew, and the Lord, the God of Heaven, I worship—he who made the sea and the dry land' [1.9].

Sasson notes that, 'Hellenistic and medieval exegetes generally thought...[of] the query to be shorthand for a full trial scene at sea in which Jonah eventually confessed his guilt to all on board.'[36] Although Sasson does not document who these 'exegetes' are, I have found his statement to reflect such a tendency among pre-twentieth-century commentators. For example, John Calvin understood that the questions were asked one at a time and that Jonah responded fully to each question in order;[37] Thomas Paine wrote that, 'the story implies that he confessed himself to be guilty';[38] and early Jewish commentators likewise understood Jonah as revealing his secret.[39]

In contrast to Sasson and Wolff, most other modern readers appear

---

34. Sasson, *Jonah*, p. 126.
35. Wolff, *Obadiah and Jonah*, p. 117.
36. Sasson, *Jonah*, p. 120.
37. Calvin, *Commentaries on the Twelve Minor Prophets*, III, pp. 49-50.
38. T. Paine, *The Complete Writings of Thomas Paine* (ed. P.S. Foner; New York: Citidel Press, 1945), p. 567.
39. For example, Malbim, Radak and Ibn Ezra as cited in Zlotowitz and Scherman, *Jonah*, pp. 96-97.

not even to notice the possibility that Jonah's full answer has been abbreviated by the narrator. For example, Halpern and Friedman suggest that, 'Jonah is also unresponsive to the irony of the sailors' first question'.[40] In fact, a few commentators explicitly reject the possibility.[41] For example, Holbert writes,

> Some critics assume that Jonah really did tell the men directly that he was fleeing from God; the author simply does not report all of the conversation. But, did Jonah 'tell them'; that he was fleeing from Yahweh? Clearly the men understood this 'partial confession' of 1.9 better than he. He told them more than he intended. They *knew* he was fleeing from Yahweh; his 'confession' of 1.9 did indeed tell them all they wanted or needed to know.[42]

If Jonah did not explicitly tell the sailors he was fleeing from the Lord, Holbert must assume that the narrator's words, 'because he had told them' (1.10), refer not to Jonah's words, but rather somehow to the pagan sailors' acute powers of inference concerning Jonah's relationship to the Lord.[43] However, this would be a very peculiar way of referring to the sailors' inference. Holbert and others, who either reject the possibility of the narrator's abbreviation of Jonah's full answer or do not even recognize this possibility, place a lot of trust in the narrator's 'reported speech'—as if the narrator were giving the reader a legal transcript of the characters' dialogue.

---

40. Halpern and Friedman, 'Composition and Paranomasia', p. 87.

41. J.A. Bewer, 'Jonah', in H.G. Mitchell, J.M.P. Smith and J.A. Bewer (eds.), *Haggai, Zechariah, Malachi, and Jonah* (ICC; Edinburgh: T. & T. Clark, 1971), pp. 1-65 (37); Holbert, '"Deliverance Belongs to Yahweh"', p. 68; Hope, 'Pragmatics, Exegesis and Translation', pp. 125-26.

42. Holbert, '"Deliverance Belongs to Yahweh"', p. 68.

43. This is certainly possible since the sailors have already learned from the lot-casting that it was on Jonah's account that the evil had come to them (1.7-8). However, why would the narrator add, 'because he had told them' (1.10), if the sailors' knowledge of Jonah's flight did not come from Jonah's telling them? Also, this narrator does not shy away from omitting or abbreviating dialogue, as is evident elsewhere; therefore, it would not be surprising for him to abbreviate Jonah's full answer here, especially since it provides the reader with no New information. Another way in which the rejection of this interpretation has been argued is to assert that 1.10 is a later addition and, therefore, should be excised from the text. See Bewer, 'Jonah', p. 37.

The Sailors' Initial Refusal of Jonah's Request (1.12-14)

The sailors have learned from Jonah that he is the cause of the threatening storm, and so they urgently ask him, 'What must we do to you for the sea to calm down for us?' (1.11). Jonah answers, 'Pick me up and cast me into the sea' (1.12). Due to the urgency and severity of the situation, one would think that the sailors would eagerly do whatever Jonah suggested; however, they refuse (1.13). Not only do they refuse Jonah's request, but they begin to execute an alternative plan by which they will put Jonah ashore. This plan defies nautical knowledge—that is, when the seas are rough, you steer the ship away from any shore to prevent being shipwrecked.[44] Why did they refuse Jonah's request? This question is answered in the sailors' prayer to the Lord. They did not want to held accountable for Jonah's innocent blood (1.14). In other words, they did not know, first, if what Jonah requested was the Lord's will, and, secondly, if their accepting his request, thereby taking his life, would save them as Jonah had suggested.

At some later point in my readings, I noticed that the narrator was presenting this dialogue between Jonah and the sailors in the exact same manner as he had presented the dialogue between Jonah and the Lord when Jonah refused the Lord's request. That is, a request is made, it is refused, the refusal is only given in the form of reported consequences, and the account for the refusal is found in a later speech to the Lord. The only difference between these two presentations of the dialogue is that Jonah's account is withheld for a long time, thereby heightening the reader's interest in learning why he refused, whereas the sailors' account is given with much less delay, thereby developing the reader's interest less by quickly answering why. This difference explains why I did not discern the omitted speech of the sailors' refusal as quickly as I had in relation to Jonah's refusal.

Although I know of no other sources suggesting that the narrator has omitted the sailors' verbal refusal, commentators generally make the first step in the process of discerning this omission by answering the question as to why the sailors refused. For example, Sasson writes,

> The seamen are bewildered, for they see themselves in a no-win situation: they are suffering because of Jonah's guilt; yet sending him to his death might well bring his god's wrath upon their heads. To overcome this double predicament, therefore, they shape separate appeals. The first, ['do not have us perish because of this person'], harks back to past actions and

44. See Sasson, *Jonah*, pp. 141-42.

the guilt that has accumulated against the sailors because of the obduracy of one man; the second segment, ['and do not assess innocent blood against us'], concentrates on the immediate future and begs God not to charge them with a crime because of what they are about to do.[45]

As this example demonstrates, the gap that was created by the narrator's omission of the sailors' verbal refusal has been filled with the information found in the sailors' prayer. The filling of this gap probably occurred, however, without even considering the possibility that the sailors' verbal refusal was omitted. This possibility probably was not considered because the information need to fill the gap is presented soon after the gap is opened, in contrast to the gap concerning Jonah's refusal. Again, not questioning the possibility of the narrator omitting dialogue reflects the commentators' naive faith in the narrator's trustworthiness.

Jonah's Reluctant Acceptance (3.3)
After the Lord has repeated his request, Jonah's acceptance is simply reported as would generally be the case with preferred seconds—that is, since preferred seconds are characteristically brief, they tend to occur in the form of reported consequences.[46] This tendency at first led me to numerous misreadings, for I assumed that here the narrator did not omit any dialogue; however, as I continued to struggle with the text, two observations convinced me otherwise. First, the narrator's presentation of Jonah's actions following his acceptance suggest that he remains reluctant and even angry at the Lord's coercing him into obedience. He gives his 'brief' oracle ('quoted' as only five words) only after he is 'hardly' in the city (3.4) and then immediately leaves the city, carrying with him tremendous rage (4.1-5). Jonah's reluctance and anger caused me to question how he would have responded verbally to the Lord's repeated request. Would he say something to express this reluctance and anger or would he simply keep it bottled up until later? Secondly, I

45. Sasson, *Jonah*, p. 132. I have substituted his translation for the Hebrew and placed it within brackets. See also Calvin, *Commentaries on the Twelve Minor Prophets*, III, p. 60; J. Hooper, 'An Oversight and Deliberation upon the Holy Prophet Jonas', in S. Carr (ed.), *Early Writings of John Hooper, D.D., Lord Bishop of Gloucester and Worcester, Martyr, 1555* (Cambridge: Cambridge University Press, 1843), pp. 473-74; Josephus, *Jewish Antiquities* (trans. R. Marcus; LCL; Cambridge, MA: Harvard University Press, 1966), 9.10.2; Limburg, *Jonah*, p. 56; and Daas Soferim, cited in Zlotowitz and Scherman, *Jonah*, p. 101.
46. See the sections 'Constructed Dialogue and Adjacency Pairs' in Chapters 1 §2 and 3 §4.

noticed that the narrator begins his report of Jonah's refusal (1.3) and acceptance (3.3) with exactly the same words (literally, 'And Jonah got up'). Since the narrator certainly does not shy away from omitting dialogue elsewhere, maybe this is a subtle clue that he is omitting something here too. These two observations led me to assume that Jonah had voiced his reluctance and anger when he accepted, under duress of course, the Lord's request. His verbal acceptance may have been something like the following: 'OK, Lord, I will go, even though I really don't want to, because I am certain that you will change your mind concerning this evil.'

One other reader of the Jonah narrative has reached a similar conclusion—that is, the narrator has omitted the reason for Jonah's reluctance. Hauser writes,

> Even though Jonah no longer has the option of fleeing, he still gives the appearance of reluctance and hesitation in carrying out his task. As in chap. 1, the writer avoids giving any *reason* for Jonah's reluctance, causing the reader to wonder.[47]

Although he does not explicitly state that the narrator omitted Jonah's (presumably verbalized) reason, Hauser's conclusion is similar in that he discerns the narrator's parallel manipulation between 1.3 and 3.3. Hauser not only reaches a similar conclusion, but he probably arrived at this conclusion in much the same way as I did. He probably also wondered about Jonah's 'appearance of reluctance and hesitation' and noticed the parallel with 1.3. Again, the possibility that a character's speech has been omitted here has previously not really even been entertained. This is probably due to the faith most readers place in the narrator's 'reported speech'.

Jonah's Oracle (3.4)

I did not consider the possibility of Jonah's oracle (3.4) being abbreviated until I came to the interrelated conclusion that the Lord's requests are constructed dialogue. Noting that the Lord's request did not include what words Jonah was supposed to speak in Nineveh, I further realized that possibly the actual words of the Lord's requests concerning Nineveh's destruction would not be as vague and ambiguous as Jonah's oracle was. If this is the case, then Jonah's doing 'just as the Lord had commanded' would require more than the five Hebrew words

47. Hauser, 'Jonah', p. 32 (Hauser's emphasis).

that are purportedly the entire contents of his oracle. Hence, Jonah's oracle is abbreviated by the narrator in order to heighten the ironic effect of his success. This would help explain how the Ninevites, who (at least as presented by the narrator) never learned the name of the Lord and continue to call him simply, 'that god' (3.9), would know what the indictment against them was ('wickedness' in 1.2; 'evil way' and 'violence' in 3.8; 'evil ways' in 3.10). The king's assessment that, 'that god will change his mind', follows immediately after his pronouncement for the Ninevites to renounce their evil, violent ways and seems to suggest that the specific indictment against their violence has been addressed in their actions. The king's assessment is confirmed when the narrator reports that, 'God saw their deeds...[and] changed his mind' (3.10).

To my knowledge, this reading is unique. Others refer to Jonah's oracle as presented in the narrative as if it were exactly quoted by the narrator. Thus, they refer to it as a brief oracle, containing only one sentence and five Hebrew words, which nevertheless has dramatic effect.[48] In fact, one commentator has claimed that Jonah 'is the most reticent prophet in the Bible'.[49] The uniqueness of my reading could be viewed as questioning the validity of this interpretation; however, I suspect that the possibility of Jonah's full oracle being abbreviated by the narrator has rarely, if ever, even been entertained.[50] The possibility of Jonah's oracle as constructed speech only representing a longer oracle occurred to me only

---

48. E.g. Band, 'Swallowing Jonah', pp. 185-87; Craig, 'Jonah and the Reading Process', p. 109; Hauser, 'Jonah', p. 33; Holbert, '"Deliverance Belongs to Yahweh"', p. 74; J. Limburg, *Hosea–Micah* (Interpretation; Atlanta: John Knox, 1988), p. 150; *idem*, *Jonah*, pp. 79-80; Marcus, *From Balaam to Jonah*, pp. 103, 135; Miles, 'Laughing at the Bible', p. 176; Sasson, *Jonah*, pp. 232-33; Trible, 'Studies in the Book of Jonah', pp. 220-21; J.D.W. Watts, *The Books of Joel, Obadiah, Jonah, Nahum, Habakkuk and Zephaniah* (CBC; Cambridge: Cambridge University Press, 1975), p. 88; Wolff, *Obadiah and Jonah*, p. 149.

49. Band, 'Swallowing Jonah', pp. 185-86.

50. Trible comes close to this interpretation:

> Nowhere in the story has YHWH given Jonah these exact words to speak. Is his prophecy, then, true or false? A contrast by omission also feeds doubt about the authenticity of the utterance. The storyteller declares that Jonah 'arose and-went to Nineveh according-to-the-word-of YHWH' (3.3a) but then does not use the phrase 'according-to-the-word-of YHWH' when reporting what Jonah 'called and-said' (3.4b) (*Rhetorical Criticism*, p. 180).

Trible's question seems to be, 'Did Jonah prophesy what the Lord commanded him?', rather than, 'Did the narrator quote Jonah's prophecy verbatim?'

when I came to similar conclusions concerning the other omitted and abbreviated dialogue.

Jonah's Omitted Answer to the Lord's Last Question (4.10-11)
The Lord has the last word in the Jonah narrative; however, Jonah's life story does not necessarily end there. What was Jonah's answer to the Lord's question? Did Jonah learn his lesson or did he continue to live with rage in his heart?

These questions are rarely entertained by modern biblical scholars, at least if their writings adequately represent their thought. Most of today's biblical scholars are primarily interested in what is *in the text itself*, as we have seen above in the literal understandings of characters' speech and the absolute trust in the narrator's presentation of the narrative in various places. However, there are some exceptions in that some modern scholars comment on Jonah's response.[51] For example, Sasson ends his comments on the text of Jonah as follows:

> We are told nothing, however, about his reaction to God's monologue. Is he skeptical about its logic? Does it drive him to further dejection? Or, on the contrary, does it restore his faith in God's justice? Pages of speculations can be written on this score; but it may be best to end these comments by revealing what took place according to a medieval Jewish homily: 'At that very moment, [Jonah] fell flat on his face saying, "Direct your world according to the attribute of mercy, as is written, 'Mercy and forgiveness belong to the Lord our God'"'.[52]

I chose Sasson as an illustration of the exception to the rule for modern biblical scholars because his comments lead us to a whole realm of readers who are likewise exceptions in that they do not limit their comments to the text itself—that is, pre-twentieth-century commentators (see Appendix 2).[53] In fact, it is probably fair to say that Sasson's own reading of Jonah was heavily influenced by this tradition, thereby explaining his reading as exceptional among modern biblical scholars, who too often ignore

---

51. For example, W.B. Crouch, 'To Question an End, To End a Question: Opening the Closure of the Book of Jonah', *JSOT* 62 (1994), pp. 101-112; Wolff, *Obadiah and Jonah*, p. 177.

52. Sasson, *Jonah*, p. 320.

53. Sasson's commentary is a wealth of information concerning Hellenistic and medieval interpretations. For example, in his footnote to these comments he refers to Midrash Yona, Josephus, *Lives of the Prophets* and Muslim traditions (*Jonah*, p. 320 n. 24).

Hellenistic and medieval commentary.[54] Here are a few of these pre-twentieth century readings that extend their discussion of Jonah beyond the strict confines of the narrative, beginning with *The Lives of the Prophets*, a first-century CE Jewish 'biography' of the biblical prophets:

> And when [Jonah] had been cast forth by the sea monster and had gone away to Nineveh and had returned, he did not remain in his district, but taking his mother along he sojourned in Sour, a territory (inhabited by) foreign nations; for he said, 'So shall I remove my reproach, for I spoke falsely in prophesying against the great city of Nineveh' (10.2-3).[55]

John Calvin wrote the following concerning the lesson learned from the book. (Note that Calvin understood that Jonah himself was the author/narrator.)

> We hence see how apposite are all the parts of this similitude, to make Jonah to loathe his folly, and to be ashamed of it; for he had attempted to frustrate the secret purpose of God, and in a manner to overrule it by his own will, so that the Ninevites might not be spared, who yet laboured by true repentance to anticipate the divine judgment.[56]

Calvin's comments on Jonah are representative in that many pre-twentieth-century commentators also understood Jonah to be the 'author' of his book. Thus, Jonah's (as author/narrator) allowing the Lord to have the last word in the narrative is the author's (Jonah's) way of expressing his consent.

Another interesting group of readings that describe Jonah's unreported response to the Lord's final question is the genre of children's Bible stories.[57] The following two examples illustrate this tendency in this genre:

> And Jonah began, at last, to understand.[58]

> And Jonah *learned* that men, and women, and little children, are all precious in the sight of the Lord, even though they know not God.[59]

---

54. This influence on Sasson appears to be the case elsewhere. For example, see Sasson's discussion of Hellenistic and medieval exegetes who assume that the dialogue between Jonah and the sailors is abbreviated in the narrative (*Jonah*, p. 120).

55. Quoted from the translation by D.R.A. Hare of 'The Lives of the Prophets', in J.H. Charlesworth (ed.), *The Old Testament Pseudepigrapha*, II (Garden City, NY: Doubleday, 1985), p. 392.

56. Calvin, *Commentaries on the Twelve Minor Prophets*, III, p. 144.

57. See Appendix 2.

58. Alexander, *The Nelson Children's Bible*, n.p.

59. L. Marshall (ed.), *The Wonder Book of Bible Stories* (1921), p. 146. Emphasis mine.

Interestingly, the genre of children's Bible stories does not limit itself to what is actually *in the text* of the Bible. Perhaps, the authors of this genre (who certainly read the biblical text) share with the pre-twentieth-century readers a concern not limited to the text itself, but rather a concern for how the text is received in their community. In other words, the confessional stance of these readers may allow them to see beyond the narrow confines of the text itself to what effects the text has on its readers, in order to augment, from their perspective of educating children, these effects for their own confessional purposes.

3. *The Narrator's Satirical Tone*

In the discussion of tone in Chapter 3, the satirical attitude of the narrator was discussed in relation to the three aspects of tone: (1) the selection and arrangement of material, (2) the narrator's voice and (3) the narrator's attitude toward the material in his point of view and judgment. It was concluded that the narrative makes Jonah look ridiculous in the four ways in which the omniscient and omnipotent narrator selects and arranges material: (1) the use of paronomasia to heighten the contrasts between the disobedient Jonah and the obedient pagans; (2) the omission of dialogue which could lessen the ridiculous portrayal of Jonah's behavior (for example, the account for his refusal in 1.3); (3) the narrator's tendency to place dispreferred seconds within the form of reported consequences, thereby creating gaps of indeterminacy; and (4) the use of flashback in order to demonstrate Jonah's success first and, therefore, make his anger look even more ridiculous. All of these combine to satirize Jonah as a prophet who in many ways is the reversal of what would be expected of a true prophet.[60]

Although the satirical tone of the Jonah narrative is generally accepted among modern biblical scholars,[61] some still hold out against this understanding[62] and, as such, stand in a long line of other readers, including most pre-twentieth-century readers.[63] Some have rejected the designation

60. See further the discussion of the text's presuppositions of 'prophet' and 'prophetic literature' in Chapter 4 §4.

61. For example, Ackerman, 'Satire and Symbolism'; Band, 'Swallowing Jonah'; Lacocque and Lacocque, *Jonah*; Miles, 'Laughing at the Bible'.

62. For example, Berlin, 'A Rejoinder to John A. Miles, Jr'; Sasson, *Jonah*, pp. 328-51.

63. The only pre-twentieth-century commentator who understands the book of

of the genre of Jonah as a satire or parody and assert another genre for the book.[64] Even though I agree that the *genre* of the Jonah narrative is a prophetic narrative, this does not preclude the *tone* of the narrative being satirical. 'Satire' does not necessarily refer to genre, but to the narrator's attitude toward the material as presented in whatever genre is chosen.

Some other scholars have rejected the satirical tone of Jonah because of the implication that this tone is a direct attack on the exclusivism of post-exilic Judaism (for example, Ezra's admonitions against inter-marriage). One such scholar is Ronald Clements, who states that the narrative cannot be satirizing these post-exilic issues because,

> [t]he entire story fails to raise any single example of those issues which we know deeply affected the relationships of Jews with non-Jews in the post-exilic period.[65]

In Clements' case, it seems as if he expects a satirist to explicitly say, 'this is what I am going to satirize', rather than assuming that the audience will easily recognize what is being satirized. However, most other scholars, who reject the satirical tone of the Jonah narrative as commenting on such post-exilic issues, pose the problem differently; this approach is exemplified in the words of Adele Berlin:

> [Miles] has not explained how a parody of prophetic writings...came to gain enough acceptance to be included in the Prophets. That is, unless Dr Miles is implying that the canonizers of the Bible did not understand the message of the book. They obviously were not alone in their ignorance; Jewish tradition regards the Book of Jonah with such reverence that it is read at the afternoon service of the Day of Atonement, hardly the appropriate occasion for a parody of the Bible.[66]

In other words, if the Jonah narrative satirizes Hebrew prophecy (and possibly, by implication, Ezra's mission), how would it have become a part of the very canon that it satirizes? In my opinion, this is the most

Jonah as satirical is, to my knowledge, Paine (see *The Complete Writings of Thomas Paine*, pp. 566, 569).

64. For example, Berlin ('A Rejoinder to John A. Miles, Jr', p. 235) defines the genre as a 'prophetic story par excellence'; Trible ('Studies in the Book of Jonah', pp. 1, 176-84), a 'midrashic legend'; G. Landes ('Jonah: A *Masal ?*', in J.G. Gammie *et al.* (eds.), *Israelite Wisdom: Theological and Literary Essays in Honor of Samuel Terrien* [Missoula, MT: Scholars Press, 1978], pp. 137-58), as a *masal*, a parable.

65. Clements, 'The Purpose of the Book of Jonah', p. 19.

66. Berlin, 'A Rejoiner to John A. Miles, Jr', p. 227.

difficult problem facing those of us who argue for a satirical tone in the Jonah narrative.

In 'Swallowing Jonah', Arnold Band addresses this question concerning the reception of a satirical text.[67] First, he gives three reasons why a reader of any satirical text may have difficulties either recognizing the satirical tone or accepting it: (1) The reader does not recognize the presence of satire in that he or she does not distinguish the narrative world of the satire from the world of that which is being satirized. (2) The reader recognizes these different worlds, but nevertheless does not comprehend the author's intention or the discrepant relationship between these two worlds. (3) The reader existentially identifies himself or herself with the world that is being satirized and, therefore, feels that he or she is also the target of the satire. To these, Band adds another reason that particularly applies to the Jonah narrative: (4) The pious reader believes that the book of Jonah is sacred Scripture and, therefore, views this narrative in the same category as some of the texts that may be the object of its satirical tone.

Band then directs his comments explicitly to Berlin's difficulty with accepting the Jonah narrative as satirical. First, he suggests that,

> [Berlin] denies that books have their history of interpretation. The book could have been interpreted as parody [or satire] before it was canonized as a serious prophetic text. [Thus] the citation of its liturgical usage as proof of its meaning at the time of composition is pointless.[68]

After dismissing Berlin's line of argument, Band nevertheless answers the question concerning how a satirical Jonah narrative could become a book in the prophetic canon: 'A sage involved in the canonizing process could "misunderstand" a text.'[69] The sage could fail to recognize the presence of satire by distinguishing the narrative's world from that which it is satirizing or could recognize these different worlds, but not the author's satirical intention or the discrepancies between the two

---

67. Band draws heavily on Margaret A. Rose's *Parody // Meta-Fiction* and, therefore, uses the terms 'parody' and 'parodied'. His definition of parody—'a composition imitating and distorting another, usually serious, piece of work' ('Swallowing Jonah', p. 179)—seems to be a genre designation which has a satirical tone. I prefer to think of the book of Jonah as generically a prophetic book with a satirical tone. Despite this different use of terminology, his comments concerning 'parody' apply well to my understanding of 'satire'.

68. Band, 'Swallowing Jonah', p. 184.

69. Band, 'Swallowing Jonah', p. 191.

worlds. Either of these possibilities would be likely for such a sage, who
not only identifies with the world being satirized but somehow accepts
the Jonah narrative as already authoritative. Therefore, Band provides
some general remarks concerning how the Jonah narrative as a satirical
work could have become Scripture.

Band's comments certainly explain in general terms how the Jonah
narrative may have been canonized, but what more can be said about
the narrative and these 'misreadings'? I suggest that the indeterminate
nature of the narrative lent itself to readings that minimized or deemphasized the satirical tone. Below, I provide two examples of gaps of indeterminacy and how these gaps contributed to readings that minimized or
deemphasized the narrator's satirical tone: (1) the omission of Jonah's
verbal refusal in 1.3 and (2) the omission of Jonah's response to the
Lord's final question.

Even though the interaction between text and reader is extremely
successful concerning Jonah's refusal (1.3) and his later account (4.2),
we have already seen above some examples of commentators who still
elaborated Jonah's account. Their elaboration was as follows: Jonah was
fearful of going to the capital of Israel's enemies, the wicked Ninevites,
whom he would naturally expect to ignore his warnings and who may
even kill him. Besides, to travel to Nineveh Jonah would have had to
cross about 750 miles of desert. In other words, we saw a tendency to
explain Jonah's disobedience in fairly normal terms. In fact, Jonah's
behavior is even described by Lacocque and Lacocque as normative:

> The commission to go to Nineveh and to proclaim the doom of the city is
> simply not reasonable. If there is any 'God' capable of such insane
> calling, one must flee as quickly as possible.[70]

In these ways, the distance between Jonah and that which he satirizes,
nationalistic prophets, is narrowed, for, after all, Jonah's disobedience in
the light of these explanations is a reaction with which any reader could
easily identify. Thus, the emphasized gap created with Jonah's refusal in
1.3, which is not closed by the negation until 4.2, forces readers to reach
their own conclusions about Jonah's disobedience in such a way that
readers become closely identified with him and, therefore, provide
'reasonable' explanations for his actions. These explanations take on a
life of their own and continue despite the reader's perception of Jonah's
own explanation given in 4.2. The persistent presence of such 'reasonable'

---

70. Lacocque and Lacocque, *Jonah*, pp. 70-71.

explanations softens the 'unreasonable' explanation given in the text itself, thereby making Jonah look less ridiculous.

The Jonah narrative ends with the Lord posing a rhetorical question which demands some response from Jonah, thereby leaving open the question as to whether or not Jonah learns the lesson the Lord is trying to teach him in the plant episode and his final question. Interestingly, there is general agreement on something that the text itself does not provide—that is, Jonah learned the lesson, repented of his ways, and then served the Lord faithfully until his death (see Appendix 2). This agreement is found among pre-twentieth-century commentators on Jonah as well as in the modern genre of children's Bible stories. In fact, to my knowledge, there are no interpretations that explicitly assert the contrary. Therefore, even if one understands the satirical tone of the narrator against Jonah, the story does not end there. That which is narrated could possibly be understood as only a prelude to Jonah's life, in which the Lord teaches Jonah his will so that Jonah can obediently serve the Lord.

In these two examples, we have just seen how the narrator's selection and arrangement of material not only contributes to the satirical tone, but also provides some opportunities for readers to interpret this satirical text in ways that minimize this tone and, therefore, make Jonah look less ridiculous. The omission of Jonah's refusal allows readers to identify themselves closely with him in their own creation of explanations for Jonah's disobedience, explanations that they themselves would have used in his situation. The omission of Jonah's response to the Lord's final question allows readers to interpret Jonah as a true, obedient prophet, who learned the lesson the Lord was teaching him and learned it well, as any true prophet would. Thus, the text itself provides some opportunities for readers to 'misread' the text or, at least, read beyond the narrative's own temporal confines. These opportunities are what Iser calls gaps of indeterminacy that require readers to fill in information from their own knowledge and experience of the narrative's world, literary tradition and the 'real' world.

4. *Flashback (4.1-11)*

The account of the Ninevites' repentance and the Lord's changing his mind immediately following Jonah's oracle in no way suggests, in and of itself, that the temporal sequence of events has been altered in the narrative. Jonah's oracle simply provoked a response. This is why I first missed the temporal frame of this episode; the Ninevites' response naturally follows. However, when reading the account of Jonah's anger and his waiting in his booth, a demanding question comes to mind: What is Jonah waiting for? The reader already knows that the Ninevites have repented and the Lord has changed his mind, so why is he waiting? These questions became even more confusing when I realized that Jonah already knew that the Lord 'would change his mind' even as far back as when he was 'still in [his] homeland' (4.2). Now the question becomes, Since *everybody* knows that the Lord has repented of this evil, Jonah must be waiting for something else, but what is it? This question itself uncritically assumes that the narrative faithfully preserved the temporal sequences of events in their chronological order. However, Jonah 'hardly' enters the city and briefly utters an oracle which is 'quoted' as only five Hebrew words. Now another question presents itself: If Jonah was so reluctant and in such a hurry, why did he wait so long before he left the city and voiced his anger? This led to my questioning of the narrative's sequence of events, for it seemed unlikely that such a reluctant character would wait around long enough for all of the events described in 3.5-10 to occur, which would have taken at least a couple of days. First, word had to reach the king from the outskirts of the city to its center, where the palace likely was, and if the city really was 'a three days' walk across' this would take at least a day. Secondly, the king would then have to issue the decree. Thirdly, the decree would then have to be proclaimed and heard throughout this large city, probably requiring at least another day. Finally, the people would need some time to change into sackcloth themselves and to put sackcloth on all of their animals. I found it very difficult to imagine Jonah just hanging around while all of this activity was going on, before he angrily addressed the Lord. I also noticed that Jonah is not present in the king's court, so the information given to the reader by the narrator is simply not available to the character Jonah. Therefore, rather than waiting around, Jonah left the city, angrily addressed the Lord for what he knew would happen (4.2), and built a booth in order to wait and see how right he was. In other words, Jonah knew all along that the Lord would not destroy Nineveh, so now he will sit outside of the city waiting to prove the validity of what he said while he was still in his homeland—that is, the Lord would change his mind and not destroy Nineveh. Jonah thus built his booth, rejoiced over the plant, requested death for a second time and heard the Lord's last question (4.1-11), even before his oracle reached its full impact in the Lord changing his mind.

Various other commentators have noticed these problems, and my solution relates closely to those of some other scholars. Other readers have also been puzzled by the sequence of events. The most striking example of another reader's puzzlement at the sequence of events occurs in Sasson's comments where he explicitly questions the narrative's chronology:

> We are told that Jonah 'left the city', a move that to many readers seems delayed for much too long. Are we to believe that Jonah remained in the city while the Ninevites grieved and prayed, fasted and clothed themselves and their animals in sack? Does Jonah share in this public piety? Does he keep on issuing the same warning throughout the vigil? If so, for how long? Moreover, how could Jonah be waiting to see what happens to the city, when whatever is to happen already has?[71]

His phrase 'many readers' refers to those biblical scholars who try to solve this problem by four different methods, which Sasson summarizes.[72] (1) Textual reconstruction: For example, Winckler followed the suggestions of some medieval commentators and argued that 4.5 originally followed 3.4. (2) Grammatical readjustment—that is, translating the Hebrew verbs so as to posit the Jonah account as a flashback: For example, the Brown–Driver–Briggs lexicon suggests a translation like, 'He sat [under the booth] until he saw what happened in the town.'[73] (3) Literary explanation: For example, Magonet understands that Jonah's leaving the city functions as a structural parallel to his flight to Tarshish.[74] (4) Traditional explanations: Jonah knows that Nineveh's repentance will not last long, so he awaits their backsliding and then the Lord's righteous destruction of the city.[75] To these, Sasson adds his own explanation: (5) Jonah did not perceive the ambiguity in his oracle concerning Nineveh's 'overturning' and now 'is consoling himself by

71. Sasson, *Jonah*, p. 287.

72. Sasson, *Jonah*, pp. 287-89. See also Trible, 'Studies in the Book of Jonah', pp. 94-102; P. Weimar, 'Beobachtungen zur Entstehung des Jonaerzählung', *Biblische Notizen* 18 (1982), pp. 86-109.

73. BDB 725 (II. a. [b.]). This translation is Sasson's, following the logic of BDB.

74. Magonet, *Form and Meaning*, pp. 58-60.

75. See Payne's discussion of the 'complicating factor' that Nineveh was destroyed before the Jonah narrative was written. This destruction would lend much support to those who piously wanted to read the narrative in such a way as to minimize its satirical tone ('Jonah from the Perspective of Its Audience', p. 7).

inventing an "I told you so"'.[76] In this way, Jonah questions the Lord's treatment of his servant the prophet, that is, Jonah himself. Thus, in Sasson's words, Jonah is 'forcing [the Lord] to acknowledge that the dignity of one individual is as precious as the salvation of a whole community'.[77]

Of these five explanations the first three are somewhat similar to my own. (1) Although I do not advocate textual reconstruction, this position is based upon an attempt to answer the problem by similarly reconstructing the sequences of events as they happened in the narrative world. Where we diverge is that those scholars who advocate textual reconstruction seem to ignore the literary device of flashback as a possibility, whereas I think that this device provides the answer. (2) Similarly, those who argue for grammatical readjustment do so in order to reconstruct the sequences as they happened and make this reconstruction explicit in the narrator's report. However, the use of flashback does not require a narrator to adjust verbal tenses accordingly and, therefore, such grammatical readjustments are unnecessary. (3) Magonet's explanation that Jonah's flight from Nineveh to the booth parallels his flight from Nineveh to Tarshish provides another literary explanation for the use of flashback.[78] These three readings, therefore, are somewhat successful and somewhat unsuccessful in their recognition of the use of flashback in the Jonah narrative.

The remaining two explanations ignore the satirical tone of the narrative, trusting in the narrator's presentation of the interactions among the characters as faithfully reported. (4) The traditional explanation, that Jonah awaits Nineveh's backsliding and eventual destruction, denies the satirical tone of the narrative by assuming that Jonah's actions are justified. (5) Sasson's explanation incorrectly assumes that Jonah's oracle was 'quoted' verbatim (even if over and over again) and that Jonah misunderstood the ambiguity in Nineveh's overturning—that is, rather than referring to destruction, 'Nineveh will overturn' (3.4) refers to the Ninevites' repentance.

76. Sasson, *Jonah*, p. 296.
77. Sasson, *Jonah*, p. 297.
78. For my literary explanation, see the discussion of the use of flashback in the narrator's satirical tone in Chapter 3 §4.

5. *Conclusions Concerning the Interaction between the Text and Actual Readers*

In the preceding discussions, we have analyzed the interactions between the text and a host of readers, broken down into somewhat abstract segments. The first segment discussed concerned the almost universally successful interaction between text and readers vis-à-vis Jonah's refusal (1.3) and his account (4.2). This segment was successful because the text exerted itself upon readers, first by producing an obvious gap in the omission of Jonah's verbal refusal and then by blatantly providing the information necessary to fill this gap according to the narrative's structure. However, the interactions of readers with other segments discussed were less successful and, oddly enough, the success or lack of success could be generalized in some instances according to whether the readers were modern biblical scholars or not. Therefore, the following discussion divides these readers into two general groups: modern biblical scholars and others, the latter category including Hellenistic and medieval commentators and modern popular interpreters (for example, writers of children's Bible stories).

Most modern biblical scholars[79] have been trained to focus upon the text itself as defined narrowly as the specific passage being studied over and against other biblical passages. This is necessary and helpful, considering the numerous text critical, source critical and philological problems. Modern biblical scholars are also taught to understand the biblical texts within their 'original' setting. This would at first suggest that modern biblical scholars are not text-bound; however, the extratextual components of the traditional historical-critical method concern material culture and historical data of the 'real' world rather than a broader understanding of the narrative's own created world. Of course, this type of material and historical information is extremely helpful in determining, for example, the text's presuppositions and historical referents. However, modern biblical scholars need additionally to look to the extratextual world that is, nevertheless, created by the text itself in its interaction with readers.

This text-bound tendency among modern biblical scholars has led to

---

79. Although to be completely fair, I probably should use the phrase, 'most scholars of the Hebrew Bible', since I have not analysed a New Testament text and its various readers.

mixed results concerning their interactions with the Jonah narrative. They have been successful in a variety of ways, including the following two examples: recognizing and filling the gaps opened by Jonah's refusal and recapturing the awareness of the satirical tone of the narrator. Both of these successful interactions can be seen as aided by a text-bound emphasis. (1) The narrator provides the information for filling the gap of Jonah's refusal within the text itself (4.2). (2) The satirical tone is only evident when scholars emphasize the text of the Jonah narrative itself as abstracted from the canon, rather than simply looking at the narrative as one of many books of Scripture. However, modern biblical scholars have also been generally unsuccessful in realizing the extent of constructed dialogue in the narrative. Few have understood that, for example, Jonah's answer to the sailors was but a small part of his full answer (1.9-10) or that the Lord's requests (1.2; 3.2) were incompletely given by the narrator. These unsuccessful interactions can be seen as limitations of a text-bound emphasis. In other words, these modern readers bring a naive assumption, based on their everyday interaction with the highly literate forms of expository prose, that everything that the narrator gives in the form of direct speech is truly a 'quotation'—containing not only the exact words, but all of the words.[80] Thus, the successful and unsuccessful aspects of most modern biblical scholars' readings can be attributed to their text-centered training, and those who are the exceptions generally borrow from other areas of literary study[81] and/or from the writings of the Hellenistic and medieval readers.[82]

In contrast to the tendency to be text-bound among most modern biblical scholars, pre-twentieth-century commentators drew from

80. S. Bar-Efrat (*Narrative Art in the Bible* [Sheffield: Almond Press, 1989], pp. 148-49) discusses some examples of 'condensation and omission' of conversations between biblical characters and Savran (*Telling and Retelling*, pp. 77-78) discusses the danger in readers faithfully assuming that a narrator simply reports the characters' speeches as they happened. It is this dangerous pit into which many modern biblical scholars have fallen in their interpretation of the Jonah narrative.

81. For example, those studies in the satirical tone of the narrator such as Band's 'Swallowing Jonah'. However, even the 'literary critics' of the Bible have missed much of the constructed dialogue in the Jonah narrative; therefore, my phrase 'modern biblical scholars' does not necessarily exclude those who see themselves as opposing the historical-critical method.

82. For example, those segments in which Sasson observes constructed or omitted dialogue—such as his discussion of Jonah's response to the Lord's final question (*Jonah*, pp. 319-20) as influenced by Hellenistic and medieval readers.

numerous texts within their own tradition whenever they interpreted a text. They assumed that Scripture not only could be used but must be used to interpret Scripture, and that Scripture itself must be interpreted within the proper context of what they understood to be the 'orthodox' tradition. This traditional tendency has also had mixed results. These commentators have been very successful in recognizing the indeterminacies of the text and elaborating upon the various possibilities for their filling. For example, even though the text gives only an abbreviated form of Jonah's answer to the sailors' four questions (1.9-10), these commentators generally recognize this abbreviated form and do not hesitate to describe further the conversation between Jonah and the sailors. In other words, these commentators are not bound to the text alone, which does not fully report this conversation, but they realize the text by filling in the blanks without inhibitions. However, this approach has also been unsuccessful because of a lack of focus upon the text itself. For example, since commentators of this persuasion interpret the Jonah narrative within the broad arena of Scripture and tradition, they do not recognize the satirical tone of the narrative, and assume this prophetic book to be much like other prophetic books. Few allow themselves to understand the narrative as satirical. Thus, the successful and unsuccessful aspects of the interaction between text and the pre-twentieth-century readers can be attributed to their emphasis upon the broader tradition rather than upon the text itself.

The most successful reading—that of the implied reader in Chapter 4—represents a combination of both approaches. This implied reader pays close attention to all of the details of the text itself and sets this text over and against others. However, he also draws upon his knowledge of the tradition, including other texts. When these two approaches are brought together in tension, the implied reader can realize fully the narrative's own world that is created in his interaction with the text. In this narrative world, more happened than the narrator chose to write down—for example, unreported conversations and Jonah's life before the Lord's request to go to Nineveh and after the lesson concerning the plant. Therefore, we as readers of the Jonah narrative can learn our reading strategies from the implied reader. We should struggle with all of the details of the text in multiple interactions *and* understand as much as possible of all the complexities of the tradition from which the text comes, in which the text participates and which our interactions with the text create.

Chapter 6

CONCLUSION

Now it once happened that the word of the Lord came to Jonah, son of
Amittai: 'Get up. Go to Nineveh, that large city, and call out against it, for
their wickedness is obvious to me.' Jonah, instead, got up to escape to
Tarshish from the Lord... And [Jonah] interjected to the Lord, 'Oh Lord!
Is this not what I said while I was still in my homeland? Therefore, I
hastened to flee to Tarshish for I knew that you are a gracious and compassionate God, slow to anger and extremely benevolent, who would
change his mind concerning the evil.'

Jon. 1.1-3 and 4.2

In my attempt to describe the interaction between the text and readers
of the Jonah narrative, I have made extensive use of conversation analysis.
In Chapter 2, the prevalence of adjacency pairs (such as question–
answer and request–refusal) in the Jonah narrative was explored.
Adjacency pairs are not only evident in the characters' dialogues given
in direct speech, but also in the dialogue that the narrator selectively
omits in the form of reported consequences. This omitted dialogue,
however, can be reconstructed from information provided elsewhere in
the text. For example, Jonah's refusal of the Lord's initial request is
simply given in the narrator's report of Jonah's disobedient actions
(1.3)—that is, the narrator withholds Jonah's direct speech from the
readers. However, the narrator then provides enough information in
Jonah's later speech to the Lord (4.2), so that his previously omitted
verbal refusal can be reconstructed as follows: 'Well Lord, I really strive
to obey your will, but I know that "you are a gracious and compassionate God, slow to anger and extremely benevolent" and I am certain
that you will "change [your] mind concerning this evil".' This is but
one example of the many adjacency pairs that the narrative contains
within a complex matrix of interactions between the various characters.

Chapter 3 built upon the observation that the book of Jonah consists
of a complex matrix of adjacency pairs by analyzing the narrative

elements of plot, character, atmosphere and tone. The plot of Jonah can be summarized by identifying the adjacency pairs involved. The narrative begins with the Lord's request followed by Jonah's refusal, followed by the Lord's response to the refusal, and so forth. In fact, very few of the events in the plot cannot be understood as a part of an adjacency pair. Thus, the narrative's plot, like conversation, is structured by the use of adjacency pairs, even though the parts may be 'hidden' in reported consequences, as is the case with Jonah's refusal (1.3).

Characterization in the Jonah narrative is developed in a variety of ways. Characters make judgments about other characters in their own words. For example, the Lord characterizes the Ninevites as wicked (1.2). The most dominant element of characterization in the Jonah narrative, however, is the interactions among the characters concerning their words and actions, most of which can be understood as adjacency pairs. For example, the Lord initiates an adjacency pair when he requests that Jonah go to Nineveh (1.2). Adjacency pairs that begin with a request are completed by either the preferred response of acceptance or the dispreferred response of refusal. Jonah refuses, thereby giving the dispreferred response. However, the Lord coerces Jonah, so that when he repeats his request Jonah reluctantly accepts, thereby giving the preferred response. These interactions between the Lord and Jonah are consistent with the overall portrayal of these characters. Jonah is predisposed to produce dispreferred seconds and initiate adjacency pairs that require the other participants to produce a dispreferred response. In contrast, the Lord (and all the other characters for that matter) is predisposed to produce preferred seconds. In addition, the Lord's omnipotence is expressed in that every request that he makes eventually ends with the preferred response of acceptance. Therefore, Jonah and the Lord (and other characters) are contrasted concerning their linguistic competence to minimize conflict by participating in adjacency pairs with preferred seconds—that is, the Lord generally participates in adjacency pairs with preferred seconds; Jonah generally does not. In this way, the characters' speech not only characterizes them according to the content of their speech, but also according to the structure of their speech.

The narrative's atmosphere concerns the limitations and conditions placed upon the characters as they interact in and with the narrative's world. In the Jonah narrative, the Lord's own will limits the choices made by all other characters. This limitation is itself expressed in the form of adjacency pairs in that all of the Lord's requests are eventually accepted. This generalized pattern includes Jonah's reluctant acceptance of the repeated request, an acceptance that the Lord coerced through his control of nature presented as requests of the obedient wind and fish. However, the Lord's omnipotence is not the only limit described in the narrative, for Jonah's refusal (1.3) and subsequent protest (4.2) assume that the Lord is prevented from acting on his vindictive judgment by his compassionate nature. Therefore, even though the Lord has ultimate control over all of creation, the Lord is nevertheless bound by his own compassion and mercy.

The satirical tone of the narrative is expressed in a variety of ways, including the narrator's selection and arrangement of material, his voice and his attitude towards the material. One example of the selection and arrangement of material that contributes to the portrayal of Jonah as a ridiculous and satirized character concerns the narrator's chosen form of presenting dialogue in the narrative. First, the narrator omits dialogue that could lessen the impression of Jonah's behavior as ridiculous. For example, Jonah's account of his refusal is omitted, thereby allowing the Ninevites' repentance, the Lord's changing his mind and Jonah's anger all to be more surprising and ironic to the reader. Second, the omission of Jonah's refusal is typical of the narrative pattern created by placing second parts of adjacency pairs in the form of reported consequences in chs. 1–3 but in the form of direct speech in ch. 4. This contrasting pattern causes gaps in the text in chs. 1–3 that are not filled until ch. 4. The gap concerning Jonah's refusal (1.3), for example, is not filled until Jonah is presented as responding to the Lord in the form of direct speech in his complaint (4.2).

In summary, Chapter 3 analyzed the narrative elements of plot, character, atmosphere and tone. This analysis was informed by the observation that adjacency pairs are the fundamental organizational structure in conversation, a structure that also plays a fundamental role in the Jonah narrative.

Chapter 4 began the discussion concerning the conversation that occurs between text and readers. This chapter started with a theoretical discussion of the reading process, drawing heavily from Wolfgang Iser's understanding of the implied reader who represents the interaction between text and reader. Iser's description of this interaction was then extended by drawing from sociolinguistics, including Grice's Cooperative Principle and preference organization (adjacency pairs). After describing the reading process, the implied reader of the Jonah narrative was identified. This implied reader is one who reads the original Hebrew, already knows or learns in the interaction all of the pertinent geo-political information (for example, Nineveh is Israel's enemy to the west, Tarshish is to the east of Israel), and receives a caricature of a typical Hebrew prophet and prophetic literature that relates closely to his own knowledge of these prophets and their books. A commentary then followed, describing the complex interaction between this implied reader and the Jonah narrative as gaps of indeterminacy are opened and filled and as the reader's viewpoint wanders from the speaker of one adjacency pair part to another.

For example, the Lord's request of Jonah begins an adjacency pair that calls for the preferred response of acceptance. Since prophets are expected to obey the omnipotent Lord, and since requests call for either the preferred response of acceptance or the dispreferred response of refusal, the reader expects that Jonah will accept the Lord's request or at least provide a convincing explanation for his refusal. However, neither is reported to the reader, thereby creating a gap of indeterminacy which the reader must fill. The implied reader, having repeatedly read the narrative before, knows that the narrator chose to omit Jonah's account for satirical purposes and fills in the gap with his own reconstruction of Jonah's account: 'Well Lord, I really strive to obey your will, but I know that "you are a gracious and compassionate God, slow to anger and extremely benevolent" and I am certain that you will "change [your] mind concerning this evil".' In this example, we see how the implied reader is guided by the text in identifying and filling the gap concerning Jonah's refusal. The gap is recognized because of the implied reader's knowledge of prophets and the Lord, as well as his acquired linguistic competence with adjacency pairs. The gap is filled because this reader recognizes the reference to the omitted dialogue in Jonah's later speech, which nevertheless has the characteristics of dispre-ferred seconds, especially including the account for why the preferred second is not being given. Thus, Chapter 4 chronicled the reader's inter-action with the text, drawing from conversation analysis as an explanatory model.

Chapter 5 analyzed misreadings—that is, discrepancies between the interpretations of the implied reader and those brought into being by numerous actual historical readers, including my own earlier readings. These misreadings break down into two general groups, depending upon the particular perspective that the various readers bring to their interaction with the text: modern biblical scholars and other readers, especially pre-twentieth-century commentators. In general, the misreadings of the modern biblical scholars can be explained by a naive trust in the narrator's presentation of the characters' dialogue. In other words, they often assume that what is given by the narrator not only represents all that was said by the characters but is, in fact, the characters' exact words, quoted verbatim, with nothing added and nothing omitted. This assumption fails to recognize the very nature of constructed speech. For example, the Lord's two requests (1.2; 3.2) are vague, both as to what the Ninevites' wickedness was and as to what exact words Jonah must use when he prophesies to them; however, most modern biblical scholars assume that the narrator has quoted them verbatim. This assumption and its related misreadings can certainly be attributed to the training biblical scholars receive which focuses strictly upon the text itself. Such a focus is extremely helpful when confronting problems concerning text criticism and sources; however, the critic can become too text-bound when analyzing narrative from such a stance.

In contrast, pre-twentieth-century commentators often elaborately interpret the characters' constructed speech. For example, Ibn Ezra and John Calvin both understood that Jonah explicitly told the sailors that he was fleeing from the Lord, even though the narrator does not report this in direct speech. These readers, therefore, do not misread the text as often as modern biblical scholars in relation to constructed dialogue; however, they misread the text in another way. They draw upon their larger tradition, including all of Scripture, in order to interpret the narrative in such a way that its uniqueness, especially its satirical tone, is missed. For example, the narrative ends with the Lord's rhetorical question to Jonah not having been answered; however, these readers often understand the narrative as implying that Jonah learned his lesson and was, therefore, a true and faithful prophet of the Lord. This understanding itself is implicit in the canonization of the narrative as a prophetic book, so it is of little wonder that readers with a confessional stance toward Scripture would read the narrative likewise. This interpretation, however, has eclipsed the satirical presentation of Jonah in the narrative—that is, the finally obedient Jonah, who 'lived' beyond the text, overcomes the reluctant, disobedient and angry Jonah who appears so ridiculous in the text itself. These confessionally oriented readers not only see Jonah as a true prophet after the narrative ends but also as a true, although disobedient, prophet within the narrative itself, thereby misreading the satirical tone of the narrator. Whereas the modern biblical scholars are often too text-bound in their interpretation of the narrative, these readers are too tradition-bound and not sufficiently text-bound in their interpretations. Ironically, they nevertheless correctly perceive the characters' speech as constructed dialogue and are not led astray to believing it to be faithfully 'quoted' material.

I hope that this study not only opens up new insights into the Jonah narrative but also provides an illustration of how a greater sense of the structure of conversation can enhance one's reading of any narrative. The structure of adjacency pairs can help explain why gaps of indeterminacy are recognized at certain places in one's interaction with a text and further explain why certain information provided elsewhere in the narrative guides the reader in filling these gaps. We have also seen that what purports to be 'reported speech' by the narrator is really constructed speech. A narrator may omit characters' speech altogether or even paraphrase their 'real' speech, but nevertheless present it in the form of direct speech. Thus, not only *how much* the narrator reports but even *that which* the narrator reports must sometimes be held suspect. This is just one reminder that the narrative's world is much larger than what is in the text itself. *The narrative's world includes all of those things that the text presupposes about its readers, that the text itself brings to the interaction, and that its readers must create in the interaction.*

Interestingly, the history of interpretation of the Jonah narrative has tended to emphasize one of these different aspects of the narrative's world and can be broken down into two general groups: modern biblical scholars, on the one hand, and pre-twentieth-century commentators, on the other. Modern biblical scholars generally emphasize what is in the text itself. Hence, they generally make great progress in areas such as text criticism, but misread the text when they begin to describe the necessarily extratextual world of narrative. In contrast, the pre-twentieth-century commentators generally place the text within its larger traditional context, including its place in the prophetic canon. Hence, they generally see the narrative's world as larger than what is explicitly given in the text, but misread those unique qualities in the narrative itself (for example, its satirical tone). These two groups emphasize the different kinds of participants in the interaction between text and reader. On the one hand, modern biblical scholars often abstract something they call the text itself as if it exists without its readers. On the other hand, pre-twentieth-century commentators often abstract the implied reader from the particular text of the Jonah narrative and make this reader synonymous with all other readers of traditional texts. Neither abstracted perspective can approach an accurate description of the entire interaction between the text and the reader of the Jonah narrative, even though each perspective can be successful vis-à–vis certain segments of the interaction. However, both perspectives, when placed within their interactive context, bring helpful insights to the interpretation of a narrative. When these two participants—text *and* reader—are understood as mutually related in the implied reader, the narrative comes alive most successfully. Hopefully, other studies of different narratives will likewise draw upon conversation analysis and succeed in describing more faithfully the interactions between other texts and their readers.

Appendix 1

THE EXPLAINING OF JONAH'S ACCOUNT (4.2)

Children's Bibles

P. Alexander, *The Nelson Children's Bible*:

> Now Nineveh was the capital of Assyria. And the Assyrians were the
> enemies of God's people. So Jonah did not mind telling the people of
> Nineveh that God was about to destroy them! 'But God is loving', he
> thought. 'He forgives people and lets them have a second chance. He
> won't destroy Nineveh. And I shall look silly.'

T.H. Gallaudet, *The History of Jonah for Children and Youth* (New
York: American Tract Society, 1833), p. 26:

> Jonah was afraid to do this. He thought it would be a difficult and danger-
> ous journey, to go alone, a great way from his own country, among
> strangers. And, when he should get to Nineveh, and begin to preach to the
> people, he feared that they would be very angry with him, and perhaps kill
> him.

J. Hastings, 'Paying the Fare [on Jonah 1.3]', in *idem* (ed.), *The
Children's Great Texts of the Bible*. IV. *Jeremiah to Matthew* (New
York: Charles Scribner's Sons, 1921), pp. 131-34 (131):

> First, Jonah paid his fare and that was right. He was an honest man and
> paid his debts. But, second, Jonah paid the fare to go to Tarshish and that
> was wrong. Shall I tell you why? Because God had told him to go to
> Ninevah, which was exactly the opposite direction, and Jonah did not
> want to go to Ninevah. He was trying to run away from God.

W. Hutton, *Jonah and the Great Fish* (New York: Atheneum, 1983):

> Jonah was frightened by the Lord's command. So he fled from the
> presence of the Lord, down to the port of Joppa.

G. MacBeth, *The Lord* (New York: Holt, Rinehart & Winston, 1970):

> But Jonah walked morosely along the black shore. He was sure in his
> pride there was nothing to be done. So he clapped his hands angrily and
> made a loud noise. He clapped his hands angrily and thought he would
> escape. 'I will go a voyage on the sea', thought Jonah.

L. Marshall, *The Wonder Book of Bible Stories*, p. 142:

> But Jonah did not wish to preach to the people of Nineveh; for they were
> the enemies of his land, the land of Israel. He wished Nineveh to die in its
> sins, and not to turn to God and live. So Jonah tried to go away from the
> city where God had sent him.

N.V. Peale, *Bible Stories* (New York: Banner Press, 1978), p. 117:

> As a good Hebrew, therefore, he despised all Gentiles. But of all Gentiles,
> he hated the Assyrians most. Therefore, when the word of the Lord came
> to Jonah telling him to go to Nineveh and turn the people away from their
> sins, he did not want to go.

A.D. Steeple, *A Child's First Book of Bible Stories* (New York: Hart,
1950), p. 87:

> When Jonah heard this, he was very afraid. He knew that the people of
> Nineveh were very strong and rich and powerful. He was afraid that if he
> went to them and told them to become better, they might be angry and put
> him in prison or even kill him. Jonah said to himself, 'God has spoken to
> me only once. Maybe if I go away somewheres, God will send someone
> else to Nineveh instead of me.'

Literary Works

P. Goodman, *Three Plays: The Young Disciple, Faustina, Jonah* (New
York: Random House, 1965), p. 199 (from the author's comments on
his play *Jonah* and its relationship to the book of Jonah):

> The perplexity in the book is the motive of Jonah's flight. The reason
> given in IV.2 must of course be accepted.

H. Melville, *Moby-Dick* (New York: Harper & Brothers, 1851), pp. 45-
46 (cited in A. Preminger and E.L. Greenstein [eds.], *The Hebrew Bible
in Literary Criticism* [New York: Ungar, 1986], pp. 467-68):

[T]he sin of this son of Amittai was in his wilful disobedience of the command of God—never mind what that command was, or how conveyed—which he found a hard command. But all things that God would have us do are hard for us to do—remember that—and hence, he oftener commands us than endeavors to persuade.

Sermons

C.R. Brown, 'What Jonah Did', in C.E. Fant, Jr and W.M. Pinson, Jr (eds.), *20 Centuries of Great Preaching: An Encyclopedia of Preaching.* VII. *Watson [Maclaren] to Rufus Jones, 1850–1950* (Waco, TX: Word Books, 1971), pp. 207-12 (208):

> Jonah did not want to go. He was a Jew and the Ninevites were Gentiles. Jews had no dealing with Gentiles.

J.W. Hamilton, 'Unwilling Missionaries [on Jonah 4.11; Gal 3.28]', in *The American Pulpit Series* (New York: Abingdon Press, 1946), IX, pp. 87-102 (87-88):

> [Jonah] didn't want to go. He was afraid that God was about to let his generosity get the better of him, that he was about to let these heathen people off; and Jonah didn't want them to be let off. So he ran away.

J.H. Jowett, 'Lulled by High Ideals [on Jonah 4.2]', in Fant, Jr and Pinson, Jr (eds.), *20 Centuries of Great Preaching*, VIII, pp. 82-86 (83):

> A man's conception of Deity is used to justify a deliberate neglect of duty.

A. Kuyper, 'Jona en Hosea [on Hos. 14.5]', in *Van de Vloeindung* (Kampen: Kok, 1930), III, pp. 77-84 (78):

> En dat nu toch Ninevé verschoond werd, maakte op Jona den indruk, dat het Heilige hier niet heilig werd gehounded, ja dat veeler inschikkelijkheid het kwaad verschoonde; en dit kon Jona niet zetten.

Pre-Twentieth-Century Works[1]

Jewish

Josephus, *Jewish Antiquities* (LCL), 9.10.2:

---

1. Works which simply mention Jonah as one of the biblical prophets and have little information about the Jonah narrative are not included here. E.g., 3 Macc. 6.8; the Sib. Or. 2.243-51; Martyrdom and Ascension of Isaiah 4.22.

This man, then, having been commanded by God to go to the kingdom of Nino and, when he arrived there, to preach in that city that it would lose its power, was afraid and did not set out, but fled from God to the city of Jope.

Pirke de Rabbi Eliezer 10 (cited in Zlotowitz and Scherman, *Jonah*, p. xix):

Why did Jonah flee? He passed judgment upon himself. He said, I know that this nation is close to repentance. Now they will repent and the Holy One, Blessed be He, will dispatch His anger against Israel. And as if it were not enough that Israel calls me a false prophet, even idolators [will do so].

Rabbeinu Bachya (cited in Zlotowitz and Scherman, *Jonah*, p. 82):

If Moses was reluctant to accept God's call to redeem the righteous Jews from Egypt because he considered himself unequal to the task; then surely I, who am being sent to wicked people, should seek to avoid my mission by fleeing to a place where God will not reveal Himself to me.

Christian
G. Abbot, *An Exposition upon the Prophet Jonah*, pp. 31, 32, 33, 35:

We need not doubt but Satan...could yield reasons enough for the hindrance of this work.

It might be, that our prophet might have a conceit, that for bringing such a message as the destruction of Nineveh, he might be murdered, or at least be much abused.

Perhaps he remembered that he did no good by preaching in his own country to men of rebellious hearts: and what good then should he do in preaching to infidels.

Thus have I touched such causes, as sense and reason yield, and the expositions on this place. The text does not contradict there, and it is not unlikely that all, or diverse of them, were tumbling at the time in the working head of Jonah. But there is one, which expressly is named in the body of the text, as appears in the fourth chapter.

J. Calvin, *Commentaries on the Twelve Minor Prophets*, pp. 28, 120:

[On 1.3]: I hence think, that Jonah disobeyed the command of God, partly because the weakness of the flesh was an hindrance, partly because of the novelty of the message, and partly because he despaired of fruit, or of success to his teaching.

[On 4.2]: Here Jonah openly declares why he bore so ill the deliverance of Nineveh from destruction, because he was thus found to have been false and lying.

J. Hooper, 'An Oversight and Deliberation upon the Holy Prophet Jonas', p. 450:

Jonas was commanded to cry and preach against the Ninivites; but being afeard, and suspecting the difficulty of the vocation, flieth another way.

Jerome, *Jérôme Commentaire sur Jonas* (trans. Y.-M. Duval; Sources Chrétiennes, 323; Paris: Cerf, 1985), p. 173:

Le prophète sait, par l'inspiration de l'Espirit-Saint, que la pénitence des Nations annonce la ruine des Juifs. Aussi, en homme qui aime sa patrie, n'est-il pas tant jaloux du salut de Ninive qu'il ne veut pas que son propre peuple périsse.

M. Luther, *Jona* (ed., G. Krause; Munich: Chr. Kaiser Verlag, 1938), p. 70:

Und wenn ihm solches alles wäre zu schenken, so ist doch das ja über die Maßen, daß er gleich seinen ersten Ungehorsam und Flucht, dafür er so greulich gestraft ist, allererst will billigen und verteidigen und die Schuld der Güte Gottes zurechnen, da er spricht: 'Ach, Herr, das ist da ich sagte, da ich noch in meinem Lande war...'

H. Smith, *Jonah the Messenger of Ninevehs Repentance*, p. 36:

[On 1.3 and 4.2]: So by urging the unkindnesse to his owne Nation and blood in leaving them to preach to strangers, as also the difficulty of doing good among such notorious sinners, and the danger of his owne person in bringing so unwellcome a message [Satan] getteth him to desist.

W. Tyndale, 'Prologue to the Prophet Jonas', in H. Walter (ed.), *Doctrinal Treatises and Introductions to Different Portion of the Holy Scriptures by William Tyndale, Martyr, 1536* (Cambridge: Cambridge University Press, 1848), p. 455:

For Jonah thought of this manner: Lo, I am here a prophet unto God's people the Israelites, which, though they have God's word testified unto them daily, yet despise it, and worship God under the likeness of calves, and after all manner fashions, save after his own word; and therefore, are of all nations the worst, and most worthy of punishment: and yet God, for love of few that are among them, and for his name's sake, spareth and defendeth them. How then should God take so cruel vengeance on so great a multitude of them to whom his name was never preached, and therefore are not the tenth part so evil as these? If I shall therefore go preach, so shall I lie and shame myself, and God thereto, and make them the more to despise God, and set the less by him, and to be the more cruel unto his people.

R. Walter, *Certaine godlie homilies or sermons upon the Prophets Abdias and Jonas* (trans. R. Norton; 1573), pp. 112-13:

First of all, it seemeth a new and unwonted thing, that a Prophet shoulde be sent forth out of the land of Israel, to go to the Gentiles...Furthermore it is certain, that feare and mistrust were stops unto him: which same also might growe of divers causes.

J. Wolfendale, *A Homiletical Commentary on the Minor Prophets* (London: Funk and Wagnalls, 1892), p. 349:

[On 1.3]: He might be influenced by fear, indolence, and unbelief. But the chief reason for his flight seems to be intense love for his own, and deep hatred to a heathen country.

Twentieth-Century Works in Biblical Studies:
Commentaries, Monographs, Journal Articles and so on

J.S. Ackerman, 'Jonah', p. 240:

[W]e finally learn [in 4.2] why Jonah had fled his divine commission.

L.C. Allen, *The Books of Joel, Obadiah, Jonah and Micah*, p. 229:

Jonah complains bitterly. 'I knew it from the beginning', he says. He could see it coming, and had done all he could to avert what was to him a theological embarrassment and a divine *faux pas*, of which he has been compelled ignominiously to be the instrument.

A.J. Band, 'Swallowing Jonah', pp. 181-82:

The compassionate, forgiving God who declares an exclusive covenant with His people, is the same God who sends Jonah on his mission to Nineveh from which he seeks to flee to Tarshish, a flight later (ch. 4) explained by Jonah in light of the possible contradictions one might infer from Exodus 34 between God's compassion and His demand from his people of an exclusive covenant.

A. Berlin, 'A Rejoinder to John A. Miles, Jr.', p. 227:

> [Miles] fails to realize that Jonah's reluctance is unlike that of Moses, Jeremiah, and others. They hesitated out of the feeling of humility, lack of self-assurance, and fear of how they would be received. Jonah is burdened by none of these feelings; his desire to evade his mission springs from a completely different source. He finally expresses it in 4:2 'O, Lord!...'

J.A. Bewer, 'Jonah', p. 57:

> It is for this reason, he tells Yahweh...that he had fled when the divine command came to him the first time. He knew Yahweh's wonderful grace, His patience and readiness to relent, too well, not to foresee that He would forgive the Ninevites if they repented.

J.M. Boice, *The Minor Prophets*. I. *Hosea–Jonah* (Grand Rapids: Zondervan, 1983), p. 244:

> He said, in effect, 'This is why I refused to go to Nineveh when you first called me; what is more, I was right in refusing'.

M. Burrows, 'The Literary Category of the Book of Jonah', p. 98:

> That, he said, was why he had rebelled against going to Nineveh is the first place (4.2).

B.S. Childs, 'The Canonical Shape of the Book of Jonah', p. 127:

> [T]he case for seeing Jonah's resistance as directed toward the inclusion of the nations is not to be dismissed as a later Christian bias, but is a genuine Old Testament witness directed against a misunderstanding of the election of Israel.

K.M. Craig, Jr, 'Jonah and the Reading Process', pp. 107-108:

> The gap which relates to Jonah's attempt to flee [1.3] is not closed until 4.2 when the reader finally learns what the prophet has kept to himself all along.

K.M. Craig, Jr, *A Poetics of Jonah*, p. 1:

> [T]he first hearers or readers would have attempted to fill one of the book's most important and extended gaps—What motivates the prophet to flee from the Lord?—with the same alacrity as their modern counterparts.

P.C. Craige, *Twelve Prophets*, I, p. 234:

> [W]hen things did not develop as he had hoped, he even remembered the
> objections of his former unregenerate days: 'is this not what I said...'

W.J. Dean and J.R. Thompson, 'Jonah', in H.D.M. Spence and J.S. Exell
(eds.), *The Pulpit Commentary* (London: Funk and Wagnalls, n.d.),
XXXI, p. 7:

> [On 1.3]: There are various impulses which may tend to drive men away
> from the all-searching eye of the Supreme. Some, like Jonah, may wish
> to avoid a service to which they cherish repugnance, for which, perhaps,
> they feel personally disqualified.

T. Eagleton, 'J.L. Austin and the Book of Jonah', p. 231:

> Why is Jonah so reluctant to go to Nineveh in the first place? Perhaps
> because hectoring a seedy bunch of strangers about their vice isn't the best
> guarantee of a long life. But in the storm scene Jonah shows scant regard
> for his own safety, and indeed by the end of the text is betraying a
> powerful death wish. The fact is that he refused to obey God because he
> thought there was no point, and tells God as much after he has spared
> Nineveh.

G. Elata-Alster and R. Salmon, 'The Deconstruction of Genre in the Book
of Jonah', *Journal of Literature and Theology* 3 (1989), p. 40-60 (50):

> In 1.3 Jonah rises and flees to Tarshish, in 4.2, he explains the reasons for
> that flight.

J. Ellul, *The Judgment of Jonah*, pp. 26-27, 73:

> He has every reason to refuse from the human standpoint. It is veritable
> folly to go to Nineveh, that great city which was always in arms against
> God and his people. To begin with, he would have to make a tremendous
> journey across the desert: about 750 miles on foot. Then he would arrive
> at a very large city with far more than 120,000 inhabitants, and he would
> be quite alone there...[T]he Ninevites...[were] a traditional foe of Israel.
> The age of Jonah was the zenith of Assyrian power...The kingdom of
> Israel where Jonah lived was an Assyrian province. God orders Jonah to
> go to the very place he could not go—a light among the darkness. In sum,
> Nineveh is the 'world' in the theological sense.
>
> Jonah incessantly tries to justify himself (4.2). It was not worth it to
> send Jonah to Nineveh to announce its destruction when God is a God of
> love who does not condemn or destroy, when he could only pardon
> Nineveh.

D.N. Freedman, 'Did God Play a Dirty Trick on Jonah at the End?', pp. 28, 30:

> While it is contrary to fact, the author gives the impression that Jonah simply sets up and departs...In fact, as we learn later, in Jonah 4:2, Jonah did in fact argue; he there says to the Lord: 'O Lord...'
>
> In short, Jonah is saying, 'I knew from the beginning what was going to happen; that's why I ran away'.

T.E. Fretheim, *The Message of Jonah*, pp. 76-77:

> Why does Jonah flee?...It is striking that the giving of the actual reason is delayed until 4:2, almost the end of the book.

H.L. Ginsberg, *The Five Megilloth and Jonah: A New Translation* (Philadelphia: Jewish Publication Society of America, 1969), p. 155:

> Jonah tries to escape from his mission of announcing Nineveh's imminent overturn...because he knows that the Lord is forgiving and often relents after decreeing punishment.

B. Halpern and R.E. Friedman, 'Composition and Paronomasia': Halpern and Friedman discuss the various uses of paronomasia which heighten Jonah's refusal.

A.J. Hauser, 'Jonah', p. 35:

> Now all is clear regarding Jonah's desire to flee from his appointed task: he had been afraid all along that God would forgive Nineveh (4.2).

E.R. Hope, 'Pragmatics, Exegesis and Translation', p. 122:

> So the GNB rendering is more justified, 'Didn't I say before I left home that this is just what you would do?' Here 'this' obviously and correctly refers to the events that have just taken place.

J.H. Kennedy, *Studies in the Book of Jonah* (Nashville: Broadman Press, 1956), p. 66:

> Accordingly, upon the sparing of Nineveh wounded pride wailed in brazen effrontery, 'Lord, I told you so!'

A. Koestler, *The Act of Creation* (New York: Macmillan, 1964) (cited in Preminger and Greenstein [eds.], *The Hebrew Bible in Literary Criticism*, pp. 472-73):

Now this very ordinary person receives at the beginning of the story God's sudden order to 'go to Nineveh, that great city, and cry against it'—which is a rather tall order, for Jonah is no professional priest or prophet. It is quite understandable that he prefers to go on leading his happy and trivial life.

W.A. Kort, *Story, Text, and Scripture*, p. 36:

[H]is predictions of the result of preaching to Nineveh were correct. 'This is why I made haste to flee to Tarshish…' (4.2). Jonah had desperately tried to keep God from the error of indiscriminate love, an error that, apparently, would subvert the meaning and value of Jonah's own life.

E.G. Kraeling, 'The Evolution of the Story of Jonah', p. 311:

In 4.2f. he launches into a prayer, but after mention of that act the hand of the author of chapters 1–2 worked in the flashback about the supposed attempt of Jonah to evade his commission by going to sea, and giving the reason (not disclosed in 1.3) why he did so.

A. Lacocque and P.-E. Lacocque, *Jonah*, pp. 61, 70-71:

Actually, what Jonah is struggling with is not so much his own unconscious—though one is never exempt from such a struggle—as with *something he already knows but refuses to accept.* As Jonah says, 'Now, Lord…'

The commission to go to Nineveh and to proclaim the doom of the city is simply not reasonable. If there is any 'God' capable of such insane calling, one must flee as quickly as possible.

G. Landes, 'The Kerygma of the Book of Jonah', *Interpretation* 21 (1967), pp. 3-31 (14):

According to 4.2, when Jonah received the divine word to go to Nineveh, he did not immediately proceed to flee to Tarshish, as 1.3 would give us to understand, but first indicated to Yahweh what unpleasant outcome this whole venture might hold for him—the deliverance of Nineveh. There is no hint in 1.2-3 that Jonah had a word for Yahweh in response to Yahweh's word for him. But obviously this is what the author wants understood, and he has intentionally delayed any account of it until all the events leading up to 4.2 have been narrated.

E. Levine, 'Jonah as a Philosophical Book', p. 243:

Jonah explicitly states why he refused to participate in God's mission: 'O Lord'.

J. Licht, *Storytelling in the Bible* (Jerusalem: Magnes, 1978) (cited in Preminger and Greenstein (eds.), *The Hebrew Bible in Literary Criticism*, pp. 476-77):

> Jonah also explains in the last part of the story why he fled to Tarshish (4.2) when first sent.

J. Limburg, *Hosea–Micah*, p. 151:

> Jonah's prayer...begins with, 'I told you so!' 'Is this not what I said...?' asks Jonah.

J. Limburg, *Jonah*, pp. 42, 89:

> Why does Jonah not want to carry out an assignment in Nineveh? His words in 4.2 provide a clue: Nineveh might repent, the Lord might forgive them, and Jonah does not want that.
>
> Jonah says, 'That is why I ran away', [in 4.2] now making clear why he tried to avoid going to Nineveh in the first place.

D. Marcus, *From Balaam to Jonah*, p. 99:

> In 4.2, Jonah purports to answer one of the major questions of the story: what was reason [sic] for his initial refusal to prophecy [sic] to Nineveh?

J. Mather, 'The Comic Art of the Book of Jonah', pp. 281, 287-88:

> Jonah not only demurs; he attempts to get away to the end of the world.
>
> He says that he knows God is merciful, and he praises God for his mercy when he is in the belly of the fish. But (understandably) he resists and increasingly resents being the butt of God's mercy—having God be merciful at his cost.

J.A. Miles, 'Laughing at the Bible', pp. 172, 177:

> The prophetic scenario calls for reluctance, to be sure, on the part of the prophet, but it also calls on him to express this reluctance in anguished eloquence...For all the texts tells us, Jonah may think himself perfectly worthy of his prophetic call. He is simply perfectly determined not to accept it.
>
> Jonah's reason for his complaint. He says (4:2): 'Oh Lord...'

M. Orth, 'Genre in Jonah', p. 260:

> Jonah's flaw at the beginning and the end is his pride or vanity—at first he fears being a false prophet, and in the end he takes the death of the plant as an insult.

D.F. Payne, 'Jonah from the Perspective of Its Audience', p. 7:

Jonah's immediate and long unexplained disobedience to God depicted in the narrative would have attracted the reader's attention, and indeed shocked him.

T. Pope, 'Notes on Selected Exegetical Issues in Jonah', p. 49:

Jonah is merely saying that he put his own plan into action beforehand, that is, instead of agreeing to go to Nineveh.

J.W. Roffey, 'God's Truth, Jonah's Fish', p. 16:

[I]nformational thunderbolts in 3.10–4.3. We suddenly learn that this prophet is not so much rebellious as only too aware of God's nature.

J.M. Sasson, *Jonah*, pp. 297, 329:

[Rewording of Jonah's confession in 4.2]: Even as you were sending me to this god-aweful city…I planned my escape to Tarshish; and I put my plan into effect because I have always known the truth about you: that when it comes right down to it, you will forgive and you will not punish: not Nineveh for its sins; not me for disobeying you. Even as the seas were raging, even as I was falling into the gaping mouth of a fish, I knew you to be full of bluster; when eyeball to eyeball, as usual you blinked first!

[Reconstruction of Jonah's speech in 1.3]: When the Lord's command to Jonah the son of Amittay was, 'Set out for Nineveh, that large city, and declare doom upon it; the wickedness of its citizens is obvious to me', Jonah prayed to the Lord saying, 'Please, Lord, I realize that you are a gracious and compassionate God, very patient and abundantly benevolent, who will relent from bringing disaster'. Thereupon, Jonah sought to escape the Lord by heading toward Tarshish.

L. Schmidt, *'De Deo'. Studien zur Literarkritik und Theologie des Buches Jona, des Gesprächs zwischen Abraham und Jahwe in Gen 18,22ff. und von Hi 1* (BZAW, 143; Berlin: de Gruyter, 1976), p. 70:

Das darf jedoch nicht auf Kap. 1 zurückprojiziert werden, denn sonst müßte bereits dort die Flucht Jonas mit dem gnädigen Wesen Gottes begründet werden.

P.M. Schumpp, *Das Buch der zwölf Propheten*, p. 179:

Nicht erst jetzt, sondern schon früher, als ihm zum ersten Male der Auftrag Gottes erteilt wurde, hat er geahnt, daß es so kommen werde. Aus diesem Grunde hat er sich damals durch die Flucht seiner Sendung entzogen; er wollte dem Erbarmen Gottes zuvorkommen und verhindern, daß durch seine Mithilfe Gottes Gnade dieser heidnischen Stadt geschenkt werde.

M. Sternberg, *The Poetics of Biblical Narrative*, p. 320:

What appeared at the time as a one-sided speech event, all too common in divine transactions, now emerges as a genuine dialogue, to which Jonah harks back in his outraged 'I told you so' or 'I knew I couldn't count on you to keep your word.'

P.L. Trible, 'Studies in the Book of Jonah', p. 231:

In our prayers the phrase introduces a sentence explaining Jonah's flight to Tarshish.

T.S. Warshaw, 'The Book of Jonah', p. 191:

But he is immediately aware, according to his later complaint, that the fatal words will not prove true and that God, being merciful, will spare Nineveh when it repents. So he decides to evade his role in the drama or condemnation of, and then the mercy to, the wicked Ninevites.

J.D.W. Watts, *The Books of Joel, Obadiah, Jonah, Nahum, Habakkuk and Zephaniah*, p. 91:

Now Jonah thinks he can justify himself for having tried to prevent this 'shameful' turn of events by avoiding God's call in the first place. He says he knew something like this would happen.

H. Werner, *Jona. Der Man aus dem Ghetto* (Exempla Biblia, 2; Göttingen: Vandenhocck & Ruprecht, 1966), p. 98:

Jona selbst bezcichnet sich der heidnischen Schiffsmannschaft gegenüber als Hebräer. Er weiß, wie wir gesehen haben, in der unter Israeliten üblichen Sprachregulierung himsichtlich dieses Wortes genau Bescheid. Seinen Landsleuten gegenüber hätte er sich einein Sohn Israels, einen Israeliten genannt. Fremden gegenüber auch war und sein Leben lang, ob er nun seine Tage in Kanaan oder im Lande Gosen in Ägypten zubrachte, geblieben ist.

H.W. Wolff, *Obadiah and Jonah*, p. 176:

In a process of hindsight, he excuses the flight described in chap. 1 (4.2a). For God's compassion came as no surprise to him: the theology of the confession of faith he quoted in v. 2b showed him that nothing else was to be expected.

A.S. van der Woude, *Jona, Nahum* (De Prediking van het Oude Testament; Nijkerk: Uitgeverij G.F. Callenbach B.V., 1978), p. 19:

In 4.2 vermeldt Jona zelf de reden van zijn vlucht.

Zlotowitz and Scherman, *Jonah*, p. xxvii.

The Sages give us two reasons for Jonah's flight: his wish to avoid an indictment of Israel and his wish to avoid personal vilification.

Other

H.H. Fingert, 'Psychoanalytic Study of the Minor Prophet Jonah', *Psychoanalytic Review* 16 (1954), pp. 55-65 (57):

Jonah did not behave as others consecrated in the Bible usually did. His behavior was in accordance with that of an emotionally disturbed person trying by flight to escape his conflict…Here is a psychic theme repeated several times during the narrative. He attempts flight to refuge. The most consistent and oldest refuge in the history of mankind is the mother. Therefore it can be assumed that Tarshish, the ship and other places of safety in this story may represent symbols for the mother figure.

R.R. Ruether and H.J. Ruether, *The Wrath of Jonah: The Crisis of Religious Nationalism in the Israeli-Palestinian Conflict* (San Francisco: Harper & Row, 1989), p. xvi:

But Jonah, knowing that God is merciful and will relent in his threatened destruction of the Ninevites if they repent, runs the other way.

Contra

Literary Works
D. Marquis, *Noah an' Jonah an' Cap'n John Smith*. In this story, Noah, Jonah, and Captain John Smith are fishing and telling fishing tall-tales. Jonah only relates his being swallowed by the fish; no mention is made of Nineveh or even the Lord.

Sermons: Jewish and Christian
J.T. Cleland, 'Jonah. A Very Minor Prophet [A Sermon for College Students]', in G.P. Butler (ed.), *Best Sermons* (Princeton: D. van Nostrand Company, 1962), VIII, pp. 279-85 (281) (Christian sermon against nationalism):

Jonah was indignant! His preaching had been, embarrassingly, too successful. He personally had hoped for, and desired, a divine wholesale holocaust following on his warning.

L. Harrison, 'The Prophet Jonah [on Jonah 1.3]', in J.F. Newton (ed.), *Best Sermons 1926* (New York: Harcourt, Brace & Company, 1926), pp. 57-64 (61) (Jewish sermon against nationalism):

[The Book of Jonah] teaches primarily that no man can successfully flee from his true mission. Whosoever runs from his duty will get into deep water. Storms will strike him. His career will be shipwrecked.

T.D. Talmage, 'Hard Rowing [on Jonah 1.13-14]', in *500 Selected Sermons* (Grand Rapids: Baker Book House, 1957), XV, pp. 369-83 (371) (Christian sermon):

[The only mention of Jonah in the sermon is as follows:] God had told Jonah to go to Ninevah to preach about the destruction of the city. Jonah disobeyed. That always makes rough water, whether in the Mediterranean or the Atlantic or the Pacific or the Caspian Sea or in the Hudson Rivier or the East River.

Twentieth-Century Works in Biblical Studies
J.S. Ackerman, 'Satire and Symbolism': A discussion focused on Jon. 2; however, Ackerman does relate 4.2 to 1.3 in his commentary. See above.

K. Almbladh, 'The Israelites and the Sea': A study limited to the imagery of the 'sea' in Israelite thought and its implications for the Jonah narrative.

R.E. Clements, 'The Purpose of the Book of Jonah': Although he discusses why Jonah was upset in 4.1 (p. 21), he does not explicitly discuss 4.2.

J. Day, 'Problems in the Interpretation of the Book of Jonah': Day discusses such issues as historicity, language, the book's purpose and so on, which do not require a discussion of the meaning of particular verses.

T.B. Dozeman, 'Inner-Biblical Interpretation', pp. 215-16 (a study comparing Jon. 3.1–4.11 and Joel 2.1-17):

Rather than employing the formula as a confession, whose aid is to avert justified divine destruction and thus provide hope that God will prolong life, Jonah turns the confession into an accusation, so that the hope for prolonged life, which is implicit in the confession, now becomes instead the motivation for his own death wish in Jonah 4.3.

J.C. Holbert, 'Deliverance Belongs to Yahweh': A discussion of satire in Jonah 1–2.

J. Magonet, *Form and Meaning*: Magonet's concern is primarily the literary structure and unity of the entire book and, therefore, he provides few close discussions of particular verses.

Other
J.L. Bull, 'Rethinking Jonah: The Dynamics of Surrender', *Parabola* 15 (1990), pp. 79-84 (79) (a discussion limited to Jonah 1–2):

Taken metaphorically, [the book of Jonah] tells of spiritual purpose denied and resisted, followed by surrender, shelter, and rebirth.

Others cited in Preminger and Greenstein (eds.), *The Hebrew Bible in Literary Criticism*: Since Preminger and Greenstein only give brief selections, I have not indicated which do not fit the pattern here.

Appendix 2

JONAH'S OMITTED ANSWER TO THE LORD'S LAST QUESTION (4.10-11)

Children's Bibles

Alexander, *The Nelson Children's Bible*:

> And Jonah began, at last, to understand.

T.H. Gallaudet, *The History of Jonah for Children and Youth*, p. 150:

> The Bible does not tell us how Jonah felt after God had reasoned with him about his foolish and wicked anger. It is altogether probable, however, that he saw, once more, how great a sinner he was; and that he again repented, and implored the forgiveness of God.

L. Marshall, *The Wonder Book of Bible Stories*, p. 146:

> And Jonah learned that men, and women, and little children, are all precious in the sight of the Lord, even though they know not God.

N.V. Peale, *Bible Stories*, p. 199:

> The story ends right there. If Jonah had anything to say, which is doubtful, the Bible doesn't record it. But every Hebrew who heard the story—and it is still read in synagogues on the Day of Atonement—understood the message: that the love of God is not confined to any one people, and that any man who hates his fellow man is really in rebellion against his Creator.

Pre-Twentieth-Century Works

Jewish

3 Macc. 6.8 (trans. H. Anderson, in Charlesworth [ed.], *The Old Testament Pseudepigrapha*, II, p. 526):

> When Jonah was pining away unpitied in the belly of the monster of the deep, you, Father, restored him uninjured to all his household.

4 Ezra 1.38-40 (trans. B.M. Metzger, in Charlesworth [ed.], *The Old Testament Pseudepigrapha*, I, p. 526):

> [List of 'leaders']: 'Abraham, Isaac, and Jacob and Hosea and Amos and Micah and Joel and Obadiah and Jonah and Nahum and Habbakuk, Zephaniah, Haggai, Zechariah, and Malachi.

Liv. Proph. 10.2-3 (trans. D.R.A. Hare, in Charlesworth [ed.], *The Old Testament Pseudepigrapha*, II, p. 392):

> And when [Jonah] had been cast forth by the sea monster and had gone away to Nineveh and had returned, he did not remain in his district, but taking his mother along he sojourned in Sour, a territory (inhabited by) foreign nations; for he said, 'So shall I remove my reproach, for I spoke falsely in prophesying against the great city of Nineveh.'

Mart. and Asc. of Isaiah 4.22 (trans. M.A. Knibb, in Charlesworth [ed.], *The Old Testament Pseudepigrapha*, II, p. 163): Jonah is given in a list of the prophets.

Midr. Shocher Tov 26.7 (cited in Zlotowitz and Scherman, *Jonah*, p. xxiii):

> The son of the widow of Tzorfas was Jonah. He was a complete *tzaddik* [righteous man].

Midr. Yona (cited in Sasson, *Jonah*, p. 320):

> At that very moment, [Jonah] fell flat on his face saying, 'Direct your world according to the attribute of mercy, as is written, Mercy and forgiveness belong to the Lord our God.'

Mish. R. Eliezer (cited in Zlotowitz and Scherman, *Jonah*, p. xxiii):

> Jonah was equal to Elijah, Elisha anointed him.

Sib. Or. 2.243-51 (trans. Collins, in Charlesworth [ed.], *The Old Testament Pseudepigrapha*, I, p. 351):

> [List of 'pious men' who will be among the resurrected]: Moses, Abraham, Isaac, Jacob, Joshua, Daniel, Elijah, Habbakuk, Jonah, and Jeremiah.

y. Sanh. 11.8 (cited in Zlotowitz and Scherman, *Jonah*, p. xxiii):

> Jonah ben Ammittai was a true prophet.

Christian

J. Calvin, *Commentaries on the Twelve Minor Prophets*, p. 144:

> We hence see how apposite are all the parts of this similitude, to make Jonah to loathe his folly, and to be ashamed of it; for he had attempted to frustrate the secret purpose of God, and in a manner to overrule it by his own will, so that the Ninevites might not be spared, who yet laboured by true repentance to anticipate the divine judgment.

Twentieth-Century Works in Biblical Studies

J.A. Bewer, 'Jonah', pp. 63-64:

> The argument is absolutely irresistible. There is but one answer possible.

W.B. Crouch, 'To Question an End, To End a Question', p. 112:

> [Crouch first provides the following reconstruction from the narrator's viewpoint:] Yes Yahweh, you have acted appropriately in showing compassion on Nineveh.
>
> [However, he then provides an answer that is] constructed to resist the intention of the narrative as follows: 'O Yahweh, do you have eyes to see but cannot see and ears to hear but cannot hear? Nineveh has not repented. They, as I in the belly of the great fish, are only afraid of dying at your hands. They have manipulated your soft heart just as I have. I remain unrepentant and so do they. O great and might Elohim, you have thought nothing about destroying countless cities through the ages—are you, in this circumstance, really that gullible?'

J.H. Kennedy, *Studies in the Book of Jonah*, p. 97:

> [T]he purpose of the book of Jonah became the purpose of the prophet Jonah.

H.W. Wolff, *Obadiah and Jonah*, p. 177:

> Yahweh's question is the narrator's final word to his reader. That reader is not spared the necessity of finding his own answer. What will Israel say, in a world in which she has to suffer herself, while the great empires flourish? Nowhere in the Old Testament is this question put so stringently and yet so kindly as in the Jonah story.

M. Zlotowitz and N. Scherman, *Jonah*, pp. xxiii, lxxiv:

> The Sages testify to Jonah's greatness; the very fact that he was a prophet and that God persevered in utilizing him for the mission to Nineveh despite his apparent recalcitrance is in itself testimony to his righteousness.

The prophet, the sailors, the Ninevites—all teach eternal lessons of repentance. From the repentance of Nineveh which was sincere by its own standards, to the dedication of Jonah whose greatness drove him to sacrifice spiritual growth and life itself for the sake of God's honor and Israel's—the Book is replete with teachings that go beyond time, nationality, and geography.

BIBLIOGRAPHY

A group from Renne, France (trans. J.C. Kirby), 'An Approach to the Book of Jonah: Suggestions and Questions', *Semeia* 15 (1979), pp. 85-96.

Abbot, G., *An Exposition upon the Prophet Jonah* (London: Hamilton, Adams & Co., 1845).

Abrams, M.H., *A Glossary of Literary Terms* (New York: Holt, Rinehart & Winston, 1981).

Ackerman, J.S., 'Jonah', in R. Alter and F. Kermode (eds.), *The Literary Guide to the Bible* (Cambridge: The Belknap Press, 1987), pp. 235-43.

—'Satire and Symbolism in the Song of Jonah', in B. Halpern and J.D. Levensen (eds.), *Traditions in Transformation: Turning Points in Biblical Faith* (Winona Lake, IN: Eisenbrauns, 1981), pp. 213-46.

Alexander, P., *The Nelson Children's Bible: Stories from the Old and New Testaments* (Nashville: Thomas Nelson, 1981).

Allen, L.C., *The Books of Joel, Obadiah, Jonah and Micah* (Grand Rapids: Eerdmans, 1976).

Almbladh, K., *Studies in the Book of Jonah* (Studia Semitica Upsalkinsis, 7; Stockholm: Almqvist & Wiksell, 1986).

Anderson, H. (trans.), '3 Maccabees', in Charlesworth (ed.), *The Old Testament Pseudepigrapha*, II, pp. 509-29.

Atkinson, J.M., 'Two Devices for Generating Audience Approval: A Comparative Study of Public Discourse and Texts', in K. Ehlich and H. van Riemsdijk (eds.), *Connectedness in Sentence, Discourse and Text* (Tilburg Studies in Language and Literature, 4; Tilburg: Tilburg University, 1983), pp. 199-236.

Atkinson, J.M., and P. Drew, *Order in Court: The Organization of Verbal Interaction in Judicial Settings* (London: Macmillan, 1979).

Baker, C.D., and P. Freebody, 'Representations of Questioning and Answering in Children's First School Books', *Language in Society* 15 (1986), pp. 451-84.

Band, A.J., 'Swallowing Jonah: The Eclipse of Parody', *Prooftexts* 10 (1990), pp. 177-95.

Bar-Efrat, S., *Narrative Art in the Bible* (Sheffield: Almond Press, 1989).

Berlin, A., 'A Rejoinder to John A. Miles, Jr., with Some Observations on the Nature of Prophecy', *JQR* 66 (1976), pp. 227-35.

Bernstein, R.J., *Beyond Objectivism and Relativism: Science, Hemeneutics, and Praxis* (Philadelphia: University of Pennsylvania Press, 1983).

Bewer, J.A., 'Jonah', in H.G. Mitchell, J.M.P. Smith and J.A. Bewer (eds.), *Haggai, Zechariah, Malachi, and Jonah* (ICC; Edinburgh: T. &. T. Clark, 1971), pp. 1-65.

Bickerman, E., *Four Strange Books of the Bible: Jonah, Daniel, Koheleth, Esther* (New York: Schocken Books, 1967).

Bishop, R., 'There's Nothing Natural About Natural Conversation: A Look at Dialogue in Fiction and Drama', *Oral Tradition* 6 (1991), pp. 58-78.

Bloom, E. (ed.), 'In Defense of Authors and Readers [Wayne Booth and others, "For the Authors"; Wolfgang Iser and others, "For the Readers"]', *Novel* 11 (1977), pp. 5-25.

Boice, J.M., *The Minor Prophets*. I. *Hosea–Jonah* (Grand Rapids: Zondervan, 1983).

Bowers, R.H., *The Legend of Jonah* (The Hague: Martinus Nijhoff, 1971).

Brewer, W.F., 'The Story Schema: Universal and Culture-Specific Properties', in Olson, Torrance and Hildyard (eds.), *Literacy, Language, and Learning*, pp. 167-94.

Brown, C.R., 'What Jonah Did', in C.E. Fant, Jr and W.M. Pinson, Jr (eds.), *20 Centuries of Great Preaching: An Encyclopedia of Preaching*. VII. *Watson [Maclaren] to Rufus Jones, 1850–1950* (Waco, TX: Word Books, 1971), pp. 207-12.

Bull, J.L., 'Rethinking Jonah: The Dynamics of Surrender', *Parabola* 15 (1990), pp. 79-84.

Burrows, M., 'The Literary Category of the Book of Jonah', in H.T. Frank and W.L. Reed (eds.), *Translating and Understanding the Old Testament: Essays in Honor of Herbert Gordon May* (Nashville: Abingdon Press, 1970), pp. 80-107.

Calvin, J., *Commentaries on the Twelve Minor Prophets*. III. *Jonah, Micah, Nahum* (trans. J. Owen; Grand Rapids: Eerdmans, 1950).

Campbell, K.S., 'A Lesson in Polite Compliance: Gawain's Conversational Strategies in Fitt 3 of Sir Gawain and the Green Knight', *Language Quarterly* 28 (1990), pp. 53-62.

Chafe, W.L., 'Integration and Involvement in Speaking, Writing, and Oral Literature', in Tannen (ed.), *Spoken and Written Language*, pp. 35-53.

Charlesworth, J.H. (ed.), *The Old Testament Pseudepigrapha*, I-II (Garden City, NY: Doubleday, 1983–85).

Childs, B.S., 'The Canonical Shape of the Book of Jonah', in G.A. Tuttle (ed.), *Biblical and Near Eastern Studies: Essays in Honor of William Sanford LaSor* (Grand Rapids: Eerdmans, 1978), pp. 122-28.

Clark, H.H., and S.E. Haviland, 'Comprehension and the Given-New Contract', in R.D. Freedle (ed.), *Discourse Production and Comprehension* (Norwood: ABLEX, 1977), pp. 1-40.

Cleland, J.T., 'Jonah. A Very Minor Prophet [A Sermon for College Students]', in G.P. Butler (ed.), *Best Sermons*. VIII. *1962 Protestant Edition* (Princeton: D. van Nostrand Company, 1962), pp. 279-85.

Clements, R.E., 'The Purpose of the Book of Jonah', in *Congress Volume, Edinburgh 1974* (VTSup, 28; Leiden: Brill, 1975), pp. 16-28.

Cole, P. (ed.), *Radical Pragmatics* (New York: Academic Press, 1981).

Collins, J.J. (trans.), 'Sibylline Oracles', in Charlesworth (ed.), *The Old Testament Pseudepigrapha*, I, pp. 317-472.

Coulmas, F., *Direct and Indirect Speech* (Berlin: Mouton, 1986).

—'Reported Speech: Some General Issues', in *idem*, *Direct and Indirect Speech*, pp. 1-28.

Craig, K.M., Jr, 'Jonah and the Reading Process', *JSOT* 47 (1990), pp. 103-114.

—*A Poetics of Jonah: Art in the Service of Ideology* (Columbia: University of South Carolina Press, 1993).

—'The Poetics of the Book of Jonah: Toward an Understanding of Narrative Strategy' (PhD dissertation; Southern Baptist Theological Seminary, 1989).

Craige, P.C., *Twelve Prophets*. I. *Hosea, Joel, Amos, Obadiah, and Jonah* (Philadelphia: Westminster Press, 1984).

Crenshaw, J.L., *Prophetic Conflict: Its Effect Upon Israelite Religion* (BZAW, 124; Berlin: de Gruyter, 1971).

Crossan, J.D., *The Dark Interval: Towards a Theology of Story* (Niles: Argus, 1975).

Crouch, W.B., 'To Question an End, To End a Question: Opening the Closure of the Book of Jonah', *JSOT* 62 (1994), pp. 101-12.

Culler, J., 'Literary Competence', in Tompkins (ed.), *Reader-Response Criticism: From Formalism to Post-Structuralism*, pp. 101-17.

Day, J., 'Problems in the Interpretation of the Book of Jonah', in A.S. van der Woude (ed.), *In Quest of the Past: Studies on Israelite Religion, Literature and Prophetism* (OTS, 26; Leiden: Brill, 1990), pp. 32-47.

Dean, W.J., and J.R. Thompson, 'Jonah', in H.D.M. Spence and J.S. Exell (eds.), *The Pulpit Commentary*, XXXI (London: Funk and Wagnalls, n.d.).

Detweiler, R. (ed.), *Reader Response Approaches to Biblical and Secular Texts* (*Semeia* 31; Atlanta: Scholars Press, 1985).

Dozeman, T.B., 'Inner-Biblical Interpretation of Yahweh's Gracious and Compassionate Character', *JBL* 108 (1989), pp. 207-23.

Drew, P., 'Recalling Someone from the Past', in Roger and Bull (eds.), *Conversation*, pp. 96-115.

Duval, Y.-M. (trans.), *Jérôme Commentaire sur Jonas* (Sources Chrétiennes, 323; Paris: Cerf, 1985).

Eagleton, T., 'J.L. Austin and the Book of Jonah', in R.M. Schwartz (ed.), *The Book and the Text: The Bible and Literary Theory* (Cambridge: Basil Blackwell, 1990), pp. 231-36.

Elata-Alster, G., and R. Salmon, 'The Deconstruction of Genre in the Book of Jonah', *Journal of Literature and Theology* 3 (1989), pp. 40-60.

Ellul, J., *The Judgment of Jonah* (trans. G.W. Bromiley; Grand Rapids: Eerdmans, 1971).

Fingert, H.H., 'Psychoanalytic Study of the Minor Prophet Jonah', *Psychoanalytic Review* 16 (1954), pp. 55-65.

Fish, S.E., 'How Ordinary Is Ordinary Language?', *New Literary History* 5 (1973), pp. 41-54.

—*Is There a Text in This Class? The Authority of Interpretive Communities* (Cambridge, MA: Harvard University Press, 1980).

Foley, J.M., *Immanent Art: From Structure to Meaning in Traditional Oral Epic* (Bloomington: Indiana University Press, 1991).

Fowler, R.M., *Let the Reader Understand: Reader-Response Criticism and the Gospel of Mark* (Minneapolis: Fortress Press, 1991).

Freedman, D.N., 'Did God Play a Dirty Trick on Jonah at the End?', *Bible Review* 6 (1990), pp. 26-31.

Fretheim, T.E., *The Message of Jonah* (Minneapolis: Augsburg, 1977).

Gallaudet, T.H., *The History of Jonah for Children and Youth* (New York: American Tract Society, 1833).

Gautam, K.K., 'Pinter's *The Caretaker*: A Study in Conversational Analysis', *Journal of Pragmatics* 11 (1987), pp. 49-59.

Ginsberg, H.L., *The Five Megilloth and Jonah: A New Translation* (Philadelphia: Jewish Publication Society of America, 1969).

Ginzberg, L., *Legends of the Jews*, IV–VI (Philadelphia: Jewish Publication Society of America, 1946–47).

Goodman, P., *Three Plays: The Young Disciple, Faustina, Jonah* (New York: Random House, 1965).

Graesser, A.C., and L.F. Clark, *Structures and Procedures of Implicit Knowledge* (Advances in Discourse Processes, 17; Norwood: ABLEX, 1985).

Grice, H.P., 'Logic and Conversation', in P. Cole and J. Morgan (eds.), *Syntax and Semantics*. III. *Speech Acts* (New York: Academic Press, 1975), pp. 41-58.

Habel, N.C., 'The Form and Significance of the Call Narratives', *ZAW* 77 (1965), pp. 297-323.

Hafez, O.M., 'Turn-Taking in Egyptian Arabic: Spontaneous Speech vs. Drama Dialogue', *Journal of Pragmatics* 15 (1991), pp. 59-81.

Halpern, B. and R.E. Friedman, 'Composition and Paronomasia in the Book of Jonah', *HAR* 4 (1980), pp. 79-92.

Hamilton, J.W., 'Unwilling Missionaries [on Jonah 4.11; Gal. 3.28]', in *The American Pulpit Series*, IX (New York: Abingdon Press, 1946), pp. 87-102.

Hare, D.R.A. (trans.), 'The Lives of the Prophets', in Charlesworth (ed.), *The Old Testament Pseudepigrapha*, II, pp. 379-99.

Harrison, L., 'The Prophet Jonah [on Jonah 1.3]', in J.F. Newton (ed.), *Best Sermons 1926* (New York: Harcourt, Brace and Company, 1926), pp. 57-64.

Hastings, J. (ed.), 'Paying the Fare [on Jonah 1.3]', in *The Children's Great Texts of the Bible*. IV. *Jeremiah to Matthew* (New York: Charles Scribner's Sons, 1921), pp. 131-34.

Hauser, A.J., 'Jonah: In Pursuit of the Dove', *JBL* 104 (1985), pp. 21-37.

Haviland, J.B., 'Guugu Yimidhirr Brother-In-Law Language', *Language in Society* 8 (1979), pp. 365-93.

—' "We Want to Borrow Your Mouth": Tzotzil Marital Squabbles', *Anthropological Linguistics* 30 (1988), pp. 395-447.

Heritage, J.C., 'Current Developments in Conversation Analysis', in Roger and Bull (eds.), *Conversation*, pp. 21-47.

Heritage, J.C., and J.M. Atkinson (eds.), *Structures of Social Action: Studies in Conversation Analysis* (Cambridge: Cambridge University Press, 1984).

Hildyard, A., and D.R. Olson, 'On the Comprehension and Memory of Oral vs. Written Discourse', in Tannen (ed.), *Spoken and Written Language*, pp. 19-33.

Holbert, J.C., ' "Deliverance Belongs to Yahweh": Satire in the Book of Jonah', *JSOT* 21 (1981), pp. 59-81.

Hooper, J., 'An Oversight and Deliberation upon the Holy Prophet Jonas', in S. Carr (ed.), *Early Writings of John Hooper, D.D., Lord Bishop of Gloucester and Worcester, Martyr, 1555* (Cambridge: Cambridge University Press, 1843).

Hope, E.R., 'Pragmatics, Exegesis and Translation', in P.C. Stine (ed.), *Issues in Bible Translation* (UBS Monograph Series, 3; New York: United Bible Societies, 1988), pp. 113-28.

Hutton, W., *Jonah and the Great Fish* (New York: Atheneum, 1983).

Iser, W., *The Act of Reading: A Theory of Aesthetic Response* (Baltimore: The Johns Hopkins University Press, 1978).

—*The Implied Reader: Patterns of Communication in Prose Fiction from Bunyan to Beckett* (Baltimore: The Johns Hopkins University Press, 1974).

—'Narrative Strategies as a Means of Communication', in M.J. Valdés and O.J. Miller (eds.), *Interpretation of Narrative* (Toronto: University of Toronto Press, 1978), pp. 100-17.

—*Prospecting: From Reader Response to Literary Anthropology* (Baltimore: The Johns Hopkins University Press, 1989).

Jauss, H.R., *Toward an Aesthetic of Reception* (trans. T. Bahti; Theory and History of Literature, 2; Minneapolis: University of Minnesota Press, 1982).

Josephus, *Jewish Antiquities, Books IX–XI* (trans. R. Marcus; LCL; Cambridge, MA: Harvard University Press, 1966).

Jowett, J.H., 'Lulled by High Ideals [on Jonah 4.2]', in C.E. Fant, Jr and W.M. Pinson, Jr (eds.), *20 Centuries of Great Preaching: An Encyclopedia of Preaching. VIII. Morgan to Coffin, 1863–1959* (Waco, TX: Word Books, 1971), pp. 82-86.

Kennedy, J.H., *Studies in the Book of Jonah* (Nashville: Broadman Press, 1956).

Kleinert, P., *The Book of Jonah*, in J.P. Lange and P. Schaff (eds.), *A Commentary on the Holy Scriptures*, 14.6 (New York: Charles Scribner's Sons, 1890).

Knibb, M.A. (trans.), 'Martyrdom and Ascension of Isaiah', in Charlesworth (ed.), *The Old Testament Pseudepigrapha*, II, pp. 143-76.

Koestler, A., *The Act of Creation* (New York: Macmillan, 1964), pp. 360-61 (cited in Preminger and Greenstein [eds.], *The Hebrew Bible in Literary Criticism*, pp. 472-73).

Kort, W.A., *Narrative Elements and Religious Meanings* (Philadelphia: Fortress Press, 1975).

—*Story, Text, and Scripture: Literary Interests in Biblical Narrative* (University Park: Pennsylvania State University Press, 1988).

Kraeling, E.G., 'The Evolution of the Story of Jonah', in *Homages a André Dupont-Sommer* (Paris: Libraire d'amérique et d'orient Adrien-Maisonneuve, 1971), pp. 305-18.

Kuyper, A., 'Jona en Hosea [on Hos. 14.5]', in *Van de Vloleindung*, III (Kampen: Kok, 1930), pp. 77-84.

Lacocque, A., and P.-E. Lacocque, *Jonah: A Psycho-Religious Approach to the Prophet* (Columbia: University of South Carolina Press, 1990).

Lakoff, R.T., and D. Tannen, 'Conversational Strategy and Metastrategy in a Pragmatic Theory: The Example of *Scenes from a Marriage*', *Semiotica* 49 (1984), pp. 323-46.

Landes, G., 'Jonah: A *Masal*?', in J.G. Gammie *et al.* (eds.), *Israelite Wisdom: Theological and Literary Essays in Honor of Samuel Terrien* (Missoula, MT: Scholars Press, 1978), pp. 137-58.

—'The Kerygma of the Book of Jonah', *Interpretation* 21 (1967), pp. 3-31.

Levine, E., 'Jonah as a Philosophical Book', *ZAW* 96 (1984), pp. 235-45.

Levinson, S.C., *Pragmatics* (Cambridge: Cambridge University Press, 1983).

Licht, J., *Storytelling in the Bible* (Jerusalem: Magnes, 1978), pp. 121-24 (cited in Preminger and Greenstein [eds.], *The Hebrew Bible in Literary Criticism*, pp. 476-77).

Limburg, J., *Hosea–Micah* (Interpretation; Atlanta: John Knox, 1988).

—*Jonah: A Commentary* (OTL; Louisville: Westminster Press, 1993).

Luther, M., *Jona* (ed. G. Krause; Munich: Chr. Kaiser Verlag, 1938).

MacBeth, G., *The Lord* (New York: Holt, Rinehart & Winston, 1970).

Magonet, J., *Form and Meaning: Studies in Literary Techniques in the Book of Jonah* (Sheffield: Almond Press, 1983).

Marcus, D., *From Balaam to Jonah: Anti-prophetic Satire in the Hebrew Bible* (Brown Judaic Studies, 301; Atlanta: Scholars Press, 1995).

Marquis, D., *Noah an' Jonah an' Cap'n John Smith: A Book of Humorous Verse* (New York: D. Appleton, 1921).

Marshall, L. (ed.), *The Wonder Book of Bible Stories* (1921).

Mather, J., 'The Comic Art of the Book of Jonah', *Soundings* 65 (1982), pp. 280-91.

Meier, S.A., *Speaking of Speaking: Marking Direct Discourse in the Hebrew Bible* (VTSup, 46; Leiden: Brill, 1992).

Melville, H., *Moby-Dick* (New York: Harper, 1851), pp. 45-46 (cited in Preminger and Greenstein [eds.], *The Hebrew Bible in Literary Criticism*, pp. 467-68).

Merritt, M., 'On Questions Following Questions in Service Encounters', *Language in Society* 5 (1976), pp. 315-57.

Metzger, B.M. (trans.), 'The Fourth Book of Ezra', in Charlesworth (ed.), *The Old Testament Pseudepigrapha*, I, pp. 517-59.

Miles, J.A., 'Laughing at the Bible: Jonah as Parody', *JQR* 65 (1975), pp. 168-81.

Miller, C.L., 'Discourse Functions of Quotative Frames in Biblical Hebrew Narrative', in W.R. Bodine (ed.), *Discourse Analysis of Biblical Literature: What It Is and What It Offers* (Semeia Studies; Atlanta: Scholars Press, 1995), pp. 155-82.

—'Introducing Direct Discourse in Biblical Hebrew Narrative', in R.D. Bergen (ed.), *Biblical Hebrew and Discourse Linguistics* (Dallas: Summer Institute of Linguistics, 1994), pp. 199-241.

—'Reported Speech in Biblical and Epigraphic Hebrew: A Linguistic Analysis' (PhD dissertation; University of Chicago, 1992).

Moerman, M., *Talking Culture: Ethnography and Conversation Analysis* (Philadelphia: University of Pennsylvania Press, 1988).

Mulkay, M., 'Agreement and Disagreement in Conversations and Letters', *Text* 5 (1985), pp. 201-27.

—'Conversations and Texts', *Human Studies* 9 (1986), pp. 303-21.

—*The Word and the World: Explorations in the Form of Sociological Analysis* (London: George Allen & Unwin, 1985).

Olson, D.R., N. Torrance and A. Hildyard (eds.), *Literacy, Language and Learning: The Nature and Consequences of Reading and Writing* (Cambridge: Cambridge University Press, 1985).

Orth, M., 'Genre in Jonah: The Effects of Parody in the Book of Jonah', in W.W. Hallo, B.W. Jones and G.L. Mattingly (eds.), *The Bible in the Light of Cuneiform Literature: Scripture in Context III* (Lewiston, NY: Edwin Mellen, 1990), pp. 257-81.

Overholt, T.W., 'The Ghost Dance of 1890 and the Nature of the Prophetic Process', *Ethnohistory* 21 (1974), pp. 37-63.

Paine, T., *The Complete Writings of Thomas Paine* (ed. P.S. Foner; New York: Citadel Press, 1945).

Payne, D.F., 'Jonah from the Perspective of Its Audience', *JSOT* 13 (1979), pp. 3-12.

Peale, N.V., *Bible Stories* (New York: Banner Press, 1978).

Pelli, M., 'The Literary Art of Jonah', *Hebrew Studies* 20-21 (1979–80), pp. 18-28.

Person, R.F., Jr, 'Restarts in Conversation and Literature', *Language and Communication* 16 (1986), pp. 61-70.

—*Second Zechariah and the Deuteronomic School* (JSOTSup, 167; Sheffield: Sheffield Academic Press, 1993).

Polanyi, L., 'Literary Complexity in Everyday Storytelling', in Tannen (ed.), *Spoken and Written Language*, pp. 155-70.

Pomerantz, A.M., 'Attributions of Responsibility', *Sociology* 12 (1978), pp. 115-21.

Pope, T., 'Notes on Selected Exegetical Issues in Jonah', *Notes on Translation* 3 (1989), pp. 45-50.

Preminger, A., and E.L. Greenstein (eds.), *The Hebrew Bible in Literary Criticism* (New York: Ungar, 1986).

Prince, E.F., 'Toward a Taxonomy of Given-New Information', in Cole (ed.), *Radical Pragmatics* (New York: Academic Press, 1981), pp. 223-55.

Rauber, D.F., in *The Bible Today* Oct. 1970, pp. 33-35 (cited in Preminger and Greenstein [eds.], *The Hebrew Bible in Literary Criticism*, pp. 473-74).

Roffey, J.W., 'God's Truth, Jonah's Fish: Structure and Existence in the Book of Jonah', *Australian Biblical Review* 36 (1988), pp. 1-18.

Roger, D. and P. Bull (eds.), *Conversation: An Interdisciplinary Perspective* (Intercommunication, 3; Clevendon: Multilingual Matters, 1989).

Ruether, R.R., and H.J. Ruether, *The Wrath of Jonah: The Crisis of Religious Nationalism in the Israeli-Palestinian Conflict* (San Francisco: Harper & Row, 1989).

Sacks, H., E.A. Schegloff and G. Jefferson, 'A Simplest Systematics for the Organization of Turn-Taking for Conversation', *Language* 50 (1974), pp. 696-735.

Sasson, J.M., *Jonah* (AB, 24B; Garden City, NY: Doubleday, 1990).

Savran, G.W., *Telling and Retelling: Quotation in Biblical Narrative* (Indiana Studies in Biblical Literature; Bloomington: Indiana University Press, 1988).

Schlegloff, E.A., and H. Sacks, 'Opening Up Closings', *Semiotica* 7 (1973), pp. 289-327.

Schmidt, L., *'De Deo'. Studien zur Literarkritik und Theologie des Buches Jona, des Gesprächs zwischen Abraham und Jahwe in Gen 18,22ff. und von Hi 1* (BZAW, 143; Berlin: de Gruyter, 1976).

Schumpp, P.M., *Das Buch der zwölf Propheten* (Herders Bibelkommentar, 10.2; Freiburg: Herder, 1950).

Smith, H., *Jonah the Messenger of Ninevehs Repentance Set Forth in His Calling, Rebellion, and Punishment* (London: 1617).

Spolsky, B., and J. Walters, 'Jewish Styles of Worship: A Conversational Analysis', *International Journal of the Sociology of Language* 56 (1985), pp. 51-65.

Steeple, A.D., *A Child's First Book of Bible Stories* (New York: Hart, 1950).

Sternberg, M., *The Poetics of Biblical Narrative* (Bloomington: Indiana University Press, 1985).

Stucky, N., 'Unnatural Acts: Performing Natural Conversation', *Literature in Performance* 8 (1988), pp. 28-39.

Suleiman, S.R., and I. Crosman (eds.), *The Reader in the Text: Essays on Audience and Interpretation* (Princeton: Princeton University Press, 1980).

Talmage, T.D., 'Hard Rowing [on Jonah 1.13-14]', in *500 Selected Sermons*, XV (Grand Rapids: Baker Book House, 1957), pp. 369-83.

Tannen, D. (ed.), *Coherence in Spoken and Written Discourse* (Advances in Discourse Processes, 12; Norwood: ABLEX, 1984).

—'Introducing Constructed Dialogue in Greek and American Conversational and Literary Narrative', in Coulmas (ed.), *Direct and Indirect Speech*, pp. 311-32.

—'The Oral/Literate Continuum in Discourse', in Tannen (ed.), *Spoken and Written Language*, pp. 1-16.

—'Oral and Literate Strategies in Spoken and Written Narratives', *Language* 58 (1982), pp. 1-21.

—'Ordinary Conversation and Literary Discourse: Coherence and the Poetics of Repetition', in E.B. Bendix (ed.), *The Uses of Linguistics* (New York: New York Academy of Sciences, 1990), pp. 15-32.

—'Relative Focus on Involvement in Oral and Written Discourse', in Olson, Torrance and Hildyard (eds.), *Literacy, Language, and Learning*, pp. 124-47.

—'Repetition in Conversation: Toward a Poetics of Talk', *Language* 63 (1987), pp. 574-605.

—'Silence as Conflict Management in Fiction and Drama: Pinter's *Betrayal* and a Short Story, "Great Wits"', in A.D. Grimshaw (ed.), *Conflict Talk: Sociolinguistic Investigations of Arguments in Conversations* (Cambridge: Cambridge University Press, 1990), pp. 260-79.

—*Spoken and Written Language: Exploring Orality and Literacy* (Advances in Discourse Processes, 9; Norwood: ABLEX, 1982).

—*Talking Voices: Repetition, Dialogue, and Imagery in Conversational Discourse* (Cambridge: Cambridge University Press, 1989).

Tompkins, J.P. (ed.), *Reader-Response Criticism: From Formalism to Post-Structuralism* (Baltimore: The Johns Hopkins University Press, 1980).

Toolan, M., 'Analysing Conversation in Fiction: The Christmas Dinner Scene in Joyce's *Portrait of the Artist as a Young Man*', *Poetics Today* 8 (1987), pp. 393-416.

—'Analysing Fictional Dialogue', *Language and Communication* 5 (1985), pp. 193-206.

—*The Stylistics of Fiction: A Literary-Linguistic Approach* (London: Routledge & Kegan Paul, 1990).

Trible, P.L., *Rhetorical Criticism: Context, Method, and the Book of Jonah* (Minneapolis: Fortress Press, 1994).

—'Studies in the Book of Jonah' (PhD dissertation; Columbia University, 1963).

Trudinger, P., 'Jonah: A Post-Exilic Verbal Cartoon?', *Downside Review* 107 (1989), pp. 142-43.

Tsui, A.B.M., 'Beyond the Adjacency Pair', *Language in Society* 18 (1989), pp. 545-64.

Tucker, G.M., 'Prophetic Superscriptions and the Growth of the Canon', in G.W. Coats and B.O. Long (eds.), *Canon and Authority: Essays in Old Testament Religion and Theology* (Philadelphia: Fortress Press, 1977), pp. 56-70.

Tyndale, W., 'Prologue to the Prophet Jonas', in H. Walter (ed.), *Doctrinal Treatises and Introductions to Different Portion of the Holy Scriptures by William Tyndale, Martyr, 1536* (Cambridge: Cambridge University Press, 1848).

Van der Woude, A.S., *Jona, Nahum* (De Prediking van het Oude Testament; Nijkerk: Uitgeverij G.F. Callenbach B.V., 1978).

Wadman, K.L., '"Private Ejaculations": Politeness Strategies in George Herbert's Poems Directed to God', *Language and Style* 16 (1983), pp. 87-106.

Walter, R., *Certaine godlie homilies or sermons upon the Prophets Abdias and Jonas* (trans. R. Norton; 1573).

Warshaw, T.S., 'The Book of Jonah', in K.R.R. Gros Louis (ed.), *Literary Interpretations of Biblical Narratives*, II (Nashville: Abingdon Press, 1974), pp. 191-207.

Watts, J.D.W., *The Books of Joel, Obadiah, Jonah, Nahum, Habakkuk and Zephaniah* (CBC; Cambridge: Cambridge University Press, 1975).

Weimar, P., 'Beobachtungen zur Enstehung der Jonaerzählung', *Biblische Notizen* 18 (1982), pp. 86-109.

Werner, H., *Jona. Der Man aus dem Ghetto* (Exempla Biblia, 2; Göttingen: Vandenhoeck & Ruprecht, 1966).

West, M., 'Irony in the Book of Jonah: Audience Identification with the Hero', *Perspectives in Religious Studies* 11 (1984), pp. 233-42.

Wilson, R.R., *Prophecy and Society in Ancient Israel* (Philadelphia: Fortress Press, 1980).

Witzenrath, H., *Das Buch Jona. Eine literatur-wissenschaftliche Untersuchung* (ATAT, 6; St Ottilien: EOS, 1978).

Wolfendale, J., *A Homiletical Commentary on the Minor Prophets* (London: Funk and Wagnalls, 1892).

Wolff, H.W., *Obadiah and Jonah: A Commentary* (trans. M. Kohl; Minneapolis: Augsburg, 1986).

Zimmermann, F., 'Problems and Solutions in the Book of Jonah', *Judaism* 40 (1991), pp. 580-89.

Zlotowitz, M., and N. Scherman, *Jonah* (Brooklyn: Mesorah, 1988).

INDEXES

INDEX OF BIBLICAL REFERENCES

OLD TESTAMENT

INDEX OF AUTHORS